GIAI PHONG!

The Fall and Liberation of Saigon

Tiziano Terzani

GIAI
PHONG!

translated from the Italian by John Shepley

The Fall and Liberation of Saigon

St. Martin's Press/New York

Library of Congress Catalog # 76-923
Manufactured in the United States of America

Designed by Riva Danzig

Library of Congress Cataloging in Publication Data
Terzani, Tiziano.
Giai phong!

Includes index.
1. Vietnamese Conflict, 1961-1975—Saigon.
2. Vietnam—History—1975-   I. Title.
DS559.9.S24T4713   959.704 '31   76-923

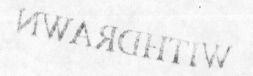

To Angela,
companion
for life

Contents

III. THE NEXT THREE MONTHS

MAPS AND ILLUSTRATIONS

All photographs by Tiziano Terzani unless otherwise indicated by captions in picture section.

Map of downtown Saigon

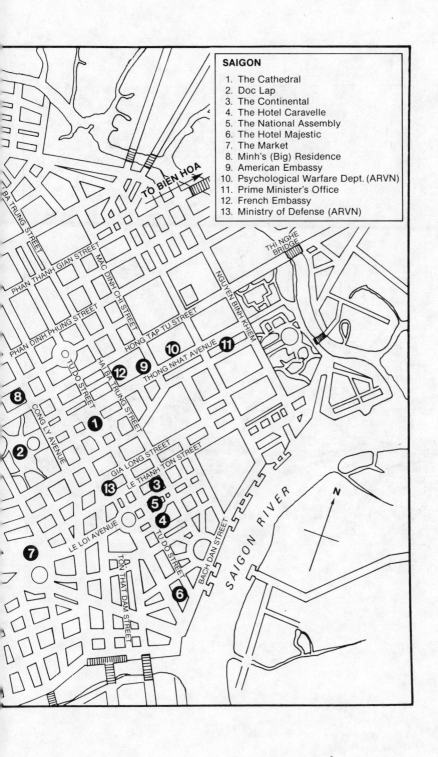

SAIGON

1. The Cathedral
2. Doc Lap
3. The Continental
4. The Hotel Caravelle
5. The National Assembly
6. The Hotel Majestic
7. The Market
8. Minh's (Big) Residence
9. American Embassy
10. Psychological Warfare Dept. (ARVN)
11. Prime Minister's Office
12. French Embassy
13. Ministry of Defense (ARVN)

TO BIEN HOA

THI NGHE BRIDGE

PHAN THANH GIAN STREET

MAC DINH CHI STREET

BA TRUNG STREET

PHAN DINH PHUNG STREET

HONG TAP TU STREET

NGUYEN BINH KHIEM

TUDO STREET

CONG LY AVENUE

HAI BA TRUNG STREET

THONG NHAT AVENUE

GIA LONG STREET

LE THANH TON STREET

LE LOI AVENUE

TUDO STREET

BACH DAN STREET

TON THAT DAM STREET

SAIGON RIVER

N

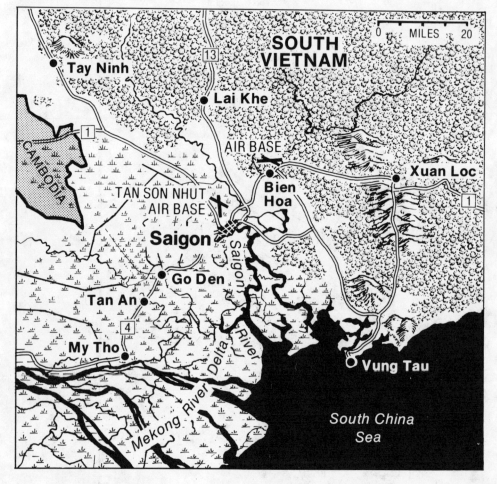

Map of area around Saigon and the Delta

GIAI PHONG !

The Fall and Liberation of Saigon

Preface

Cao Giao flung open the door of Room C-2 in the Hotel Continental where I had just arrived, and we hugged each other excitedly, both of us happy to be together again in Saigon.

It was Sunday afternoon, April 27, 1975. I had unjustly feared that he, in an irrational moment of panic, had left with the Americans. He had thought that I, having been escorted to the airport for the second time in two years by Thieu's police, would not succeed in returning before the end.

He was not only my interpreter and guide. To him, and to Buu Chuong, a former political prisoner freed at the end of 1971 who had since accompanied me across the war-torn country and into a liberated area in the Delta, I owed everything I knew about Vietnam that was not to be found in books.

Cao Giao came from a literary family in the North. For nine generations his ancestors had spent their lives writing commentaries on the *I Ching*, the great Chinese *Book of Changes*. nis father had been a district judge in the French colonial administration, and from the time he was a small boy, Cao Giao had been brought up in the country by a Communist patriot assigned by the French, after years of prison, to forced domicile in his home.

He had come to the South in 1954, and had lived his *rage d'être vietnamien*, as he called it, by working as a journalist, consultant, and interpreter for the foreign press. He spent nights studying, translating documents, making notes for people who like myself arrived for a limited period and wanted to see and understand everything.

Some of his American acquaintances, fleeing Saigon in the last fearful week in April, had urged him to take his family and go with them to the United States.

"You know languages, you never sleep, you could easily get a job as a night clerk in a hotel," they had told him.

That wasn't the reason he had stayed.

"Inside every Vietnamese there's a mandarin, a thief, a liar who sleeps—but there's also a dreamer," he said to me.

"The revolution sets me to dreaming, and I want to see it with my own eyes."

I too had wanted to see it.

I had been thrown out of Vietnam in mid-March, shortly after the fall of Ban Me Thuot. Nguyen Quoc Cuong, the head of the "Press Center" of Thieu's Information Ministry who later fled with the Americans, had told me that in one of my articles, just published, I had insulted the chief of state and thrown mud on the Republic of Vietnam.

Nguyen Ngoc Bich, director of the government press agency, Vietnam Press, and who was also to flee with the Americans, had repeated the same things to me. I was expelled.

It left me feeling desperate. I had followed these events for four years and did not want to miss out on the end which I, like everyone else, saw as imminent. I was well aware that should I try to return, I would be arrested and put back on the first departing plane. The only thing to do was to arrive on a plane that would not depart: the last one.

I was lucky. When the Air Vietnam jet arriving from Singapore landed at Tan Son Nhut airport, almost all the immigration police had already fled and no one bothered to look at the "blacklist" with my name. I was in Saigon.

Shortly after Cao Giao's arrival, Buu Chuong also came to look for me at the hotel, and I asked them to help me, as in the past, to record everything that happened, everything we saw and heard.

We would move around everywhere in the city, talk to as many people as possible, collect every sort of documentation and eyewitness testimony. Every evening we would get together to compare our experiences and transcribe our notes. And so we did.

During the war years I had already passed through the lines and gone to the other side of the front in an effort to meet the Vietcong and "the other Vietnam," and this fact surely helped me to establish contacts with the new authorities once the guerrilla forces had gained power.

I was invited several times to Doc Lap Palace, and obtained the first interview with Nguyen Huu Tho, president of the National Liberation Front and in effect Thieu's successor as head of state; I had long and unique conversations with officers of the Liberation Army and responsible members of the Party. Along with Nayan Chanda of the

Far Eastern Economic Review, I was the first Western journalist to leave liberated Saigon, to tour the Delta provinces, to witness reeducation courses for onetime "puppets," and later to make the reverse journey from the South to the North of the country.

Three months after the Liberation I left Vietnam by way of Hanoi, where I stayed several days and in a series of encounters learned the other version of events I had experienced on only one part of the front. I carried in my suitcase fourteen notebooks, twenty tape cassettes with interviews, recorded speeches, conversations with people in the street, and bundles of newspapers, documents, and translations.

It is from this material that the book that follows has emerged.

I cannot have written the whole truth, for even if there were such a thing I would certainly not have seen it in its entirety. But I have done my utmost to see that everything I have written is correct, since I am convinced that even if there is no single truth, there is certainly falsehood.

Every incident, every sentence, every name I have reported has been checked to the greatest extent possible in a situation that was both difficult in itself and often chaotic. There was no reason to invent, or have recourse to the imagination for even a single detail: in a story like this one, nothing is more fantastic than the reality.

I work for a magazine, *Der Spiegel,* that allowed me to stay in Vietnam as long as possible and which has always left me free to write as I pleased. For this, Thieu's men had called me "a Communist"; the Vietcong, after knowing me a few months, "a bourgeois receptive to change."

I make no claim to be objective. I myself have my prejudices, principles, sympathies, and emotions, which certainly have influenced the choice of the very things I saw and recorded. Here they are.   T.T.

Saigon, April-July
Florence, August-October 1975

I. THE DAYS BEFORE

A city besieged

The sky was the only route left. Now there was no other way to enter or leave Saigon. High above, dense and blue; toward the sea, clear and luminous, with light fluffy clouds tinged with burning oranges and whites. Stationary, reflected in the waters of the river; changeable with the passing of the hours.

The roofs of the city were decked with flags as though in celebration. After the 1973 ceasefire, every house and public building had had to hoist the banner of the Republic, three red stripes on a yellow background, as an oath of fidelity to Thieu's regime, which a week before had become Huong's regime and was ready to become someone else's, anyone else's, provided it was not the Communists', not the Vietcong.

The Vietcong. For three days an unusual, restless silence had hung over the battlefields. It was as though they were already gazing from across the river at the two pointed bell towers of the cathedral. Close by. People felt them breathing down their necks. It could not be the usual Sunday, with large crowds attending afternoon mass and later the promenade on Tu Do Street and along the quay, to eat dried squid grilled in the stalls on charcoal and served with hot sauce, and to look at the ships moored at the docks.

No one went promenading the afternoon of April 27 in Saigon. People hurried, in cars loaded with relatives and suitcases, on foot with packages and bundles: those trying to leave; those moving in search of a more secure house for protection against an attack that could be felt in the air; those returning to the market to stock up on rice, dried fish, canned meat. Fresh produce was no longer available because the road from Dalat was closed, as was that from the Delta.

Those who had no bundles carried their fear like a pack on their backs. People crept along the walls, bent over slightly, as though to avoid something that might fall on their heads—perhaps a rocket.

Four rockets had fallen at dawn. One had crashed through the roof of the Hotel Majestic, gutting the empty

VIP suite and killing an employee. The others had struck
in Phan Chu Tinh Street, creating havoc among a group
of hovels and refugees. They were the first missiles on Saigon since December 1971 and were not a real attack, only
a warning by the Vietcong to say they were there.

Like these, others might arrive, all of a sudden, and
people kept their ears cocked to catch every sound. But in
the sky one heard only the continual roar of jets loaded
with fleeing Americans and South Vietnamese.

The president of the Republic, Tran Van Huong, had
convened an extraordinary session of the National Assembly for late afternoon. Every hour Radio Saigon repeated
the call: members of the two chambers were to meet in the
Senate at six o'clock. The first order of business was "to
choose a political personality to replace the head of state
and negotiate with the other side."

After an agonizing week of juridical disputes over pro-
cedural details of constitutional interpretation while Vietcong troops were massing unopposed around the capital,
the political situation seemed to have finally loosened up.

But wasn't it already too late?

The resignation of Nguyen Van Thieu on Monday,
April 21, and his departure—demanded for months by the
PRG (the Vietcong Provisional Revolutionary Government)
as a condition for opening negotiations with Saigon—had
given rise to the hope that a new southern "peace cabinet,"
composed of persons not linked to the old regime, might
put an end to the war.

People had thought Huong's succession to Thieu would
be only a formality and that the new president would immediately yield power to the man who by now everyone
had singled out as the only acceptable figure, both to the
Vietcong as a negotiator and to the remnants of the Republic as head of state: General Duong Van Minh. But after becoming president Huong gave no sign that he might
resign; indeed he gave the impression of wanting to stay
on for as long as possible.

In his swearing-in speech Huong vowed to fight on "until the troops are dead or the country is lost." And to a
Western diplomat who had gone to his office to urge him
to resign the new president, asthmatic and suffering from
arteriosclerosis, had pompously replied:

"Thieu has fled destiny. Destiny has now come to me."

So began an endless and exhausting game of passing the

buck, justified in the name of "respect for the Constitu-
tion." Huong said that if the Assembly no longer wanted
him as president, it was up to them to vote him out of office; the Assembly replied that it was up to Huong to resign.

On Saturday, April 26 the two chambers, meeting jointly
in a scene typical of the end of a regime, had spent ten
hours in pathetic and heated debate on how to resolve this
constitutional problem, which was becoming increasingly
irrelevant in the face of the Communist forces now press-
ing at the gates of the city.

On the 24th, General Minh had refused the post of
prime minister which Huong, in an attempt to quiet his
opponents but without giving up power, had offered him.
The general had shut himself up in his villa to await "the
nation's call."

Minh was convinced that his accession to the presidency
would halt the advance of the Communist troops, that
there would be a ceasefire, which would be followed by negotiations with the PRG for the creation of a coalition government as described in the 1973 Paris Accords. He was so
sure that the PRG would agree to negotiate with him that
he had already designated Nguyen Phuoc Dai, a woman
lawyer, to head the Saigon delegation to Paris for the re-
sumption of political talks.

Minh envisaged taking power not as the representative
of a fading, indefinable Third Force that pointed to him as
its candidate, but rather as Thieu's successor, representing
the first force on a par with the PRG. It was no accident
that he kept his distance from the more leftwing elements
in the so-called "third component," such as Mme. Ngo Ba
Thanh, who was never consulted by the general. She and
others refused to recognize the legality of the previous regime, and demanded the destruction of the whole military,
police, and juridical apparatus of the administration—
whose continuity would be guaranteed should Minh become Huong's constitutional successor.

Though he had never had any contact with the PRG,
Minh was convinced that he was the man the Communists
would accept in power in Saigon. The man who had persuaded him of this was Jean-Marie Merillon, one of the
most brilliant and open-minded diplomats of the Quai
d'Orsay, whom Giscard d'Estaing had dispatched as French
ambassador to Saigon barely one year earlier. Before and
after the fall of Thieu, Merillon (everyone familiarly called

him "Memé") had been tirelessly shuttling between the
presidential palace, the American embassy, and every politician of any say in the South Vietnamese capital.

"The PRG asserted that it wanted to negotiate, and that
was the solution we favored. France wanted to play an
honest role; it was a kind of duty for us to avert a bloodbath in Saigon. We simply conducted ourselves like the
Swedish consul who saved Paris by staying put and medi-
ating with the Nazis who wanted to blow up the bridges
and set fire to the city," Merillon told me some weeks later.

Actually France's game was more subtle and ambiguous.
The French, by offering themselves as mediators in the
name of the Paris Accords — invoked by everyone, but no
longer of any value since the situation had changed so
greatly — were pushing toward a quick agreement on a coalition government. The idea behind this policy was simple:
the Vietcong represented an indisputable reality in South
Vietnam. It was better to give them a slice of power at
once and so prevent them from taking all of it in a little
while.

Merillon carried forth his government's policy by personally weaving a network of contacts that extended from
American Ambassador Martin to President Huong to such
pro-French generals as Tran Van Don, Thieu's deputy
prime minister and later minister of defense.

Behind the official meetings had been a number of discreet nightly rendezvous in a villa on Le Van Duyet Street,
made available by Chan Ngoc Thai, first private secretary
in all previous governments and a man with close ties to
the French.

A final meeting had been set up between President
Huong and General Duong Van Minh for the afternoon
of Saturday the 26th inside the Mai Xuu Xuan plantation
on the outskirts of Saigon, but again no agreement was
reached. That afternoon Huong's car had to return to the
city by secondary roads, since thousands of refugees,
afraid of being caught in the midst of a battle and fleeing
toward Saigon before the Communist advance, had
jammed the highway from Bien Hoa.

ARVN Rangers and paratroopers, brought in to defend
the capital, set up roadblocks to prevent the column of refugees from entering the city and spreading panic, as had
happened at Da Nang, Hue, and Nha Trang.

Huong's constitutional resistance was obstructing every
solution that offered hope for a ceasefire.

"My God, don't these people realize that thousands of human lives are on razor's edge?" Merillon remarked to a journalist on the evening of the 26th.

He was not the only one convinced that for Saigon, now surrounded, it was only a matter of hours.

Waiting

By now it seemed inevitable: if negotiations did not begin at once Communist troops could no longer be stopped, and the war would end in a final grand and bloody battle in the streets of Saigon.

For days many in the underground had been getting ready secretly.

Groups of students had stocked rice and medical supplies in various parts of the city and hidden weapons and mimeograph machines in "friendly houses." Their center was Van Hanh, the Buddhist university in Truong Minh Giang Street, a complex of badly finished yellow cement buildings on a courtyard of beaten earth that turned into a sea of mud in the rainy season.

"We chose Van Hanh because it was in a working-class neighborhood; most of the people around were for the PRG and would help us," I was told some weeks later by Nguyen Huu Thai, the student leader I had met years before and often encountered again in brief periods of freedom between one prison term and another.

Since they were well aware of the city's deep anticommunist vein, and in order not to arouse suspicion and also to work more effectively, the students decided to present themselves as part of the "Third Force". They began by calling themselves "Buddhist Student Committee" and wearing green armbands with a red cross as identification. These were almost but not quite the colors of the Front. The students were to change their image as the situation developed. Once the battle had begun Van Hanh was expected to function as a receiving center for the wounded, but the students' real objectives were: 1) to weaken resistance in the ARVN, and 2) to spread the idea of peace among the population.

Their liaison man with the National Liberation Front

was a student who was in daily contact with a group of
Vietcong leaders in the city.

Infiltrators were everywhere. Some had arrived separately,
one by one, by trucks and buses in the first wave of refugees.
Others had come on foot or on Hondas, passing the regular
ARVN and police roadblocks with false identity cards.

All were volunteers. Many came from Hanoi. Though
they did not know Saigon, they had studied it minutely
from maps and memorized the streets to take, the addresses at which to present themselves. Once inside the
city, they reconstituted themselves in groups of ten to fifteen men. Each group had an objective: a barracks, a munitions dump, a police station. Their common assignment
was to protect the bridges at all costs. It was expected that
the ARVN would try to withdraw within a defensive perimeter inside the city at the moment of attack, and attempt to block the entrance of the Vietcong infantry and
armored columns by blowing up the bridges.

As high-ranking officers who had been responsible for
the offensive explained to me some months later in Hanoi,
fifteen hundred Communist commandos had infiltrated
themselves around Tan Son Nhut Airport as early as April
25th. With the help of local cells of the Front that had
survived the Tet offensive and the Phoenix elimination
program, they had even succeeded in transporting four
105-mm. cannons, in pieces. The Communist Military
Command for the Saigon Region had been set up in the
seventh district of the capital, and placed under the orders
of a brigadier general. Even the members of the Central
Committee of the Party responsible for the city were all
present on the evening of the 26th.

"Saigon was like a sponge," Cao Giao's brother told me a
few days later. He had entered the city with a group of
North Vietnamese journalists assigned to document the
battle that was expected to ensue. A television operator
had carried his movie camera and rolls of film with him,
hidden in a sack, all the way from Hanoi.

In Camp Davis, an enclosure in the middle of Tan Son
Nhut Airport, two hundred PRG soldiers were waiting.
Their situation, like so much else in this war, was one of
incredible absurdity.

They had arrived on January 30, 1973, by the terms of

the Paris Accords, and had been stationed right in the heart of the Saigon war machine, in quarters previously assigned to American officers. They had whitewashed the barracks, dug up the strips of ground between the asphalt, and planted banana palms and papaya trees. The ceasefire for whose application they had come to negotiate with representatives of Thieu and of the United States had never become a reality, and as the months passed by their trees had borne fruit.

Formally the PRG delegation at Camp Davis enjoyed diplomatic immunity, but naturally the Saigon authorities did everything they could to send them back to the jungle where they had come from. Their telephone lines, water supply, and electricity were periodically cut, but the Vietcong did not abandon what they called the first "liberated" area in Saigon; every Saturday Vo Dong Giang, a bony colonel and member of the Central Committee of the Communist Party who was also a brilliant debater, held his press conference, interrupted each time by the roar of South Vietnamese jets taking off on their way to bomb the approaching Communist positions.

The last press conference had been on Saturday the 26th. Someone had asked if the Communist forces were really about to attack Saigon, and Giang had answered:

"Our troops continue to advance."

He knew a good deal more than that. The previous evening a coded message from Loc Ninh, administrative capital of the PRG, had warned the delegation at Camp Davis that the all-out attack on Saigon was imminent. It was by now impossible to come get them out without revealing these plans to the enemy, and the delegation would have to fend for itself. "Good luck. See you in Saigon, comrades," the message ended.

"We started digging bunkers under the barracks," Giang told me a week later, "but we had to do it at night so it wouldn't be noticed. We had no proper tools, and we used our shirts to carry away the dirt."

Camp Davis was isolated in the middle of Tan Son Nhut. Not far from the DAO (U.S. Defense Attache Office), which had become the center for the American evacuation, it was surrounded by ARVN troops beginning to disband. Rumor had it that elements of the South Vietnamese air force were planning a quick stroke against the two hundred Vietcong sitting on their doorstep. To wipe them out would have been child's play.

The man who had first led the delegation at Camp Davis and who had left for the guerrilla war zone after three months of futile talks about how to achieve a ceasefire, was once again in the immediate vicinity of Saigon.

Tran Van Tra, the legendary Vietcong who had conceived and conducted the 1968 Tet offensive, now commander in chief of the Liberation Army, had arrived north of Bien Hoa with his mobile headquarters on the night of April 25.

Five divisions under his orders were closing in on Saigon, with others coming full speed down Highway 1 along the coast, heading for the capital.

North Vietnam had declared general mobilization. Five army corps, each with three divisions, and each division with at least ten thousand soldiers, were now committed in the South.

On March 28 an important strategical decision had been taken in Hanoi and communicated to Tran Van Tra: "Prepare to take Saigon."

The order had been passed along to the troops on April 17.

That very day instruction began for the soldiers who would be involved in the attack on the capital. The political commissars of the various units had explained that it would be a long hard battle, one that might last for weeks and even months, but that it was important to pursue the enemy into his last entrenched camp.

On April 19 the "great Ho Chi Minh campaign" for the liberation of the capital was launched. One of the watchwords was "Once the bamboo is notched, one blow is enough to break it."

The final session

More than any argument from the diplomats or his advisers, it was the four warning rockets which fell on downtown Saigon on Sunday, April 27, that convinced Tran Van Huong it was time to go. Had he insisted on remaining president, the capital would have become, as he himself had cynically predicted a week before, "a sea of fire and a pile of bones."

He spent the morning in Doc Lap Palace consulting with dignitaries of the regime, then sent a letter by military courier to the president of the Senate, Tran Van Lam, who was waiting in General Minh's villa, a letter that ended as follows:

". . . once the Assembly meeting in joint session has chosen a personality to whom to entrust the sacred task, I am ready to hand over to him all presidential powers of the Republic of Vietnam. The sooner this is done the better."

Senators and deputies had been urgently summoned by radio.

Some began arriving around five o'clock at the old Senate building, built by the French on the Bach Dang river embankment, next to the National Bank. The atmosphere was very tense. In the corridors, on the steps leading from the central hall to the gallery, little groups of people spoke anxiously among themselves. A senator said to me in the taproom:

"All right, we're accepting Minh because the Communists want him. But are they still prepared to negotiate?"

Why should they be? By now they had Saigon by the throat.

Old lawyers, professors, former military men turned politicians, young technocrats trained in the United States, social climbers and pushers raised to power by the mafia of Thieu's nephew Hoang Duc Nha, legislators of the regime, all of them used to publicity and accustomed to American television cameras, now sought out journalists not to make statements, but to ask,

"Is there still a chance? How much time do we have?"

When at 6:45 Tran Van Lam rang the bell and called the Assembly to order, senators and deputies found themselves in a half-empty chamber. They looked around with dismay and took a count: of the 219 who should have been there, there were only 136. The others had already chosen to save their skins by fleeing.

Tran Van Lam was brief. He declared the session open and announced that it would be held "behind closed doors."

While the journalists and public left the gallery, General Cao Van Vien, ARVN chief of staff, General Nguyen Khac Binh, chief of police, and General Nguyen Van Minh, military governor of Saigon, entered the chamber, followed by soldiers with bulging briefcases of maps and documents.

Tran Van Lam had asked them to prepare a report on the military situation for the Assembly.

They painted a picture of disaster.

Since the start of the offensive launched by the Communist forces in South Vietnam on the night of January 1 — simultaneous with the Khmer Rouge offensive in Cambodia, which had already ended on April 17 with the capture of Phnom Penh — South Vietnamese troops had suffered one reverse after another.

Phuoc Binh had fallen on January 7. The city had no strategic importance, but it was the first provincial capital to be taken by the Vietcong after the Paris Accords. From the Communist standpoint, it had been a means of testing the American reaction. There was none.

Thieu, for his part, had neither defended the city adequately nor employed his reserve troops to take it back. He had probably let it fall as a form of blackmail against the United States. It was as if to say: "Look, if you don't help us, if you don't give us more dollars, things are going to end badly here." The blackmail tactic hadn't worked.

On March 10, after pretending to concentrate their troops around Pleiku and Kontum, the Vietcong had attacked Ban Me Thuot in the Highlands. The city with its ninety thousand inhabitants, 250 kilometers north of Saigon, had fallen in one night.

Thieu had gone to Phan Rang to talk with General Phan Van Phu, and there, on the evening of March 14, without consulting the other generals, he had decided on his own to evacuate all the Highlands and concentrate his forces along the coast, where he thought the Vietcong would have to pass if they were planning to push toward Saigon.

It was a hideous blunder. The ARVN troops, setting out on the march with three thousand vehicles and with tens of thousands of civilians who believed they would be safer and could avoid air force bombings by following the troops, were bottled up on Highway 7 by Vietcong units and decimated.

Quang Tri fell on March 19, An Loc on the 20th — two cities that in 1972 had been defended by the ARVN at a cost of thousands of dead and their total destruction.

There was something incredible about the rapidity and harshness of these defeats, and in Saigon a rumor spread that the Americans were giving the Communists what they had promised them in a secret agreement signed at the time of the Paris Accords.

No one could prove this or that Thieu was in on the game. Certain strange coincidences, however, began to be noticed in Saigon: that, for instance, many American military advisers had gone on leave and left the country right after the fall of Ban Me Thuot. The Saigonese then remembered what Kissinger had told his associates in Paris — that the American task in Vietnam was now to guarantee a "decent interval," after which the inevitable could happen.

Had the "decent interval" elapsed exactly two years after the Paris Accords? Many thought so when, on March 26, the old imperial capital of Hue was also taken by the Vietcong and the story of its abandonment was recounted by those who had succeeded in escaping. It was learned that Colonel Nguyen Huu Due, the provincial chief, received on one day the order to resist at all costs, and on the next the order for an immediate withdrawal. Bewildered, he jumped on a helicopter and flew to Da Nang to see General Ngo Quang Truong, commander for the entire First Military Region.

"Saigon is betraying us," Due had said. "We must do something."

Al Francis, the American consul in Da Nang, who was present at the meeting, took him aside and said:

"Colonel, orders are orders. Follow them and we'll have occasion to meet again."

They did meet again. Upon his return to Hué, Due collected his troops, covered the sixty kilometers to the sea, where the embarkation point had been set up, and was rescued. During the march the Vietcong did not fire a single shot at the retreating column.

Probably the "American plot" existed only in the imaginations of the South Vietnamese generals and politicians who had to find an excuse for their own mistakes.

Another truth underlay what had happened in the first months of 1975: the Vietcong and North Vietnamese were taking militarily what they would have obtained politically if Thieu had honored the Paris Accords.

Tan Ky fell on March 24, Quang Ngai on the 25th, Da Nang on the 29th. Half of the oft-cited million ARVN troops defending the South were lost, along with half their weapons, tanks, planes, and munitions.

On April 1 Qui Nhon fell, on the 3rd Nha Trang, on the 4th Dalat. Every day people in Saigon whispered of a coup d'état, but no one even attempted it.

Thieu had planned to set up something like a Maginot Line just north of Saigon, to defend a region that would have been more or less the old French Cochin China, comprising the capital and the Mekong Delta. All fleeing refugees carried along with the southern troops in their retreat would have been settled in this area.

A group of generals—among them Nguyen Van Minh, Tran Van Trung, and Admiral Chung Tan Cang—had made plans to withdraw eventually even beyond Saigon and set up a government of resistance at Can Tho. But the Communist advance continued to outstrip all forecasts, with a speed that persistently took the ARVN by surprise.

Phan Rang fell on April 16, Phan Thiet on the 19th, and on April 20, after the only real attempt at resistance by the ARVN, the city of Xuan Loc fell, the last obstacle on the road to Saigon. Thieu resigned.

The report made by the three generals to the joint session of the Assembly held in the Senate chamber on the evening of April 27 concluded with an examination of the situation in Saigon. The ARVN now had sixty thousand soldiers in the city, but no possibility of sending for reinforcements. The Vietcong had an equal number of troops, but these were increasing hour by hour.

At 8:45 Tran Van Lam called for a show of hands. He read from a sheet of paper:

"Who agrees that President Huong should hand over presidential powers to General Duong Van Minh so that the latter may seek a way to restore peace in Vietnam?"

All raised their hands.

Minh was president by unanimous vote. His inauguration was to take place next day.

After the senators' and deputies' cars drove off along the Bach Dang embankment and dispersed themselves in the city, the streets were deserted. A curfew had been in effect since eight o'clock. The radio immediately broadcast the result of the voting, and repeated it several times. The announcement was directed especially at the Vietcong forces.

The people of Saigon, locked in their homes, awaited an answer from the sky, in the form of rockets that could come from one moment to the next.

But the night was calm, and this rekindled the· hope that if Minh were to hasten to put together a government and come up with a peace plan of his own, this city now stifled by uncertainty might gain a breathing spell.

II. THE THREE DAYS

April 28

In search of a government

General Duong Van Minh had trouble putting together a government, and his inauguration, announced for eleven o'clock in the morning, was postponed first until three, then until five in the afternoon.

All morning long spokesmen of the Saigonese political world, generals, businessmen, profiteers, and friends presented themselves at the back door of his villa at No. 3 Tran Quy Cap Street, a stone's throw from Pasteur Street. Some had been summoned for consultations, others had come simply to offer themselves or their unsolicited advice to the president designate. By now people habitually entered Minh's home by the back entrance—the front door had been closed ever since the general, after becoming president in the 1963 coup d'état against Diem, had in turn been deposed barely four months later by his colleague General Khanh.

Knots of people stood in the courtyard facing the green gate, which opened from time to time to let in the expected guests, deputies, senators, the curious. They spoke of opening negotiations with "the other side," of preparing the defense of Saigon, but most of all, of doing something quickly. There was no desperation, indeed there was a certain optimism. No one spoke of surrender.

Vanuxem, a retired French general who had fought as an officer in the French expeditionary corps twenty years before and had lost his first war against "*les viets*," as he called the revolutionaries, moved, obese and sweaty, from one group to another. He was trying to convince everyone that Saigon could still win, that "*les viets*" were extremely weak, that he had it from a reliable source in Paris that the Russians and Chinese did not want a Vietcong victory and that so this was an auspicious moment to counterattack.

Vanuxem had arrived in Vietnam two months before at the invitation of Thieu, who had wanted him as a military adviser, and had stayed on, getting himself accredited as correspondent for an obscure French publication, *Carrefour*.

At the gate Ly Qui Chung, a brilliant young opposition

deputy who for years had worked for General Minh and was to be his information minister (the Republic's last), did the honors of the house.

Minh received his guests in the drawing room on the ground floor, seated on a long blue divan, in the midst of his large aquaria full of colorful tropical fish. The veranda opened onto the garden overflowing with orchids. These were the general's great passion during the years when, fallen into disgrace and forgotten by the Vietnamese, he was kept alive politically by those observers (most of them foreigners) who continued to point to him as the only alternative to Thieu, as the only man who could restore peace to the country.

The Paris Accords, by proposing a coalition government that would bring together the Saigon administration (First Force), the Vietcong administration (Second Force), and a group vaguely defined as the third component or Third Force, had helped to assign Minh this role of a man of destiny awaiting his turn. Without ever having declared himself, and without the Third Force, if it ever effectively existed, having recognized him as such, Minh automatically became the symbol of the neutralist and non-Communist "third component" that wanted to put an end to the war and apply the Paris Accords.

Actually he represented an equivocation, but an equivocation convenient to everyone. To Thieu, who had nothing to fear from Minh, he was a general without troops and a politician with no electoral base. To the Americans, who knew Minh (the CIA had helped him out during his 1963 coup) he could be counted on as a sort of ace in the hole for a more moderate and acceptable regime in Saigon. To the Vietcong, who let it be understood they would agree to negotiate with Minh, he was a means of pushing Thieu out of the presidential palace. To the Third Force, which was disorganized, divided, persecuted, and without a charismatic leader, Minh was a suitable figure, a meeting point, a cover that each faction intended to manipulate in its own way at the proper time.

Unlike so many of his colleagues—cowardly and turncoat generals who were constantly being accused of corruption and were involved in the most shady deals—Minh was an honest soldier. Respected by the troops he had commanded, he was physically courageous and had a traditional sense of honor. When he was a French officer and the Japanese tortured him for days, knocking out all his teeth, he did not give in. "My country is well worth a set of dentures," he once said to me, recalling that episode.

He liked publicity but did not enjoy exposing himself, and when his followers expected him to make a pronouncement or take a position in moments of crisis, he always backed out with ambiguous statements that neither satisfied nor irritated anyone. His indecision was often taken for prudence, for shrewdness, but actually his silences, for all the great significance attributed to them, were only the sign that the general had nothing to say. He was the opposite of an intellectual: a man without ideas, without visions.

"His greatest quality is his height," a Vietnamese friend once told me. Those five feet eleven inches, exceptional for an Asian, earned him the nickname "Big Minh," but they also gave him that imposing air that accounted for his distinction. Were it not for a group of young intellectuals like Ly Qui Chung and Nguyen Van Ba, who placed themselves behind him and directed him, Minh would not have been president designate of the tottering Republic of Vietnam, reduced by that Monday afternoon to little more than the republic of Saigon.

After four days of relative calm on all fronts, fighting had violently resumed on the outskirts of the city the morning of the 28th, and the sound of mortar and cannon fire could be heard clearly all the way to Tran Quy Cap Street. The Vietcong had seized the approach to the Newport bridge on the Bien Hoa highway, only five kilometers from the center of Saigon, and showed no signs of being dislodged. Saigon troops had dispatched an armored unit, but the first vehicles had been hit by B-40 rockets and were burning on the asphalt, blocking the road to those coming up behind.

In Minh's drawing room, amid the aquaria, one caller followed another, and during these meetings the time went by. The general had found a vice-president, a prime minister, and a few others, but the list was not complete. Those he wanted did not accept or were undecided, and those who offered themselves he did not want in his government. But now the swearing-in ceremony could not be postponed a third time, and at 4:45 Minh, dressed in a dark blue suit, prepared to leave for the palace with whatever government he had.

Enter Big Minh

Doc Lap, or Independence Palace, built of concrete and glass with American dollars after Diem's neighboring one had been half destroyed by cannon fire in 1963, had become the quintessence, the symbol, of Thieu's regime: gray, isolated, heavy, barricaded, cut off from people even while in the heart of the city.

The presidential palace lies some two hundred yards from the red brick cathedral, on Thong Nhat (Unification) Avenue, which runs perpendicular to Tu Do Street, the Rue Catinat of French times. Thong Nhat Avenue, very wide and lined with old trees and others more recently planted, extends from the botanical garden and the zoo at one end to the large, impertinent iron gateway, the entrance to Doc Lap, at the other. Along that route of little over a half-mile stood the American embassy, white, compact, windowless, like a fortress bristling with antennae, with a small Protestant church next to it where former Ambassador Bunker used to go, during the war he himself was directing, to read the Gospels on Sunday. There too were the Psychological Warfare Command, the offices of the prime minister, the British embassy, and the secondary entrance to the French embassy.

Doc Lap Palace lies in the middle of a small park whose large trees have a reddish bark; in Thieu's day it was impossible even to approach the gate: rolls of barbed wire, fences, iron barriers blocked the avenue and all the surrounding streets. Soldiers in battle garb, with rifles on their hips, were stationed every twenty yards, and if anyone stopped merely to look a policeman whistled and ran up to chase him away.

Thieu preferred to move around by helicopter, and there were always two of these big ugly birds squatting in two grass clearings alongside the palace. Among the trees were hidden anti-aircraft batteries, a dozen armored vehicles, and the tents of the palace guard.

Thieu had always feared a sudden attack by the Vietcong or a coup d'etat by his own generals. Neither one nor the other was ever attempted, and Thieu departed from his palace on April 21, leaving the presidency to the seventy-one-year-old, asthmatic, and half-blind Tran Van Huong.

On the afternoon of April 28 Doc Lap became accessible for the first time in its history. The south gate on Nguyen

Du Street was open, and you had only to present yourself and a policeman, without checking your credentials, would point to the side stairway that led up one flight to the large open hall adjoining the conference room. Conspicuously planted in the middle of the blue carpeting was a very high iron scaffold on which men were working.

They were repairing the damage caused by the bombardment of April 8. In broad daylight, out of the calm sky, an A-37 South Vietnamese air force jet had darted between the two bell towers of the cathedral and dived on the presidential palace one, two, three times, releasing a bomb load originally intended for the Communists. Saigon came to a halt. Sirens sounded the signal for immediate curfew and the streets emptied, while columns of smoke rose from the palace. Thieu emerged without a scratch and the plane, piloted by Lieutenant Nguyen Thanh Trung of the South Vietnamese air force, disappeared in the direction of the north where the Liberation Army by now controlled a large part of the country.

"It has nothing to do with me. It's not a coup d'etat by the air force," Marshal Cao Ky declared.

"It was the individual act of a criminal, a rebel," Thieu said, but took the precaution of forbidding all planes to fly over the city from that moment on. Saigon newspapers reported that the pilot was deranged, and to give a somewhat patriotic slant to the affair added that the lieutenant had gone berserk because he had been unable to rescue his family from Da Nang before the Communists arrived — his gesture was a protest against the loss of the northern part of the country.

Three months later, talking in Hanoi with Colonel Tran Cong Man, editor of *Quan Doi Nhan Dan*, the armed forces newspaper, I heard a quite different version of this incident:

"Nguyen Thanh Trung has been a Party member ever since he was a student. It was the Party that ordered him to join the Saigon air force and go to the United States where he obtained his pilot's license. Such a man was important for a crucial occasion, and for this reason Trung did not reveal himself and had never been used before. The bombing of Doc Lap Palace was a blow well worth the trouble. The air force was Thieu's trusted weapon, one of the foundations of his power. With the bombs of April 8 we wanted to destroy that trust, to spread suspicion within the air force itself. The attack succeeded magnificently."

From the top of their iron scaffold the workmen looked down curiously at the unusual crowd gathering in the great hall of the palace and the colonnade opening on the garden. Deputies, senators, judges of the high court arrived one by one, to be welcomed by aides of the outgoing and incoming presidents. The army officers assigned to the palace looked awkward in their starched and ironed green field uniforms, their pant legs stuck in leather boots, without weapons and without guard belts so that their shirts drooped at the waist. They went to meet the older and limping guests, and helped them to their seats.

A violent thunderstorm was about to erupt; a strong warm and humid wind had risen and now rolled through the corridors of the palace, swept through the hall, making the long light curtains of white muslin of the French windows in the big reception room flap spectrally in the air. The room was illuminated as for a celebration, and two soldiers were arranging the last red damask armchairs.

Dignitaries of the regime, and members of the outgoing government (at least those who had not yet fled) sat in the first two rows; behind them came the others. The armed forces were represented by two young generals in full uniform, complete with ribbons, medals, and a gold cordon on the right shoulder. Missing was Cao Van Vien, the chief of staff. With his wife and children, his officers and all their families, he had already gone to Tan Son Nhut to take a plane for the United States, without even bothering to hand in his resignation.

On a large lacquered panel on the back wall a medieval Vietnamese commander on horseback hurled himself against a horde of the usual enemy invaders of Vietnam: the Chinese.

Underneath in the center was a podium with two microphones. To the sides two of the yellow flags with three red stripes, the colors of the Republic.

Tran Van Huong, president for a week, spoke first. Bent, old, trembling, with large dark glasses that made him even blinder than he was, supported by an aide, he introduced General Minh to the assembly, then turned to him and concluded:

"Your responsibilities are great, General." Dragging his feet and cane, he left the stage.

The podium remained vacant. Minh did not stir. A soldier entered the beam of light from the reflectors, took down the two flags, and carried them away. He came back and removed the coat of arms of the Republic from the podium, and another soldier attached in its place the white and blue image of a flower with five petals enclosing the Chinese yin-and-yang sign, symbol of the opposites that constitute the unity of the universe.

There was a long murmur in the room. The Republic had changed its face.

Minh slowly approached the podium, measuring his steps, his look grave. The scene was charged with emotion, and two strokes of lightning that flashed nearby with a roar of thunder marked for everyone the historical significance of the moment.

Minh spoke amid the splashing of heavy rain that fell on the palace, on the garden, on an expectant Saigon.

"I can make you no promises. In the days ahead we will have nothing but difficulties, terrible difficulties. The decisions to be taken are grave and important, our position is a difficult one." We thought for a moment that he was about to announce surrender as he continued, "I have thought for some time that the use of force is not a good solution for us," but then he went on.

"The order to our soldiers is to stay where they are, to defend their positions, to defend with all their strength the territory remaining to us.

"I accept the responsibility for seeking to arrive at a ceasefire, at negotiations, at peace on the basis of the Paris Accords. I am ready to accept any proposal in this direction."

So Minh was not giving up. What he was proposing had already been bypassed, rejected by the PRG; there was nothing new in his speech, nothing to encourage hope for an immediate solution that evening.

Minh spoke slowly, reading word for word from a written text. Then he folded it, put it in his pocket, and in a new tone of great emotion and sincerity that explained his position better than any other words, said:

"Citizens, brothers, patriots! In these difficult hours I can only beg of you one thing: be courageous, do not abandon the country, do not run away. The tombs of our ancestors are here, this is our land, it is here that we all belong." The roomful of people applauded.

Minh introduced the Catholic ex-president of the Senate Nguyen Van Huyen as his vice-president, assigned to conduct the negotiations, and Vu Van Mau, leader of the Buddhist opposition, as his prime minister. He said the full cabinet would be presented next day. Again there was brief applause. The ceremony was over. It was 5:50, and we crowded toward the exit.

Standing on the steps, senators, judges, deputies, high functionaries in the various ministries waited for their white-uniformed servants to open the rear doors of their official cars, which were beginning to edge slowly along the brief rise at the main entrance to the palace.

They were a collection of solemn men, all in dark suits with neckties except for a priest in a wide cassock and a bonze in dark brown. They had been overtaken by what was happening in their country, but they still kept conferring, took each other by the arm, and whispered private secrets into each other's ear. The color of its flags might change, but the old world of Saigon was still there, with all its compromises, its little conspiracies, its government deals.

The storm had shifted and the sky was rent by the last rays of the sun, which gilded the tall trees on the square and the roof of the cathedral. The odor of damp soil gave the air an unusual freshness. Saigon was calm, like a normal city filling up its streets again and resuming its pace after a downpour.

Along with a few colleagues, I set out for Tu Do Street. The news vendors were selling the first copies of the *Saigon Post,* dated the following day, April 29. The headlines were: "Big Minh at the Helm," "Ceasefire Likely," "Saigon Residents Feel a Sense of Relief, Hope." Three cars went by with colorful signs on their sides announcing the programs of the downtown movie theaters: at the Capitol, *La CIA mène la danse* ("The CIA Leads the Dance"); at the Rex, *La maison du diable* ("The Devil's House"); at the Eden, *La belle et le clochard* ("Beauty and the Tramp").

We heard three booming sounds. We stopped. One of us, looking at the still cloudy sky, said, "It's thunder!" Then came another three, four, five, and we felt the thunder coming to us from the earth, from under our feet. "They're bombs!"

From whom? At whom?

The Doc Lap anti-aircraft batteries began firing madly. All of a sudden machine guns, rifles, all Saigon were firing. We heard the bullets pattering on the roofs of the houses like hailstones. As I scurried into the offices of Reuters I saw policemen, bent down on one knee and with outstretched arms, firing their pistols toward the cathedral.

A coup d'état? But by whom?

The sirens wailed, giving the signal for immediate and permanent curfew. The streets emptied in a twinkling. Cars stopped at the curb, and people crouched in doorways. Some, bent over motorcycles, sped for home. Ships moored at the waterfront had opened fire with their heavy guns and the sky was furrowed by the red traceries of the projectiles.

"It's an air raid, an air raid, we have the alarm from Tan Son Nhut," an officer on guard at Doc Lap Palace responded excitedly on the telephone.

Five South Vietnamese air force A-37s, captured by the Vietcong, were making repeated passes over the airport, over the hangars and munitions dumps, over the parking areas where thousands of people were waiting to board American planes for Guam. Lieutenant Nguyen Thanh Trung was making his second air strike, as the colonel in Hanoi was later to explain to me:

"The planes took off from and returned to Phan Rang. Trung was the squadron leader. He had a good knowledge of the airport and its defense system. For a week we'd been training the other four pilots, since they were accustomed to Migs. During the attack they maintained radio silence, so they would not be discovered. Surprise was important. We thus succeeded in hitting many enemy planes still on the ground. The puppets thought we could never attack the airport because our comrades were still at Camp Davis. In fact we thought about it a long time before giving the signal for the operation, but we had to do it. The air force was Saigon's last defense, and it was indispensable to attack Tan Son Nhut and Bien Hoa."

After fifteen minutes the wild shooting lessened, stopped; but Saigon had had a taste of what might turn out to be a street-by-street, house-to-house battle. The relief felt over Minh's accession to the presidency had lasted for little more than a moment. Now it seemed too late for anything. Minh did not yet have a government, and the other side seemed unwilling to accept him as a negotiator. How could he negotiate? How could he stop a war machine that already seemed to be moving in to crush Saigon?

Listening that night to Radio Giai Phong, the Liberation Front station, we shuddered. Commenting on the new president's confirmation, the radio spoke of the "Minh-Huyen-Mau clique," which was stubbornly prolonging the war in the hope of maintaining American neocolonialism. Then at the end of the news broadcast came the clear notes of "Rise up, Indomitable Saigon!"

"It's the signal for the attack," said Cao Giao, "The same thing happened on the eve of the attack on Da Nang, Hué, Nha Trang. . . ."

"It's just propaganda, they're doing it to save face. There may already be a general agreement," suggested someone else.

The hope that there might still be negotiations, that a massacre in Saigon could be averted, died hard.

Was it really an illusion? The answer would come soon. If the Vietcong accepted Minh's invitation to "lay down arms and sit down at a table to negotiate," the night would be calm. Otherwise the rockets would arrive. The Vietcong were said to have thousands of them encircling the capital. What was there to do against rockets?

I went to bed, covering myself with a mattress.

April 29

Sunrise on the wrong side

I had fallen asleep thinking of the rockets, and in my sleep I heard them land close by, with a muffled crash, in salvos of four or five at a time.

I ran to the window and saw the square in front of the National Assembly and Tu Do Street deserted. There was only the policeman on guard, seated at the foot of the steps with his M-16 between his legs, motionless at his post, gazing at the black sky toward the river.

It seemed like one of the usual Saigon nights, with its roar of cannons, the war not far off but never actually there, with people sleeping quietly, convinced that after all the capital would not be touched.

And yet that night Saigon—silent, holding its breath—did not sleep. In that silence broken by the crash of bursting rockets thousands and thousands of persons were reckoning with their lives, making plans that would be carried out at dawn, seeking someone from whom to get help—ready to betray family, friends, and all the ties of years if only to find a way to escape. Escape. But how? Only a very few knew how.

More rockets fell, much closer it seemed, and the policeman, crouching, ran to take shelter under the entrance arch of the Assembly building. To the west, behind the geometrical outlines of the houses, you could see a rising halo of light that climbed, grew, and expanded with a reddish glow. It was still the dead of night, but it was as though that morning the sun were rising over Saigon ahead of time, and from the wrong side.

"Everything here is in flames. About thirty rockets have fallen on the runways and ammunition dumps. They look like 122s. Whiskey Joe, Whiskey Joe, do you hear me? Over."

"O.K. Whiskey Joe here. Roger."

The whole hotel was awake by four o'clock. In the corridor someone had succeeded in tuning in on the security circuit of the American embassy with an ordinary FM radio, and we were hearing the excited voice of a marine speaking from the United States DAO (Defense Attaché

Office) at Tan Son Nhut Airport.

The corridor filled up with people. It was perhaps the safest place in the whole hotel in case a rocket struck the building. The only guests by now were journalists, mostly Americans, and a few Polish members of the International Commission for Control and Supervision, which had been set up after the Paris Accords. We stood there glued to the radio, while under our feet the floor trembled with each new shock. The radio went silent, then a metallic buzz indicated that the circuit had been reopened. Again the voice from Tan Son Nhut:

"They're still falling all around here. Two marines are dead at Gate 4. What do we do with the bodies?" There was no answer.

The attack on the airport was very serious. For days military experts had been saying that a Vietcong move against Tan Son Nhut would be the signal for the attack on Saigon; if the airport fell, the capital was finished. The American evacuation now seemed inevitable. Imminent.

Some of the journalists rushed to their rooms to pack their bags. An American colleague, who had his telex in the hotel, came to show everyone a strip of paper.

"My office in Washington has heard it from the Pentagon. The evacuation is set to begin in two hours."

Someone called the American embassy for confirmation. No one knew anything about it. Voices on the radio were talking about an emergency meeting set for six o'clock; once again the airport was calling Whiskey Joe, and the problem was still what to do with the bodies of the two marines.

"Take them to the Seventh Day Adventist Hospital," came the reply from the embassy.

A Polish colonel, who had taken his walkie-talkie up to the third floor of the hotel to communicate with his officers trapped in their residences at Tan Son Nhut, came down the stairs saying:

"There's a battle along the outskirts of the airport. My men say they can hear AK-47 rifle fire."

Were the Vietcong launching an infantry attack? If so, evacuation by air would be impossible. Even if marines were to arrive from the Seventh Fleet and set up a safety cordon along the runways, the Vietcong were now able to hamper landing and take-off operations. While we talked, confirmation of this came from a new voice calling Whiskey Joe:

"This is Jacobson. The situation is serious. The evacuation plan has to be changed. Changed. Options 1-2-3 are no longer valid."

The Americans and other "whites" who had decided to leave knew what this meant. Evacuation by helicopter.

For the past few days the American embassy, and other embassies that had obtained Washington's guarantee of help in evacuating their citizens, had been distributing "extremely confidential" instructions to be followed in case of an emergency evacuation. Each person had been given addresses to which to go in order to be picked up and taken by helicopter to the aircraft carriers of the fleet cruising off Saigon.

On Monday the 28th Dr. Schostal, first secretary of the Italian embassy, reminded me that since I had no visa I had entered the country illegally and would have to come to an immediate understanding with the authorities. After instructing me to leave with the American evacuation because the Italian embassy, even were it to remain open, would be unable to shelter me ("that kind of assistance is not the job of diplomatic missions"), he handed me the following document with repeated admonitions about its confidentiality. It was similar to those issued by other embassies.

In case of emergency, Italian citizens should do as follows:
1) put their own passports and those of their wives and children in their pockets. These must obviously be Italian passports.
2) go with the greatest dispatch to one of the following assembly points, bringing along no more than one suitcase of modest size:
   a) to No. 192 Cong Ly for those who live in the vicinity of the Embassy;
   b) to No. 22 Gia Long for those who live in the vicinity of the Hotel Continental;
   c) to No. 2 Phan Van Dat for those who live in the vicinity of the Hotel Magestic.
How to recognize the state of emergency.
The ambassador and the first secretary will be notified by telephone, assuming that the telephones are working.
The ambassador will telephone Colonel Andrei, who in turn will notify Marshal Pimpinella, Dr. Schostal if he has not already been advised, and Signor Esposito.

He will send his driver with Signor Venuti to notify the other employees.

Dr. Schostal will notify the journalists at the Hotels Majestic, Continental and Caravelle. If the telephones are not working, he will go there in person.

In case, however, the situation should take a sudden turn and the telephones no longer function, everyone should provide himself with an FM radio to listen for a message that will be broadcast by the American radio in Saigon. The message will consist of a weather announcement: "105 degrees and rising". . . . After thirty seconds there will be a song: "I'm dreaming of a white Christmas". . . . The message will be repeated every 15 minutes for two hours. In all probability, all this will happen at night.

Should this occur, each person will have to get to the nearest assembly point by his own means, without counting on the help of anyone but himself.

Remember to carry sums of money in your pocket, in piasters and dollars, to give to the police blocks if necessary. Do not forget to carry your passport on your person. Only by showing your Italian passport will you be able to avail yourself of help.

N.B. The above is to be considered highly confidential. No interested party should speak of it to anyone else. Neither to a Vietnamese nor to a foreigner of another nationality. *Above all, should he have Vietnamese relatives, he will refrain from communicating it.* [Underlined in text.]

Dawn came, and now an orange ball of fire and black columns of smoke rose over Tan Son Nhut. The ammunition dumps struck by rockets were exploding. We saw two F-5s take off and go to bomb Communist positions before disappearing over the horizon to the south. An old DC-3 came down slowly on Tan Son Nhut and vanished behind a row of trees. A small L-119 observation plane exploded in the air, struck by Communist anti-aircraft fire that crackled in the sky like fireworks.

In the hallways of the Continental there was now great confusion. Those who had decided to leave carried their suitcases to the lobby and distributed bottles of wine and champagne, typewriters, bulletproof jackets, and helmets to those remaining. Many stayed glued to their transistor radios, awaiting the order to leave.

In recent hours the old message, "105 degrees and rising," had been changed because by now all Saigon knew it.

The new one was to be "Mother wants you to call home." But the American radio continued to broadcast music.

One group was still listening to the communications between the American advisers and marines at the airport and Whiskey Joe.

About every fifteen minutes since five in the morning, a voice had been heard saying:

"I'm Father Devlin, Father Devlin of Yen Do Street, when is the evacuation?" Whiskey Joe replied regularly:

"No instructions for now. Call back."

About seven Father Devlin called back desperately:

"Tell me, when the evacuation comes, how do I get to a helicopter emplacement? I'm in Yen Do Street; there's a curfew twenty-four hours out of the twenty-four; how can I move? Tell me what I should do!"

He got no answer. While the usual voice was speaking from the airport, we could hear a telephone ring on the radio. Then:

"Hello, Watanabe here, Japanese embassy. Any news on the evacuation?" Whiskey Joe told him to change frequency, and in the hotel the Americans and the others waiting to leave were worried.

There was panic when we heard the voice of Jacobson, the American embassy adviser, saying to Whiskey Joe:

"Pay close attention. Tell the ambassador to proceed toward Tan Son Nhut with extreme caution."

Was the evacuation already in progress? Was Ambassador Martin going and leaving the journalists behind?

The hotel switchboard was in total chaos. The old night clerk Annamalay, an Indian who even in his rare moments of sobriety had never succeeded in transferring a call from the desk to a room, had abandoned his post, leaving the task of inserting and pulling out the proper plugs for calling the embassy to an anxious group of colleagues.

Someone succeeded. No, the evacuation had not yet begun, nor was it yet decided on. Everyone should stay close by their radios. Martin, not trusting his collaborators, whom he had always accused of being defeatists and Cassandras, was putting on a final show of arrogance by going to Tan Son Nhut to take personal stock of the situation.

From the eight o'clock news bulletin we learned that President Ford had summoned an urgent meeting of the National Security Council for nine o'clock, Saigon time. There was nothing to do but wait. The telephone rang continuously. The callers were simple Vietnamese asking how to escape, newspaper colleagues in other hotels wanting to know what we knew, diplomats seeking out their fellow nationals to warn them to be ready.

While the hotel waiters were still folding up the cots on which they had slept as always, and putting on their white jackets—frayed but well pressed, with the initials CP, Continental Palace, in blue on the front—a nervous, frightened, excited group of guests assembled in the garden for breakfast.

Everyone in the bloodbath

Joseph, one of the old employees of the hotel, forty-five years in service but by occupation still simply "boy," with his twenty words of French and an absurd, out-sized pair of black pointed shoes left to him by some guest years before, shuffled among the tables taking orders for breakfast and explaining to his distraught customers that morning that there were no brioches and that they probably wouldn't arrive later either.

"Why not?" someone asked.

"Peut-être aujourd'hui c'est finir la guerre," he answered.

An American journalist with very broad shoulders, wearing a white jersey and sneakers, a former marine turned war correspondent for a Chicago daily, likewise went from table to table, taking the names of colleagues who wanted to leave.

For each hotel, the American embassy had named a group leader who would be responsible for the evacuation of foreign journalists. In case of emergency, the escape order would come to him, and he would lead the rush to the assembly point.

Many were undecided. Some were still entertaining the possibility of a ceasefire and a coalition government. An Englishman kept repeating:

"The Americans can't allow Giap's tanks to parade through Tu Do Street. These attacks are only a diversion. There must already be an agreement."

Fear and uncertainty made some people terribly loquacious, others silent and sweetly smiling.

"There'll probably be a single, total evacuation," said the

journalist and group leader, who had just spoken by telephone to someone in the embassy. "Anyone who doesn't give his name now runs the risk of being left in the lurch."

His list grew as breakfast went on.

For thousands and thousands of Vietnamese these were hours of terror. With the rockets falling on Tan Son Nhut they understood that they had lost their "ticket to salvation" forever.

The evacuation of persons thought to be on the "Vietcong blacklist" to refugee camps on Guam at the rate of seven thousand a day, was begun by the Americans barely a week before and now had to be discontinued. For hours no one had heard the roar of the giant United States Air Force C-141s, which had been landing and taking off in a continuous cycle over the past days and nights. The runways were impassable. For many people who had already sold all their possessions and organized every detail for their departure, this was equivalent, they believed, to a death sentence.

The bombardment by the five "Vietcong" A-37s the previous evening had turned Tan Son Nhut into a nightmare. Thousands of persons were encamped in the DAO mess-hall and gymnasium when the jets—which at first everyone took to be friendly—struck the buildings one by one. Hundreds of others, embarkation cards already in hand, were in the helicopter parking area.

The bombs fell, and some struck in the middle of the terrorized crowd loaded with baggage and children. It was a massacre. Two planes that were already on the departure line took off; a military plane rose with its doors still open and people running after it. More than five hundred people died in the slaughter.

The evacuation was suspended, but the survivors stayed on; they did not give up. For hours on end they stayed on the asphalt, amid corpses and shattered suitcases, their ears cocked in the darkness of the night, their eyes straining in the clear sky of dawn, waiting for another airplane that would come back to get them. It didn't come, and the rocket fire created new victims among the desperate.

The people of Saigon were so convinced in those days that the arrival of the Vietcong would mean a terrible massacre that they were ready to run any risk, carry out any sort of madness, in order to escape.

For months the Americans had been talking about the

great "bloodbath" that would take place in Saigon if the
Vietcong were to enter the capital. According to their calculations there would be between 150,000 and 200,000 victims of Communist reprisals.

The idea of the massacre was so widespread among the
population that it was not only officers of the ARVN,
the police who had collaborated with the "imperialists,"
and the soldiers who had fought against the Vietcong who
feared for their lives. Secretaries, clerks in American
agencies, bar girls, prostitutes who had lived on American
dollars, maids, cooks, drivers who had worked for American families, doctors, engineers, and young people who
had merely studied in the United States likewise felt themselves "marked."

The advance of Communist troops from the Central
Highlands to the coast, and from north to south, had been
accompanied by hair-raising rumors of wholesale slaughter
and revenge.

In Da Nang twelve South Vietnamese policemen were
marched naked through the streets and then beheaded
one by one; the Catholic bishop of Ban Me Thuot had
been captured by the Vietcong and cut in three pieces; the
father and rest of the family of the head of Thieu's palace
guard living in the Central Highlands had been impaled
and exhibited for days to the population. A bonze told of
having seen three hundred people beaten to death with
sticks on the market square of Ban Me Thuot. All Saigon
knew and repeated these stories.

No one would then have believed that the bishop would
arrive in the capital a few days later, free and all in one
piece; that there were three hundred dead in Ban Me
Thuot but that they had been victims of the aerial bombing ordered by Thieu after the liberation of the city; that
the relatives of Thieu's palace guardsman were safe and
sound, having themselves been the ones to start the rumor
so as to escape to Saigon more easily with all their money.

All these rumors were regularly confirmed by military
spokesmen in Saigon, and corroborated by Washington.

On April 16, James Schlesinger, Secretary of Defense,
had told Congress that at least 200,000 Vietnamese might
be killed in the event of a Communist victory. On the
18th, Colonel Robert Burke, a spokesman for the Pentagon, had declared that according to secret reports, bloody
reprisals were being carried out in Communist areas and
that the details of certain incidents were "horrifying."

On the same day, Kissinger, speaking before the House Committee for Emergency Aid, had said that in recently occupied areas in Vietnam, "We expect the Communists to try to eliminate all possible opponents. There will be a lot more than a dozen executions."

Stars and Stripes, the American armed forces newspaper in the Pacific, carried a resounding headline in one of the last issues to arrive in Saigon: "At Least a Million Vietnamese Will Be Slaughtered."

"It will be a hundred, a thousand times worse here than in Hué during the Tet offensive in '68," people in Saigon said — not knowing that many victims of the Communist "massacres" in the old imperial capital were actually caused by American bombing, and that many of the bodies filmed, photographed, and mourned in the common graves uncovered with such publicity when the city was retaken by American marines and Thieu's troops were Vietcong soldiers buried there alongside civilians by the retreating Communists.

The terror of a bloodbath had increased day by day as the war drew close to Saigon. At the time of the fall of Ban Me Thuot a girl in a travel agency in downtown Saigon, who wore her hair in a long black braid down her back, had asked me:

"Do you think the Communists will cut off my hair?"

Six weeks later that same girl and thousands of others like her were convinced that the Vietcong would pull out their fingernails one by one, simply because they were lacquered.

Women who had had children by the Americans were persuaded that the Communists would take the children and kill them, because this, it was said, was what had happened in all the areas they had occupied. After the Liberation I met two young mothers who were desperate because in the panic they had put their half-caste children on an orphan flight. They had counted on catching up with them later and finding them in the United States but had been left behind.

The capture of Phnom Penh by Khmer Rouge partisans on April 17, and the first vague and never confirmed stories of the massacres and violence that were said to have taken place in Cambodia, made the front pages of the Saigon newspapers for days, again giving the public an idea and new evidence of what was supposed to happen here, but on a much larger scale and in a more methodical way.

The people of Saigon were already imagining that, once the city had fallen, squads of Vietcong assassins would go from house to house with lists that had long been ready (so it was said) searching out victims for the firing squad. Everyone thought he knew at least one reason why it would happen to him.

"They'll kill me, I'm sure of it," a forty-year-old woman had told me in mid-March. In the past she had worked for two years as a switchboard operator in the Australian embassy.

Catholics were among the most terrified. It was said that those who had fled from the North in 1954 would be forced to retrace the same path in the opposite direction, on foot, through the jungle, along the Ho Chi Minh trail; it was said that girls would be obliged to marry the blind men, cripples, and disabled veterans of North Vietnam.

In the first weeks after the Liberation this rumor continued to circulate insistently, and the churches barely had time to celebrate the mass marriages of young girls who hastily took any husband at all so as not to find themselves pushing the wheelchair of "half a Vietcong."

The stories and rumors of massacres, the "bloodbath" theory was invented and spread by American propaganda and that of Thieu to discredit the enemy, to strengthen the spirit of resistance of the population and the South Vietnamese army, and to persuade a reluctant American Congress to appropriate new billions to save Vietnam—or at least the greatest number of Vietnamese—from the "Communist yoke." It ended up rebounding on the authors themselves, and became one of the factors that accelerated the rout, breakdown, and chaos in the South.

The Americans had had plans ready for some time for the evacuation not only of the entire American colony and their local relatives, but of all Vietnamese whose lives would be in danger once they fell into Vietcong hands, because of their activities as collaborationists.

The CIA section of the embassy had prepared enormous lists of persons, with varying priority depending on the danger each would be in: the first to be evacuated would be high officials, ministers in office or retirement, espionage agents, those in charge of the secret police, and anyone who had been involved in the Phoenix Program, which had been launched in 1968 to eliminate systematically from the cities and villages any person who was even suspected of having ties with the Front.

Then there were the lists of provincial leaders, district chiefs, senators, deputies, high officials of certain ministries, retired generals and diplomats, plus other lists of persons in one way or another connected with American policy in Vietnam.

The State Department had figured on a minimum of 130,000 persons to be evacuated. Other supplementary lists brought to 200,000 the number of Vietnamese whom it was indispensable to get out of the country if the United States was to keep its word to its "allies" that it had undertaken to fight the war for them.

The lists had long been ready, a whole fleet of airplanes allocated by the Pentagon, but Ambassador Martin in Saigon and Kissinger in Washington had steadfastly refused to give the signal for the operation, fearing that this would provoke the premature end of an already tottering regime.

When the Communist offensive began to pass from one success to another the embassy, while still not announcing the evacuation, sent away resident American families discreetly, without attracting undue attention.

"Every morning we discovered that another villa had been abandoned, that nothing was left in an apartment but furniture with empty drawers," I was told by a *tiba*, a cleaning woman, in a quarter inhabited chiefly by foreigners, near Mac Dinh Chi cemetery.

Defense Secretary Schlesinger wanted all "nonessential Americans" to be removed from Saigon as soon as possible whatever the cost, but Martin continued to say there was no such need and insisted that all American departures be in accordance with Vietnamese laws. For many who had local wives and children this meant paying up to two or three million piasters under the counter to obtain exit visas. Martin was so convinced — or wanted to convince others — that the situation was not precarious that he even refused to pack and ship his own furniture, china, and personal library.

Things speeded up with Thieu's resignation. The evacuation was officially announced, but instead of the seven thousand Americans thought to be still in Vietnam, the embassy was stormed by old deserters, businessmen, and pensioners whom no one had taken into account. Along with their families and Vietnamese relatives they came to another thirty-five thousand persons. Bureaucratic formalities were put aside and in the movie auditorium of the DAO complex, which had once been MACV (Military As-

sistance Command, Vietnam), headquarters of the United
States expeditionary force, embarkation cards were issued
at a steady pace for the "Freedom Birds," planes leaving
for Guam or the Philippines. To silence the Vietnamese
immigration authorities, the embassy promised that all airport guards and police would also be allowed to take refuge in the United States.

The evacuation started off accompanied by an anti-
Communist and humanitarian publicity campaign that was
supposed to camouflage the defeat and the American
flight. Hundreds of children, orphans or otherwise, were
loaded onto military planes taking off across the Pacific to
the United States. President Ford went to greet the first
planeload and have himself photographed on the ramp,
smiling and holding in his arms the first child "saved from
Communism."

There can be no doubts about the intentions of this ba-
bylift. On April 2, Dr. Phan Quang Dan, minister of social
affairs in Saigon, had written to his prime minister, Khiem:

> The departure of a considerable number of orphans will
> cause a profound emotion in the world, and especially in
> the United States, that will be all to the benefit of South
> Vietnam. The American ambassador will assist us in every
> way possible, since he himself is convinced that the evac-
> uation of hundreds of thousands of war victims will help to
> sway American public opinion in South Vietnam's favor.
> When the children arrive in the United States the press,
> television, and radio will give ample publicity to the matter
> and the impact will be enormous.

The Vietnamese themselves reacted in part with scorn
for this kidnapping operation. When a United States Air
Force Galaxy exploded in the air while taking off from
Tan Son Nhut, a disaster in which 206 of the orphans on
board lost their lives, a South Vietnamese official told the
New York Times correspondent who was at the airport at
the moment:

"Its nice to see you Americans taking home souvenirs of
our country as you leave—China elephants and orphans.
Too bad some of them broke today, but we have plenty
more."

According to American calculations, the evacuation was
to last until May 13. When however it became clear that it
might be interrupted much sooner, the embassy went over

its plans, revised the lists, and changed the priorities. Many persons who had received assurances and promises that they would be able to leave and had sold everything they possessed and exchanged their last piaster for dollars on the rising black market, found themselves ruined and abandoned.

An ex-colonel, who had worked for years in the office of the prime minister, told me what had happened to him:

"They had given me an address and an appointment. The instructions were precise: bring only one suitcase per person and only your very closest relatives.

"I went with my wife. It was a beautiful villa. I left my car in front of the door. An American received us, led us into the drawing room. There were other families. They gave us envelopes with all the documents and told us to wait. They would come to get us with a bus after dark. With the curfew and the streets deserted we would attract less attention.

"Toward midnight the American came back, saying that something had gone wrong, the schedule was changed. We had to go home. When I went out, my car wasn't there any more; someone had realized what was happening and had gone off with it."

I saw the colonel several times again after the Liberation. His greatest worry was that someone might find out he had tried to leave.

Gradually, as the days passed and the prospect of a "bloodbath" came nearer, the embarkation cards distributed to the Vietnamese by the American embassy became increasingly precious. By now there was a permanent and very long line of people at the embassy waving papers, certificates, and letters of recommendation. On the Saigon open market, which had always bought and sold everything, the cards rose from a thousand to two and three thousand dollars apiece.

A clerk at USIS (United States Information Service), instead of distributing the cards to the people in his department, sold them for fifteen hundred dollars each. He was unable to enjoy his small fortune however, because in order to stay in the business up to the last moment, he never made it to his plane.

General Cao Hao Hon, Thieu's palace adviser, obtained fifty places for his staff, but preferred to put them up for sale at one thousand dollars each.

At the beginning of the evacuation, an American who

wanted to take along one or more Vietnamese to whom he
was not related had to present the required documents
and sign affidavits; in the end it was enough to take them
with him to the right place at the right time.

When a marine at the DAO exit called for "Smith" to
embark, he was presented not only with the usual big
blond youth, but with a small crowd of Vietnamese
"Smiths" whom the American had simply declared to be
his relatives, and who filed up the ramp of the plane behind him. Some, in making these hasty declarations, ac-
knowledged people older than themselves as their
children.

The rumor spread in Saigon that every American could
take with him up to ten Vietnamese in this manner, and a
thriving market in desperation and fear began.

Former GIs who had remained in Vietnam as pimps,
failed contractors, bar managers, small drug pushers and
brothel owners repaid themselves in a few hours all the
dollars they had squandered in years of drunken nights in
the dark nightclubs of Saigon.

Well-to-do families who had not been able to escape in
any other way bought themselves "their American," who
would take them away for five to ten thousand dollars a
head.

My Linh, the madam of a small brothel near the Tran
Hung Dao monument, gave four thousand dollars to her
American "boy friend"; he told her to pack the suitcases
while he went to get the papers. He never came back. The
same thing happened to dozens of girls like her in the
various bars on Tu Do Street.

Others kept their word so as not to spoil the market for
themselves. One American was discovered and arrested at
the embassy while trying to obtain embarkation cards for
his "family." He had already shuttled three times between
Saigon and Guam, each trip netting him thousands of
dollars.

The owner of the "Giao Sport" shop in downtown Saigon was more fortunate. He found an American who for
six thousand dollars put him on a list of important CIA
agents. The Americans came to get him with a car and
took him under escort to Tan Son Nhut together with
other real agents.

Even Indonesians and Iranians on the International
Control Commission profited by the situation. On their last

planes out of Saigon on Sunday the 27th, they took the families of their local subordinates for three hundred dollars a head.

Fear of the Vietcong had made Saigon lose its wits. Panic, like fire left smoldering in a hayloft, had exploded and now clung to everyone. People spoke of nothing else; to get out had become an obsession.

Beggars in Tu Do Street used the new argument to arouse the pity of passersby. One of the orphan bootblacks who lived in the Eden passageway and who had "adopted" me, came up to me every day stretching out his hand and saying:

"Papa, you give me money, I go America."

As the hours went by, the fear of a "bloodbath" had begun to infiltrate even the group of journalists who on the morning of the 29th were having breakfast in the garden of the Continental under foliage heavy with white jasmine blossoms.

When I tried to explain to a British colleague that I had never shared the principles and policies of the Americans' intervention in Vietnam and therefore saw no reason now to share the risks and emotions of their flight, he said to me with surprise:

"But haven't you ever worked for the Americans? Haven't you ever shared your news with them?" He was one of the ones who left.

Weeks after the Liberation, the new authorities let it be known that, among the dossiers the Americans and South Vietnamese had not had time to destroy, they had found files on certain journalists who had "collaborated."

One of them, a former member of the Peace Corps who spoke Vietnamese well, had remained in Saigon. In his file they found a handwritten report by Tom Polgar, head of the Saigon CIA, covering his activities as an "informer," first in Thailand, later in Cambodia and Vietnam. Nothing happened to him. The Vietcong summoned him to the Foreign Ministry, where they told him he was an enemy of the Vietnamese people and that therefore he would have to leave. He protested, saying he didn't understand, and the official who had communicated the expulsion order to him said:

"Think about it. Go to America. Think back on everything you've done, read over what you've written, compare it with what you've seen, and then write to us, let us know. Maybe some day you'll be able to come back and we'll talk about it again."

Time went by and the radio continued to broadcast music; the announcement that Mother wanted you to call her at home didn't come.

The lobby of the hotel was filling up with frightened people, and Joseph came to say that there were some Vietnamese who were looking for an American.

"Who? What American?"

"An American, any one at all."

To whom it may concern

One had been the driver for an American colonel, one an interpreter with the Special Forces, one had worked as a file clerk. The others had similar stories.

There were six of them, tired and scared; in rudimentary English with a strong American accent picked up from the GIs, they asked for help. From inside their shirts they drew packets of documents in cellophane, letters with large American eagles, diplomas from American schools. The "interpreter," who later said he had actually been an interrogator of Vietcong prisoners for the Green Berets, had a "security clearance" certificate on a United States Defense Department letterhead. All of them had a standard letter addressed "to whom it may concern." It read:

"The bearer of this letter has served and fought under my command. He is a person who believes firmly in the values of democracy and the free world. If he should fall into Communist hands, his life would be in serious danger because of the services he has performed. You are urged to give him all possible help and assistance." There followed the scribbled signatures of high-ranking American officers.

The six men were between twenty-five and thirty years of age. They were strong, with plump, hard faces, but they showed us their letters with docile looks of hope and panic. Each of these letters could be a ticket to salvation or, a few hours later, a death sentence.

They had come from the American embassy, where they

had spent the night in the midst of the desperate crowd besieging the building. They had found no one who would listen to them. The marines were blocking all the entrances, and had stationed themselves with fixed bayonets along the white enclosure wall.

By now only Americans were allowed to enter. A few Vietnamese had also managed to get in, by putting rolls of hundred-dollar bills in the hands of the "incorruptible" leathernecks. The marines struck the empty hands of the others with their rifle butts as they clung to the railing or tried to climb the wall.

Some people rolled on the ground in fits of hysteria; some screamed the names of Americans, colonels, generals with whom they had been friends. Elegant women with large pieces of Samsonite luggage between their feet and children in their arms sobbed as if in a daze. There were officers in uniform who tried to get themselves recognized by someone on the other side of the railing and simple bar girls who had come only because they had once had a few American boy friends.

General Huynh Van Cao, a senator and one of Thieu's most faithful followers, wept impassively, with his wife holding onto his arm. The millionaire Le Trung Nghia, who had been an intimate of Westmoreland at the time of the great American war, tried to elbow his way through. Ngo Khac Tinh, Thieu's cousin and former minister of justice, was turned back when he had already reached the gate.

Seeing that they stood no chance, the six men had thought of the American journalists, who would surely take them along to the embassy.

"Sorry, very sorry," repeated my American colleagues, knowing the most they could take in the evacuation would be their typewriters and a small suitcase.

I discovered later that at that moment in Saigon thousands of persons were in search of a recipient for their to-whom-it-may-concern letters. In the course of their departure during the past few days, American military men, contractors, representatives of private firms, and officials had each signed dozens of similar pieces of paper as part of the process of discharging their subordinates, and in the hope that someone at the embassy would honor their recommendations.

But in the confusion of the final hours, among the orders and counterorders, the personal tragedies, disappointments, and professional failures, the embassy had lost its head. All promises went up in smoke.

The departing Americans forgot even their own last dead, the two marines killed at Gate 4 at Tan Son Nhut. Someone had taken them to the morgue in the Seventh Day Adventist Hospital, as the embassy had ordered, and they stayed there until the Vietcong began bringing in their own dead.

The Americans left behind 250 Filipinos who had worked for them; they abandoned 12 South Korean diplomats, a group of Chinese from the Taiwan embassy, and still worse, the whole staff of Lon Nol's Cambodian embassy, which had placed itself under American protection after the liberation of Phnom Penh.

It was the Vietcong who discreetly put many of these people on the first planes leaving Vietnam for Laos, in order to avoid the embarrassing choice of keeping them in prison or (in the case of the Cambodians) handing them over to the new Khmer Rouge government.

The story of "Radio Red Star" was typical of the mindless haste with which the last Americans abandoned Vietnam.

For years the CIA had been operating, at No. 7. Hong Tap Tu Street, a clandestine radio station that imitated the call letters, music, and language of Radio Giai Phong, the voice of the National Liberation Front, and transmitted on almost the same frequency. Its purpose was to create confusion in enemy ranks by spreading false news reports, interpolated with speeches by Vietcong leaders whose voices it imitated.

It was this broadcasting station, for instance, that had reported the death of General Giap in December 1972 under an American bombing of Haiphong, a story later taken up by the whole international press; it was this station which, after the fall of Da Nang and Hué, broadcast the news of a coup d'état in Hanoi, and of the withdrawal of three North Vietnamese divisions from the South in order to confront a Chinese invasion of North Vietnam. In April, Red Star had once again announced Giap's death, but this time only one Saigon daily, *Chin Luan,* had picked it up in its edition of the 27th.

The Americans had always employed their best agents and experts on the Communist world in this clandestine radio operation, and all South Vietnamese secret intelligence services were connected with it. In preparing its evacuation plan therefore, the Hong Tap Tu Street staff decided to remove the less important clerks and secretaries first and allow the others to keep working until the last moment. As a result only the secretaries got out. The files, the collections of documents, the lists of informers, and the best agents were left behind. Among them was the famous composer Pham Duy, who before putting himself at the disposal of the Americans had been a member of the resistance.

The rocket and artillery attack against Tan Son Nhut continued, and American jet planes were beginning to dart through the sky. Arriving from aircraft carriers off the coast, they were preparing to protect the air corridor through which evacuation helicopters would later pass.

At nine I telephoned the Italian embassy, which up until the previous evening had seemed determined to stay on, as did the French, Belgian, Swiss, and Japanese. Ambassador Rubino confirmed:

"We're staying, Terzani. We're staying."

By now Vietcong forces were attacking on all sides of the capital, and the roar of battle could be heard from every direction.

The population of the outlying quarters was fleeing toward the center of the city. People had begun to abandon their homes at dawn, especially around the airport. Cong Ly Avenue was now the backdrop for the classic Vietnamese scenes from which Saigon had so far always been spared: thousands and thousands of people running, dragging carts loaded with their belongings; men with mattresses on their shoulders; women with clusters of children; shouting, weeping, explosions.

The Saigon Military Command feared that what had caused the fall of Da Nang, Nha Trang, and other cities on the coast, would also happen here — that the refugees would carry the Vietcong along with them, and that the wave of refugees would spread panic. It had therefore ordered troops to block the entrance to the large thoroughfare leading to the center of the city.

The soldiers had set up a barrier at Yen Do Street. People pushed and hurled themselves against the barbed wire, while the troops held their machine guns by the barrel and swung them like cudgels; others fired in the air, over the heads of the fear-crazed crowd.

A French television crew trying to reach the airport to film the exploding ammunition dumps was stopped by some Saigon Rangers. Lined up against the wall, they barely had time to show their passports.

"If you'd been Americans, we would have shot you. They've made us fight this war for years and now they leave us here to get our throats cut by the Vietcong. Pigs!" the officer cursed.

Another group of journalists had managed to get through Vo Thanh Street to staff headquarters. The soldiers took away their cameras and whatever money they had.

From the roof of the Hotel Caravelle, which had become the crowded observation platform for the war, with all television cameras of the world pointing their lenses at the horizon, one could see that Saigon was doomed. A ring of black and white smoke from the explosions marked the city limits. The fighting at the Newport bridge could now be followed by the naked eye, as well as the puff of mortar shells fired at close range.

The Vietcong had already entered the Phulam radar station on the outskirts of Cholon. The curfew imposed the previous evening was still in effect, and below us the streets, squares, and gardens were deserted.

How much longer would it last?

The psychological war goes on

In headquarters, in barracks, in the offices of the General Staff and in the police stations, all they talked about at that moment was escaping. Escaping. Those who had not yet succeeded counted the number of missing colleagues, of empty desks. By now the list was very long.

General Cao Van Vien had left with his whole staff on the morning of the 28th. Marshal Nguyen Cao Ky, along with four hundred other officers, had sworn the previous Saturday not to leave the country. Three days later he had sent off his wife, and at dawn on the 29th someone who went to look for him found his villa at Tan Son Nhut empty.

Almost all the officers who lived in residences near the air base like Ky had succeeded in fleeing with the Americans.

Gone was former police chief General Loan, renowned for the photograph made during the Tet offensive that showed him firing a pistol into the head of a Vietcong prisoner whose hands were tied behind his back. Gone was Colonel Ngoan, airport chief of staff, along with 1,600,000 dollars. Gone was General Nguyen Van Manh, in charge of security, his suitcases full of gold.

Others, in the fear of being left behind by the Americans, had seized ten Air America helicopters parked on a landing pad and flown off toward the sea in search of the American fleet. The exact position of the aircraft carriers had been kept secret, and some of these helicopters ran out of fuel and disappeared beneath the waves.

All the higher cadres and many pilots of the South Vietnamese air force had also fled. The Americans, not wanting their sophisticated fighter bombers like the F-5E to fall into Vietcong hands, put their UTAPAO base in Thailand at the disposal of anyone wishing to land there. More than 150 jets were thus "saved," along with their crews.

Admiral Chung Tan Cang, former commandant of the Saigon region and later head of the navy, escaped.

General Ngo Quan Truong of the First Military Region, the man who had directed the flight from Da Nang from a ship and whom Thieu had placed under surveillance in Cong Hoa Hospital, probably with the intention of putting him on trial, was picked up with a helicopter by the Americans and taken away on the afternoon of the 28th.

General Phu, on the other hand, remained in bed with "nervous exhaustion." Three days later he was to commit suicide with a strong dose of Novakin, pills against malaria.

General Tran Van Don, Thieu's deputy prime minister, who had gone personally by helicopter to give the order for withdrawal at Phan Rang—mainly to make sure that his boat was ready to flee from Vung Tau—preferred at the last moment to entrust himself to the Americans.

The only group from which no one had yet deserted was the Psychological Warfare Command led by General Tran Van Trung. When on the 27th his officers suggested drawing up a general evacuation plan, Trung replied that everyone's duty was to stay and fight to the end:

"All you can do is send away your families." He himself had put his wife and two children on board an American plane.

Since the Psychological Warfare Command was located right next to the American embassy on Thong Nhat Avenue, they all perhaps hoped that they would be able to leave at the last moment with the Americans.

"As soon as I heard the rockets on Tan Son Nhut I went into the office, where I found Colonel Hien and Captain Anh. They had been there all night," Colonel Do Viet told me after the Liberation. He had been one of two military spokesmen—the other being Le Trung Hien—who for years had put forth from the press room podium the most outrageous fabrications about the progress of the war, enemy losses, and the victories of the ARVN. They called it a press conference, the journalists had dubbed it "the four o'clock follies."

After the American withdrawal two conferences were held: one in the morning and one in the afternoon. After the ceasefire, they were devoted to the denunciation and tally of "Communist violations," now risen to five- or six-digit figures.

The press conference was supposed to take place even that morning, April 29. It had been ordered by General Trung, and Colonel Hien said to Do Viet: "You take care of it this morning."

"I went, but no one was there, so I was spared the embarrassment. I had nothing to say; we had received no reports on military operations from outlying commands that morning, and I didn't even know exactly what was happening at Tan Son Nhut.

"When I went back to the office—and it was all I could do to get through the crowd milling in front of the American embassy—Hien and Anh were still there talking. There were also two photographers who had come to protest the theft of their cameras and money in the vicinity of Tan Son Nhut. I took care of them. I telephoned the headquarters of the Fifth Division. No one answered. I called the press office of the Chief of Staff, but no one answered there either.

"After several attempts, I finally got a certain Lieutenant Hoanh, but as soon as I began to explain the case, he said, 'Colonel, this is no time to bother about journalists, there's no one here any more,' and hung up."

The offices of the General Staff had been emptied, the phones rang in a void, the fans blew on abandoned papers. General Vinh Loc had agreed to succeed Cao Van Vien as chief of staff only so as to be in a better position to flee. On assuming the post, he made a speech, broadcast by radio to the troops, in which he said:

"Obey orders and don't run away like rats." Then he got on a plane and left, many other officers along with him. I met one who, while refusing to give me his name that day, said:

"It's certainly no honor to stay, but to leave is worse— it's dishonor." And he stayed.

"At eleven o'clock—"Do Viet went on to relate, "a telephone call came for Colonel Hien. I saw his face change from yellow to green. He said something to Captain Anh. I saw them both take some papers out of their desks, I saw them take off their uniforms and put on suits that they had in plastic bags. 'We're going to eat,' Hien told me. I never saw them again."

At National Police headquarters there was also great confusion. The cells were full of prisoners, some of whom had been under interrogation for months. The chief of police, General Nguyen Khac Binh, had left without even handing over his post, and no one knew what to do.

Binh had gone to the airport, escorted to the end by his bodyguards. Standing in front of the plane that was to fly him to Thailand he had taken some bundles of piasters out of a large briefcase to pay off his gorillas—but they, suddenly realizing that he did not intend to take them along, had turned their pistols on him. Binh had no choice but to take them all away with him.

When his successor, Trieu Quoc Manh, named by the new President Minh, arrived in his office, a delegation of policemen came to ask him what sort of evacuation plan he had. His only answer was to order them to free the prisoners held in central police headquarters.

"There are only a hundred," he was told by the officers, who reckoned perhaps on killing the other two hundred or bargaining with their lives.

Manh calmly convinced them that it was better to do as he said. Once he was sure all three hundred had been freed, he went back to General Minh and handed in his resignation. He had performed his most important task as chief of police.

President Minh

Minh, in his villa, could hear the rockets falling on the airport. After being sworn in on Monday, the general had returned home and summoned Vice President Huyen, Prime Minister Vu Van Mau, and his young collaborators for the following morning.

"We held a very modest meeting in General Minh's drawing room. It was a question of organizing the government, but most of all of letting the other side know that we wanted to negotiate," Huyen told me a week after the Liberation. "All of us had agreed to take power in order to move the country toward reconciliation, toward peace. We believed that negotiations were still possible, but we didn't know what the other side wanted of us. It seemed to me that the simplest thing would be to go and ask the PRG delegates who were at Camp Davis."

At eleven o'clock on the morning of the 29th, a jeep with four of Huyen's trusted associates, escorted by soldiers of Minh's guard, started out for Tan Son Nhut. The troops blocking Cong Ly Avenue and still holding at bay the wave of refugees trying to reach safety in the center of Saigon, let them through, but the Vietcong soldiers guarding Camp Davis would not even open the gate.

"What do you want?" asked a captain.

"We've come on behalf of Vice President Huyen. . . ."

"We have nothing to say to you. Our position is clear, our conditions are contained in the declaration of April 26. . . ."

The four men looked at each other in embarrassment. No one knew what the demands were—no one had seen this declaration.

Even Huyen and Minh were bewildered when the delegation brought back the message to the villa. One of the young assistants resolved the enigma:

"On the 26th they demanded the end of all American intervention in Vietnam and the dismantling of our army and the police."

Vu Van Mau picked up the telephone and called Ambassador Martin. The Government of the Republic of Vietnam asked the Americans—all Americans—to leave the country. Within twenty-four hours. It was noon of April 29.

The Americans had already decided to leave. Since

11:20 a.m. a line of black smoke had been rising from the chimneys of the building. They were burning secret documents.

Good-bye, America!

The password arrived on the roof of the Hotel Caravelle even before the radio began broadcasting the messages agreed upon and the voice of Bing Crosby intoned, "I'm dreaming of a white Christmas."

An American television reporter, the group leader responsible for the residents of the hotel, who was keeping in contact with the embassy by walkie-talkie, shouted, "We're going!" The words rebounded from floor to floor, crossed the square in front of the Assembly building like a flash, and reached the Continental.

There was chaos in the two hotels. There was the slamming of doors, the calling out to one another and shouting in the hallways, the dragging of suitcases, and running, running. The fear of those who were leaving dissolved. That of those remaining curdled, became sharper. I came to understand the mechanism of panic. My neighbor next door left, the one across the hall left; it seemed to me that everyone was leaving, and for a moment I too thought of fleeing.

There in the noonday sun on silent, deserted Tu Do Street the hurried parade began: American journalists, officials, businessmen, and contractors carrying their suitcases or packages as they streamed toward the assembly points. The cashier of the Caravelle went running after two of them who in the confusion had forgotten to pay their bills. Joseph and the other waiters at the Continental had gone out on the sidewalk; from the windows the Vietnamese, incredulous, astonished, but also terrified, looked on. If the Americans were leaving it was really the end. The end. What would happen now?

The flight of the Americans was pathetic, frightening, and we who followed it from afar held our breath. The Vietcong, who by now were on the outskirts of the city and were known to have infiltrated some thousands of sabo-

teurs everywhere, could have bombarded the assembly
points and landing pads with their mortars, could have
easily brought down the helicopters with their "Strella"
missiles as they lifted off. They did not. Partisan troops did
not fire a single shot against the helicopters for as long as
the evacuation lasted.

But more frightening still than enemy hatred was the
rage, despair, and frustration of the "friends" who felt
themselves betrayed and abandoned. The old, latent anti-
Americanism of the Vietnamese "allies" might have burst
forth suddenly and dreadfully at any moment.

A group of ARVN soldiers fanned a few machine-gun
blasts at the first busloads of people going toward Tan Son
Nhut, but the American marines escorting the convoy dispersed them. These were isolated incidents; the spark that
might have provoked a massacre did not ignite.

All the weight, danger, and responsibility for a doubly
mistaken policy fell suddenly on these last escaping Americans. Ten years ago it had been intervention, now it was
abandonment. Suddenly the mere fact of being an American in Vietnam became a sin, like being a German in the
presence of a Jew, and we who stayed behind rushed to
make little flags for ourselves out of pieces of cloth with
the colors of our countries, to wear on our shirts or display
on the windshields of our cars.

Among those leaving were some who had not shared
their country's policy. They had criticized the war, had had
nothing to do with the American government in Vietnam,
did not believe in the "bloodbath," and had decided at first
to stay on.

These representatives of the American press, who in the
past had played an important role in shifting public opinion in their country away from narrow-minded reactionary
positions, were still in Saigon on the morning of April 29.
Among them were H. David Greenway of the *Washington
Post,* Loren Jenkins of *Newsweek,* and Malcolm Browne of
the *New York Times,* who by 1965 had already exposed "the
new face of war" in a book of that title. There was photographer Mark Godfrey of the *Magnum Agency,* who like the
others had risked his life dozens of times to go to the battlefields in search of the truth of the conflict, which certainly did not emerge from the communiqués and official
photos. They too left. Someone at the embassy had persuaded them that the departure of "all" Americans was a
condition for avoiding the battle of Saigon. In reality, Mar-

tin did not wish to leave behind too many witnesses of what was going to happen, of what was to give the lie to all his daydreams. Washington had turned the page on Vietnam.

Once again I telephoned Ambassador Rubino.

"We're leaving," he said, embarrassed. "I'm not much convinced, but the Ministry has given us carte blanche."

The flight was precipitous. Papers, photographs, and the documents of an Italian who had asked to marry the Vietnamese woman with whom he had lived for years in order to take her out of the country remained in disorder on the first secretary's desk. The personnel of the Italian mission waited for hours in the sun at No. 192 Cong Ly Avenue before the Americans finally came to pick them up along with a group of Vietnamese.

The news of the total American evacuation shook the city. No one bothered any longer to respect the curfew that had been imposed the previous evening. On Tu Do Street cars began to pass loaded with people and baggage, military jeeps driven by officials in civilian clothes with their families, motorcycles carrying four and five persons.

All were on their way to the waterfront, in search of a ship, a boat, anything that floated and that would take them away.

The waterfront military police had thrown up a barrier at the Hotel Majestic. For a while the troops held fast by firing over the heads of the crowd; then they saw that people were getting through anyway, that hundreds of their colleagues were piling onto moored motor launches behind them, and they fell in with the surging crowd and ran toward the pier.

Two white cars from the International Red Cross, with large fluttering flags, crossed the center of the city, and the Swiss representatives made the rounds of the hotels to announce to foreign guests that they were making Red Cross Headquarters a neutral area where anyone who wanted could come take shelter.

In the international community only the French were organized. They had reserves of water and rice in their embassy, and the Grall Hospital, which they ran, was equipped to take care of some hundreds of refugees in the event of a siege lasting days or weeks.

The other foreigners—Chinese, Koreans, Japanese, and Europeans—were abandoned to themselves, and their great fear was that if the Vietcong did not attack and take the city in a hurry, disbanded troops of the ARVN would (as had already happened in Da Nang and other cities) put

Saigon to fire and sword, pillaging the residential quarters, looting the stores, and indiscriminately killing anyone they found in their path. The hunt for the foreigner would begin. The Continental and the Caravelle were symbols of the wealth and prosperity of the Americans, the whites, and might well be among the first objectives of such reckless bands in a city under cannon fire and fallen into anarchy.

The Red Cross is situated at the end of Hong Tap Tu Street. The Vietnamese section is on one side of the street at No. 201; on the other, at No. 406, is the headquarters of the International Committee. There was a great bustling of people coming and going around the two offices. Men were unloading from trucks large sacks of rice to be distributed in case of siege; groups of youths in white shirts with Red Cross armbands practiced removing and putting back stretchers in a dozen ambulances that had been readied to collect the city's wounded. A medical captain of the ARVN arrived in a jeep. Obsequiously, helmet in hand, he introduced himself to the Swiss representative.

"You must save me. You must hide me here with the rest of my family; we haven't been able to get away; we're all in danger of being killed; you must help us get away; we want to go to France. . . ." He was the son of the owner of the Hotel Miramar. "We're rich, we can pay."

The telephone rang continually. Other officials called, other people asking for help, asking to be protected.

A senator demanded that a Red Cross car come and pick him up at his home because the Vietcong in his quarter would kill him.

The medical captain insisted, he wanted guarantees, he wanted to hide with the Red Cross, and the Swiss representative lost patience and burst out:

"We're not here to evacuate people. . . . When it's all over, I'll give the list of those who've taken shelter here to the authorities, the new authorities. . . ."

"And what if they're the Vietcong?" asked the captain.

"Then I'll give it to them!"

"But do you guarantee. . . ?"

"All I can guarantee you is that here there will be no summary executions, no one will be killed without a regular trial. . . ."

The medical captain departed. Already he could see himself before a people's court.

I wanted to go back to the center of the city, so I went

out onto the street to find a lift. No one stopped. People on motorcycles passed in a hurry, bent double to make themselves as small as possible, as though sheltering themselves from the rain. Cars honking their horns madly and jeeps with their headlights on sped along toward Cholon; later I saw them go by again in the opposite direction. They were trying to leave Saigon by Highway 4 toward the Delta, but it too was occupied by the Vietcong a few kilometers away. So they came back in search of another way out. There was none.

Highway 1 was cut, as well as the road for Bien Hoa. The way to the sea had been cut off the night before. It was now impossible to get to Vung Tau. Saigon was a trap, closed, blocked, besieged. When would they get here?

Finally a man of about thirty, in civilian clothes, with dark glasses and a red cap, stopped his Honda for me.

"Are you going toward the center?"

He answered yes, but added that we would have to go by way of the market, because at the beginning of Hong Tap Tu Street army deserters were stopping traffic, robbing passersby, and taking automobiles.

The sky had clouded over, it was about to rain, and the city had a funereal look. We went through a working-class neighborhood, through narrow streets, swerving to avoid heaps of garbage that now no one bothered to remove. Standing in doorways or in groups on the sidewalk, people looked at me with curiosity. Some pointed at me and laughed. Someone yelled, *"My, My"* (American, American); a boy ran after the motorcycle and threw a stone.

"Don't worry, I have a pistol," said my driver, and he made me feel the bulge under his shirt on the right side. He was a policeman; he had thrown away his uniform.

"Where are we going? To the embassy?"

"No," I answered. "To the Hotel Continental."

He was almost ready to shoot me. He had taken me for an American and had picked me up with the sole thought that by joining me he would be able to save himself.

The actual evacuation began at three in the afternoon.

The "Jolly Green Giants," marine helicopters arriving from aircraft carriers, alighted on the DAO landing pads, took on the first groups, and lifted off heavily from the ground. Smaller helicopters descended on the roof of the embassy, stayed three or four minutes, and then left.

The black and gray helicopters of Air America, the company financed by the CIA, went to other parts of the city to pick up the last "important Vietnamese" with their families.

The men who had organized the evacuation had chosen high buildings with roof terraces or some elevated structure, a water tank for instance, on which the helicopters could alight. The addresses had been kept secret, but by now they were well-known not only to those who were supposed to leave.

From the top of the Caravelle you could see clusters of people here and there on the roofs fighting and pushing their way up iron stairs that led upward to these improvised landing places: so many stairways to the sky, all loaded with people.

Some had paid fabulous sums in the last hours to be on those helicopters; some had simply given a thousand-piaster tip to the doorman of the building and asked him to show them the way to the roof.

About five in the afternoon Martin emerged from the American embassy with a group of marines forming a circle around him, and went on foot to say good-bye to the French ambassador, Merillon.

"He didn't want to leave. He would have stayed to the end, he would have stayed in the city to wait for the Vietcong, if that was what had to happen," Merillon told me later. "Martin left because the State Department ordered him to leave."

The meeting between the two was brief. They no longer had much to say to each other. What they had worked for—a solution that would not give the Vietcong everything they were now about to take—had not been achieved. Both had failed utterly. For Merillon it was a political, professional matter; for Martin it was something personal as well.

He had come to Vietnam at the end of his career ("I accepted because I felt it to be a mission," he had told me in the course of a long conversation in January). His son had been in the army and was killed by the Vietcong, and he had come to carry on his war. An anti-Communist in the style of the 1950s—"the last of the cold warriors," one of his colleagues had called him—he had come here with the belief that the weight of American power could keep the South from falling into the hands of the "reds," as he called them. He had been defeated.

Still on foot, he went from the French embassy to his house, a short distance away. He left everything behind — furniture, prints, books — and took only a suitcase and his dog.

He went back to the embassy, and from his huge office with its yellow wall-to-wall carpeting he took the American flag that he kept beside his desk, folded it up, and put it in a paper bag. Then he went up on the roof, and a helicopter carried him away.

The scene was a repetition. Two weeks before, John Gunther Dean, his colleague in Phnom Penh, had left in the same way, with the flag under his arm, escorted by marines who pointed their machine guns at a crowd of terrified Cambodians: both men ambassadors of a great power who were now reduced to the role of false medieval heroes, swept away by history.

Of all the empires that had faded out in Indochina, the one attempted by the Americans ended the most indifferently, with neither form nor style. The French, beaten, had left Hanoi in 1954. On the Doumer bridge, which crosses the Red River, the disarmed officers and men of the expeditionary corps filed in front of the Vietminh troops entering the city. A Communist soldier kicked a French officer in his ass. The latter turned and gave a military salute. The Vietminh returned the salute by raising their hands to their foliage-covered helmets.

Martin and the Americans left equally defeated, but without receiving any military honors. The American dream ended with the roar of the big flying machines that were to have pacified this country of Asian rebels and which instead served only to carry their supposed pacifiers to safety.

The Americans! They had wanted to annihilate a revolutionary movement, but instead they nourished it. They had come to put things in order and they left them in chaos. They had come to build and had destroyed. They had come to protect a people who they said had been attacked and they went away protecting only themselves from these very same "friends."

Ten years of tragedy for nothing.

Dollars to the people

The departure of the Americans unleashed pillage.

It began in the early afternoon with neighbors entering abandoned houses to poke around, with someone taking a chair, another struggling to load an air conditioner on a motorcycle.

In a flash it became an orgy of people opening drawers, ripping down curtains, emptying refrigerators, taking sheets, blankets, dishes. The whole city was turned upside down. The Americans had hardly left before their houses, apartments, villas, and offices were invaded, devastated, gutted.

The dwellings of Vietnamese who had fled suffered the same fate. Pictures, rugs, television sets, radios, sewing machines, typewriters, tables, clocks, and stereo equipment, all were carried away; fans, chandeliers, and even electric wires were ripped from the ceilings and walls.

From the PX, the emporium "for Americans only," came merchandise still in its shipping cartons, carried out on people's shoulders: cases of whiskey, soap, batteries, crackers. . . .

From the slums, from the buzzing and squalid hovels of Khanh Hoi, came breathless, seething groups of barefoot, ragged people, running to the center of the city. Some realized that their hands alone would be insufficient and hurried back to get carts and small wagons.

It began like a spontaneous popular celebration and ended in a macabre division of spoils. From time to time, amid the shouting, laughing, and cursing, shots could be heard.

On Hai Ba Trung Street, I saw a man's corpse, a bullet in the chest, lying in the middle of a pile of empty cardboard boxes.

On Lam Son Square, in front of Brinks, the abandoned residence of unmarried American officers, thousands of persons pushed and trampled each other to get through the narrow gate of the building. By now it had been stripped room by room, down to the last nail, by a triumphant crowd that appeared at the windows to show its trophies and throw down from the upper floors anything it was unable to transport by the stairs. Many contented themselves with pawing through the heaps of scraps and broken pieces.

It was an impressive show of rage, frenzy, and joy by people bent on plunder.

I saw children who fell down trying to drag away cases of beer that were too heavy for them, and pairs of policemen who helped each other to transport air conditioners. I saw women walk away with enormous sides of frozen meat, still wrapped in white butcher's gauze, from the deep-freeze storage rooms of the building; I saw a cripple scoot away on his little wheeled cart with a roll of blue carpeting over the stumps of his legs, and a uniformed army colonel on a motorcycle with his wife on the back seat holding a velvet-covered armchair.

"At last American aid reaches the people," said Cao Giao.

In the drizzly sky, the deafening dance of American helicopters shuttling between the embassy and other assembly points continued. Higher up, to provide protection, "Cobra" helicopters circled with machine guns.

I made a brief tour of the city and everywhere I saw the same scene. Streets were littered with trash, old newspapers, photographs, and letters that people threw from the windows of looted houses or emptied from the drawers of the furniture they dragged away on their backs. Cars went by loaded with mattresses, tables, and dismantled beds.

On Tran Hung Dao Street a convoy of military trucks passed at top speed, headlights on, loaded with sacks of rice: an officer was on his way to sell his battalion's supplies to Chinese receivers in Cholon.

In certain sections around Le Van Duyet Street, looters had also begun to attack the shops and houses of rich Vietnamese, the homes of government officials. Some well-to-do families hastily abandoned their dwellings to take refuge in other parts of the city.

The only policemen I saw in the whole city were those who, pistol holsters open, were claiming their share of plunder in the middle of the throng of other looters, or rushing away on their Hondas loaded with merchandise.

Like a puppet no longer supported by its strings, the whole government apparatus of Saigon was collapsing. There was no order, no army, no authority other than that of the guns and weapons that many, a great many still had and were using.

The city that evening of April 29 was a chaotic mass of people robbing, fleeing, or fighting for a place on the stairways to the sky as they waited for the helicopters.

Come, brothers

At 5:30 on that confused and fearful afternoon of April
29, a car emerged from the villa at No. 3 Tran Quy Cap
Street, turned left on Cong Ly Avenue, and drove full
speed toward Tan Son Nhut Airport.

The three men inside, however, were not fleeing. They
were representatives of the Third Force on their way to
ask the PRG delegation at Camp Davis what they could do
to avoid the battle, the destruction of the city, and the
thousands and thousands of victims that would result, now
that an attack on Saigon seemed imminent.

They were the lawyer Tran Ngoc Lieng, imprisoned by
Thieu and released just three days before; Professor Chau
Tam Luan; and Chan Tin, the Redemptorist priest who
for years had been devoting himself to political prisoners,
and in Thieu's last months had led street demonstrations
for peace and the application of the Paris Accords.

In their pockets the three carried a pass signed by President Minh to get them through the roadblocks that the
ARVN had erected along the way. But no one stopped
them.

In Minh's villa, the whole day had been spent discussing
the formation of the government and the possible participation of the Third Force. But the situation had not improved a bit from the previous evening, when the general
had had to present himself at the palace without the complete list of his ministers.

The problem was simple: the Third Force did not know
what to do. Up until the week before, neutralist elements
of this third component had been ready to participate in a
government under Minh. Men who claimed to belong to
the PRG in Saigon had suggested this solution, and General Minh had had assurances from French Ambassador
Merillon that the PRG would accept a government of his
with the Third Force included as a participant in the negotiations for a settlement of the crisis.

Then there had been the interminable week of Huong's
presidency, supported by the Americans. The situation
had rapidly changed, the PRG's position had stiffened, and
the Vietcong radio had called the new government "the
Minh-Huyen-Mau clique."

"By succeeding Huong, General Minh becomes the First
Force, not the Third," said some neutralists who, now
afraid of getting burned by joining a government that like

all previous ones was called "puppet" by the Vietcong, preferred at the moment to remain outside.

Others instead were still prepared to collaborate with the general, but wished to contact the PRG in order to ask for time and to ascertain Communist intentions.

This is what they had been discussing in Minh's villa when at five o'clock Father Chan Tin arrived to ask the new president for a written permit to go free the political prisoners in Saigon jails.

Minh had suggested instead that he accompany the two other representatives of the Third Force to Camp Davis to speak with the Vietcong. The three agreed to go.

"Tan Son Nhut looked deserted. We saw only a very few ARVN soldiers," Father Chan Tin told me a few days later. "Only in the area of the DAO was there great confusion.

"The American marines had set up a defense perimeter all around the building and helicopters were coming down on a landing pad. We heard the sound of incoming mortar shells, and huge columns of smoke were rising from the runways and exploding fuel dumps. . . .

"We asked the PRG officer who came to receive us at the gate of Camp Davis to speak to Colonel Vo Dong Giang; we were coming in a personal capacity, and not as a delegation from Minh."

The Vietcong let them in. Giang and the three had never met before, but they knew each other by reputation. In recognition of his work on behalf of political prisoners, Colonel Giang had sent Chan Tin a small lacquer from Hanoi on the occasion of Tet.

"I know that you come as friends, and for this reason I welcome you. The official delegation has already been here," said Giang. And as he shook their hands and accompanied them hastily toward a bunker, he called them "brothers."

"We're sure that Saigon is about to be attacked. What can we do to prevent a massacre in the capital?" asked lawyer Lieng.

"We've stated our conditions and Saigon has not replied. The order to attack has already been given. It's up to Minh to see the situation clearly. It's not a question of surrendering, but of accepting the outcome of this great struggle of the Vietnamese people against foreign domination.

"Minh should not order the troops to resist, as he has

done; by now he should allow our two armies to shake hands and embrace. There are no more victors or vanquished. It is the Vietnamese people, all the Vietnamese people, who have won, and America, only America, that has lost," said Giang.

As they spoke, a salvo of Communist rockets fell very close to the camp, and the four of them went to take shelter in one of the underground tunnels that had been secretly dug on previous nights.

The conversation continued for another half hour, after which Chan Tin and the others wanted to go back and tell Minh to declare Saigon an open city. But Giang advised them to remain. The airport was under fire; to reenter the city would have been extremely dangerous.

The Camp Davis telephone lines were cut. There was no longer any way to communicate with the villa in Tran Quy Cap Street. Minh waited in vain for his three informal emissaries to give him word of what was happening.

"Giang asked us to stay. For supper we ate dry rice biscuits," Chan Tin told me later. "We spent the whole night in the tunnel. After every artillery salvo there were long periods of silence.

" 'Now our soldiers are advancing,' Giang explained to us.

"We weren't able to sleep a wink. We stayed there all night pressed close to the ground, talking and getting to know each other, but above all hoping that the end would come soon."

The night of the helicopters

Terrible and blood-chilling, night fell on a city in the grip of apprehension and fear, on thousands and thousands of people who felt themselves caught in a trap, who fully expected to be massacred at dawn.

It was known that the Communists had brought their deadly 130-millimeter cannons within a radius of ten kilometers. When these began firing Saigon would become a slaughterhouse, and they were expected to begin from one moment to the next. There was a rumor that the Vietcong had stockpiled 300,000 rounds for the capital.

At eight o'clock Radio Saigon, now under the control of Minh's followers, no longer spoke of "Vietcong" in delivering the news. The announcer said:

"This morning our brothers on the other side attacked the airport of Tan Son Nhut. . . . Our brothers on the other side are now attacking on all fronts. . . ."

Was there still a glimmer of hope for negotiations?

The sky was overcast. Toward nine o'clock it began to rain. There was no electric light and the city was plunged in gloomy darkness. From the windows of the ninth floor of the Caravelle—where journalists, Chinese from Hong Kong and rich Vietnamese who had taken refuge in the hotel ate by candlelight an excited and noisy supper served by impeccable waiters in jackets and black bow ties—one could see from time to time the red flames of sudden explosions in the direction of the airport.

People said these were special squads of American saboteurs come to destroy South Vietnamese air force jets that had not succeeded in leaving for Thailand and that were not to be allowed to fall into the hands of the approaching Communist troops.

In these brief flashes of light one could discern on the roof of the American embassy the black shapes of people scurrying under the rotating blades to board the helicopters.

The evacuation was continuing. All night the sky's black void was punctuated by the intermittent red lights of these strange birds of prey that lowered themselves slowly onto the roofs, oriented themselves by throwing a long white ray of light at intervals from their single eye, alighted for four or five minutes, then slipped away loaded with people, taking pains each time to avoid the tall radio antenna above the post-office building and the two pointed bell-towers of the cathedral.

It was an obsessive, deafening dance of macabre monsters, ghosts of the past, last specimens from a prehistory that was about to be swept away.

Bands of wandering, drunken soldiers circulated with machine guns through the deserted streets of the city, in search of a way to escape or another bar to loot.

In front of the Hotel Majestic, which the night clerks had bolted shut for fear of attack, an American guest was locked out for the whole night: he had been delayed because he had wanted to go to his room and get his passport before leaving from the embassy. As company he had an ARVN colonel who kept a pistol trained on him, repeating:

"Either we're saved together or we die together." They both stayed in Saigon.

The students at Van Hanh University, after listening to the evening news broadcasts from Radio Hanoi and the Front, were convinced that the final attack on the city was imminent and decided to stay in the buildings. There were about a hundred of them. They divided the few weapons they had among themselves and set up guard shifts at the two main entrances.

In outlying sections of the city where they had infiltrated in recent days, groups of guerrillas emerged from the friendly houses that had hidden them and went to occupy certain selected police stations, neutralize self-defense units, and protect the bridges on the principal roads leading into the city.

"We took the barracks on Dong Binh Street with only a megaphone," Cao Giao's brother recalled after the Liberation. He was a member of one of these commando units in the seventh sector of the city.

"There were only eleven of us, but in the dark we made the puppets believe that we outnumbered them, and so they surrendered without firing a shot."

In the clandestine cells of the Front, political cadres prepared for a "popular insurrection."

Thousands of red and blue flags with a gold star in the middle were prepared or taken from secret storerooms and distributed to members of the local revolutionary committees.

In many neighborhoods, young people in self-defense groups were persuaded to surrender and hand over their weapons.

Saigon was unaware of it, but from the General Mobile Command of the Liberation Forces, situated that night north of Bien Hoa, General Tran Van Tra had given the order to his troops to march on the capital, and under cover of darkness the various units were moving to occupy the positions from which they would make their final assault in the morning.

April 30

A deafening silence

Day came suddenly, but the terrors of the night did not vanish.

In the livid light of dawn Saigon was a ghost city. Huge gray clouds rolled slowly over the silent extension of houses, buildings, monuments, and hovels, and were lost in the limpid remoteness of the sea that no one could reach any longer.

It was as though an unforeseen pestilence had swept away three million inhabitants. Large rats scoured through piles of sweetish, putrid garbage on the sidewalks. Every so often a jeep full of soldiers crept along the wet pavement of the broad avenues, their rifles leveled at the shuttered stores, the bolted doors and windows. Gusts of wind raised eddies of waste paper and scattered packets of documents, newspapers, and letters left on the streets by the looters.

Only around the American embassy was there still turmoil. At 7:30 the marines standing guard at the outside wall retired, in battle formation, their bayonets pointed at a desperate crowd of Vietnamese who were now climbing over the gate, invading the lawn, and bursting with shouts into the building to rob and destroy. The retreating marines ran along the roof, firing tear gas into the stairwells. Other marines went to the safe, sprinkled a can of gasoline on the piles of hundred-dollar bills constituting the funds of the embassy, and set them on fire.

The crowd had arrived at the third floor. Furniture, filing cabinets, and desks were overturned. Everyone tore out what he could. Policemen from the nearby station pushed through the crowd and went to the safe; they put out the fire and carried away armfuls of dollars. Others ran out carrying pictures of presidents, typewriters, curtains, armchairs, and air conditioners.

On the floor of the lobby, near the plaque commemorating the marines who had died defending the embassy during the Tet offensive, lay a sentence from Lawrence of Arabia that American military advisers loved to recite and which someone in the embassy had had framed:

"It is better that they do it imperfectly than that you do

it perfectly. For it is their war and their country and your time here is limited."

At 7:45 a green helicopter alighted on the roof. The last eleven marines flung themselves through the open doors and the helicopter lifted off.

Tongues of flame emerged from the loopholes of the modern fortress building, now enveloped in a pink and black cloud of smoke and tear gas.

From a nearby house at the lower end of Thong Nhat Avenue, ARVN soldiers discharged their rage and their machine guns at the iron belly hovering in the gray sky. The helicopter swerved abruptly and they missed it. The sound of the churning blades dissolved in the damp sultry morning air, and a moment later the helicopter was a diminishing speck on the horizon. It was the last. The last.

A despairing silence fell on the city.

At the embassy a rumor spread that the marines had placed dynamite charges in the cellars, and the mob of thieves, policemen, looters, and would-be fugitives dispersed leaving only stripped machines, furniture, bookshelves — like jackals scampering away from a carcass.

Groups of people, still clustered on stairways to the sky, continued to wait, listening for the now impossible hum of a distant engine. Then these knots of heads and bodies broke up; people sadly descended the stairs and disappeared over the rooftops.

The silence had become deafening.

Stand by for an announcement

Two hundred yards beyond the American embassy, on the other side of Thong Nhat Avenue, General Minh and Vu Van Mau were meeting in the Prime Minister's office with their associates when an ARVN officer brought the news that the evacuation was over.

"It's time to make the announcement," said Ly Qui Chung.

Since the previous evening the young information minister had been upholding the idea of declaring an unconditional surrender, but General Minh was opposed, insisting instead that the list of ministers be completed so that he could announce it that day. Discussion continued over the two plans of action.

At Van Hanh University, the students who had occupied the buildings had reexamined the rapidly changing situation and decided to alter the name of their committee.

For "Buddhist Students" they substituted "Patriotic Buddhists." Two hours later they changed it again to "Revolutionary Committee," and with this name as their heading they began to mimeograph hundreds of sheets that would serve as permits to circulate in the city, and as identification documents for ARVN soldiers whom they would persuade to surrender.

The leader of the students, Nguyen Huu Thai, had spent the night in the house of a friend, along with the political cadre who was the Front's liaison man with the university. At seven o'clock in the morning he had driven alone on a Honda to the An Quang pagoda.

"To avoid a battle in Saigon it was necessary that Minh declare surrender, and the only man who could persuade him was venerable Tri Quang," Thai told me some days later. "The Buddhists wanted to avert a bloodbath in Saigon at all costs. In the final week they had tried to contact the Front for assurances that the neutrality of ten Buddhist centers, where the faithful would assemble, would be respected during the fighting, but they got no answer. Trich Tri Quang agreed to intercede with Minh and telephoned him."

Minh hesitated; he said that if he surrendered too many people would condemn him, that Saigon would really run the risk of a massacre, since many ARVN units would disobey orders and barricade themselves in the capital.

Minh handed the phone to Vu Van Mau. Trich Tri Quang and the senator who had become prime minister two days ago had known each other for a long time, and for years Mau had been the An Quang pagoda's political man.

Mau said he was ready to surrender; all he asked was that the Front accept two conditions:

1) that certain persons in the government be allowed to leave the country (who and how many was not specified);

2) that field commanders of the two armies meet to set up the procedures for surrender.

"I was following the conversation on the telephone," Thai went on, "and I told Trich Tri Quang this was impossible now. The attack on Saigon had begun, and at best

I could get in touch with a representative of the Front around noon. That would be too late."

The venerable Buddhist explained the situation, and Mau repeated it to General Minh, who seemed convinced.

"Certainly there's no longer any way to contact the other side. The delegation I sent yesterday afternoon hasn't come back," he said.

While Thai was on his way back to Van Hanh, Minh and the others in the prime minister's office set to work preparing a statement.

At nine o'clock Radio Saigon announced:

"Citizens, stand by. The president will shortly deliver an important speech."

From the top of the Caravelle I looked out over a deserted, motionless Saigon. Time passed with exasperating slowness. At 10:20 I saw the hotel staff gather around the radio; I recognized the slow, awkward voice of General Minh, but the only words I understood were those of a waiter:

"*C'est fini! C'est fini!*" he shouted at me. The president was saying:

"I believe firmly in reconciliation among Vietnamese. To avoid needless bloodshed, I ask all soldiers of the Republic to put an end to all hostilities and remain where they are. The Military Command is ready to make contact with the Army Command of the Provisional Revolutionary Government to achieve a ceasefire. I furthermore ask our brothers of the Provisional Revolutionary Government to cease hostilities on their side. We are waiting here for their representatives to come and discuss an orderly transfer of powers."

After recording the speech in the prime minister's office, Minh had gone with all members of his government to Doc Lap Palace.

The surrender broadcast had been delayed for five minutes because at 9:50, just as Minh was about to send one of his officers to the radio station with the recording, General Vanuxem, that relic of colonial France, had arrived. Once again he tried to persuade the president not to surrender, but to launch an appeal to the Chinese and Russians to intervene. Minh had listened to him, then saying, "All right, all right," had ordered the officer to leave.

The Saigon I saw from the roof of the Caravelle did not react. It still lay there, silent and motionless as before.

Barefoot soldiers passed on Tu Do Street, with rifles on their backs and sacks full of goods on their shoulders. A group of paratroopers, dismayed and insolent, sat down in the empty armchairs on the terrace of the Continental.

Then I saw a policeman walking erect toward Thieu's monstrous Monument to the Unknown Soldier, in front of the white palace of the National Assembly. I saw him stand at attention, take his pistol from its holster, and fire a bullet into his temple. He lay there in a pool of blood, alone, for a few minutes. Then a soldier on a motorcycle stopped, took the pistol, and drove off; another took his watch.

Announcement of the surrender dissolved the army.

Front-line ARVN units emerged from blockhouses and trenches, abandoned their heavy weapons, and turned back toward Saigon. Those in city barracks opened the doors, took off their uniforms, and went in search of civilian clothes.

Groups of armed soldiers stopped the rare automobiles loaded with baggage in which some people were still trying to flee, made everyone get out, and drove off, firing shots in the air. Others, by now without rifles, robbed passersby, and made people open the doors of their houses by threatening to throw hand grenades that they held with the safety catch off.

A hasty disrobing began everywhere—in the streets, alleys, gardens of villas, and courtyards of ordinary houses. Thousands and thousands of soldiers and policemen removed their belts, jackets, shoes, helmets, and stood in their underwear, barefoot, with their shaved heads. From the windows people threw them old pants and shirts.

At the Tan Thuan bridge a captain threatened to shoot the fleeing soldiers; he was knocked down.

At Quang Trung Recruiting Center, where the officers had disappeared the night before, twenty thousand soldiers undressed together, and the expanse of uniforms, helmets, rifles, and boots abandoned on the road and in the rice paddy remained an impressive sight for days.

At the Psychological Warfare Command on Thong Nhat Avenue, where General Trung had come in the morning to make the usual arrangements for the nine o'clock press conference, a unit of paratroopers who had withdrawn from the Thi Nghe bridge invaded the courtyard.

"An officer went into the storeroom and distributed all

the cigarettes there were. The soldiers dropped their uniforms on the floor and ran out," Colonel Do Viet told me.
"Two *paras* aimed their machine guns at each other's stomach, counted one-two-three, and fired. They were Catholics and didn't want to commit suicide."

In Cholon and Gia Dinh, Front cadres who had lived in
hiding for years emerged armed into the streets and occupied the police stations; flags of the Front began to flutter
over the wooden huts along the canals.

At the announcement of the surrender a student ran
shouting with joy from Van Hanh University to give the
news to people in the neighborhood. A policeman shot
and killed him with an M-16.

About a hundred Rangers retreating along Truong
Minh Giang Street entered the university building, and a
colonel tried to organize a line of defense there. The students and his younger officers persuaded him to desist.
The Rangers relinquished their weapons and received civilian clothes in exchange.

The students recorded the names and units of those
who surrendered and distributed little mimeographed yellow slips that read: "Brother . . . of the . . . division has
handed over these weapons. . . . He has promised to obey
the revolutionary authorities and is authorized to return to
his family. Signed: Students' Revolutionary Committee."

With the new weapons recovered from the soldiers, the
students reinforced their sentries around the building. A
group of fifteen went to occupy the Agricultural Faculty, a
few yards from the radio station on Nguyen Binh Khiem
Street.

"I left my comrades at the Faculty and went to look for
Ly Qui Chung. With him we'd be able to enter the radio
station without having to fire on the soldiers who were still
defending it," Thai told me after the Liberation. "I found
Chung at Doc Lap Palace, but the chauffeurs were afraid
and refused to drive us to the radio station. So I stayed at
Doc Lap."

Some ARVN units, retreating in orderly fashion from
the front lines, tried to blow up the bridges behind them,
but squads of Liberation Army soldiers who had infiltrated
the city were already stationed along the main thorough-
fares, protecting the munitions and gasoline dumps and
the bridges. They let the retreating ARVN and armored
units go by, but they fired on sappers who were trying to
plant their loads of TNT.

In many ministerial, police, and immigration offices, office workers remained who were trapped by the curfew or had gone for shelter, hoping to be taken out by the Americans. Those who tried to destroy compromising documents, to burn the files before surrendering were stopped—colleagues whom no one had ever suspected stepped forward, declared themselves members of the Front, and took charge.

The same thing happened at No. 5 Bach Dan Street, an old colonial villa painted entirely white, headquarters of the notorious CIO (Central Intelligence Organization), the espionage agency that had been one of Thieu's most important instruments of terror. Upon announcement of the surrender four employees (three men and a woman) took out pistols, herded all the others out, and barricaded themselves inside the building, thus saving all the dossiers that had been compiled over the years by the secret police in collaboration with the American CIA.

Giai Phong! Giai Phong!

In downtown Saigon the announcement of the surrender was received with dismay by the foreign colony, which had gathered in the large hotels, the Grall Hospital, and in some of the closed and shuttered shops on Tu Do Street.

The Republic that for years had sustained and defended them all, behind which they had done their business and trade, was finished forever. The new one coming made them fearful, but it was even more fearful at that moment to have to wait for it.

"The Vietcong will let the city fall into chaos, they'll let the ARVN put everything to fire and sword, so that when they arrive they will be welcomed as liberators," said the owner of a French restaurant.

Suspicious-looking soldiers crept along the walls, barefoot and with rucksacks full of stolen goods or hand grenades; a pair of them darted away on a Honda with pistols in their hands.

"Let's hope they get here soon. Better *les viets* than these criminals," said a French lady in the lobby of the Continental, which was crowded with Europeans.

By now they all had no other wish than to be considered neutral. The war that was ending had suddenly become an affair in which they wanted no part, as though they had never been involved in it. All at once to be French seemed a protection; the tricolor was hoisted on the flagpole of the Continental, and within a few minutes it was waving over all buildings owned or inhabited by the French. Indian merchants on Tu Do Street and Le Loi Avenue put out their own flags.

The roar of cannons had ceased from the moment of surrender. One heard only isolated bursts of machine-gun fire, and single shots from individual weapons. Then, a little before noon, came the approaching sound of a new weapon and a rumble of engines that Saigon had never heard before.

"They're tanks!" said someone.

From the corner of the Caravelle I saw, coming down from the direction of the cathedral, in the middle of deserted Tu Do Street, a large flag of the National Liberation Front on an American jeep, with eight youths in civilian clothes with red armbands, hands in the air, shouting, *"Giai phong! Giai phong!"* (Liberation! Liberation!). It was 12:10.

I started running. The jeep went as far as the Hotel Majestic and turned back toward the cathedral. I ran after it. At the corner of Gia Long Street I saw two big Molotova trucks bearing down on me from the right loaded with Vietcong, in green uniforms and jungle helmets, crouching on the back; I dodged the first, which had a heavy machine gun in the middle, camouflaged with palm branches. I grabbed on behind the second. The soldiers stared at me, astonished and smiling. I think I said, *"Bao chi, bao chi"* (journalist, journalist). They were all very young, sixteen to eighteen; one of them made a sign to me to crouch, to stay down. They were going to take the Ministry of Defense.

Arriving at the corner of Pasteur Street, the trucks halted and the soldiers jumped out. Running bent over, they slipped past the empty sentry box; one of them stayed on the truck and held the heavy machine gun aimed at the building.

Next to the flagpole in the courtyard, where Thieu's "three-banded" flag still flapped, a colonel tried to kill himself. The soldiers stopped him. I saw his pistol waving in the air, his arm held by a dozen hands. In a moment it was all over, and the flag of the Front was flying over the building.

In front of the cathedral, a jeep full of fleeing ARVN soldiers had smashed into a tree. The soldiers had taken off their uniform jackets, thrown their rifles on the grass, and hoisted a white shirt on the radio antenna.

On Thong Nhat Avenue a long line of tanks flying the colors of the Front rumbled toward Doc Lap; southern soldiers in underpants ran to meet them, and from the tanks covered with dust and branches, youthful Vietcong smiled and waved greetings with their hands.

The entrance to the palace was wide open. The big iron gate had been knocked down in one piece, and on Thieu's well-kept lawn there were deep ruts from the heavy tank tracks. Three tanks stood at the foot of the steps; the one in the middle, with the number 843 in white on its turret, had been the first to arrive. Others stood in a semicircle or along the fence. A large red and blue flag with the five-pointed yellow star in the center waved gently on the roof of Doc Lap.

The thirty-year war was over. The insurrection begun 117 years before to drive the foreign invaders from Vietnamese soil had won, and the Vietnamese people were once again masters of their own destiny.

Go seven blocks and turn left

The order to attack had arrived by night from the General Mobile Command of the Liberation Army on the outskirts of Bien Hoa. Four armored columns were to move simultaneously at sunrise and enter Saigon from different directions. The infantry would follow.

The Western Column, on the Tay Ninh road, was to aim for Tan Son Nhut and enter Bay Hien Street; the Northern, on Highway 13, was to leave Phu Nhuan and go down Hai Ba Trung Street; the Southwest Column, from Road 4 in the Delta, was to enter Cholon by Luc Thinh Street; the Eastern Column, with the hundred tanks, armored cars, amphibious vehicles, cannon, and anti-aircraft of Brigade 203 already positioned at Ho Nai, was to cross the great "Saigon bridge," divide into two columns, and enter the city by Phan Thanh Gian Street and its parallel, Hong Tap Tu. The appointment for them all was: "To Doc Lap Palace as soon as possible."

Brigade 203 knew already by the afternoon of April 23 that its final mission was to take Saigon, but by then only two tank squadrons had arrived at Suoi Cat near the capital; the others, with which they had begun the drive southward, occupying Hue and Da Nang, had barely reached Phan Thiet and Phan Rang on the coast, and the soldiers of the advance guard had to wait.

In Tank 843, a Soviet-made T-54 which the soldiers had covered with coconut-palm branches to camouflage it, there was great excitement on the night of the 29th. The crew was made up of volunteers. The tank leader was Bui Quang Than, the driver Lu Van Hao, the first gunner Thai Ba Minh, the second Nguyen Van Ky. All were young men from the North; none of them had ever been to Saigon, and, awaiting the signal for departure, they repeated to each other the brief and precise order given them by Bui Van Tung, political commissar of the Brigade:

"Cross the Thi Nghe bridge. Proceed straight ahead on Hong Tap Tu Street. Go seven blocks and turn left. Doc Lap is right in front of you."

The tanks set out at five o'clock, in closed formation. At the center of the column was the General Staff of Brigade 203, with Commander An and Commissar Tung. The advance on Saigon was later recounted as follows by Nguyen Trung Tanh, one of the participants:

"Puppet artillery had been firing at us all night from Thu Doc Military School, the Police School, and from behind Ha Tien Cement Factory. Our cannons returned shot for shot while our engineers repaired the bridge in the Buy district, which the retreating puppets had had time to blow up.

"We started at five o'clock. We no longer had anything to fear from the air force, and we kept all our anti-aircraft batteries with their sights lowered. That way we made our way. By six the Long Binh bridge was already behind us and we had destroyed four of the puppets' M-113 armored vehicles. At the Rach Chiec bridge some enemy tanks held us up a little by firing antitank missiles, but our leading squadron destroyed them one by one. At eleven we were on the Thi Nghe bridge.

"The door to Saigon was open in front of us. The first three tanks were already rolling down Hong Tap Tu Street when two enemy M-41s blocked our way, firing like mad. Our Tank 390 pierced one of them with a shell, the other went up in flames, hit by Bui Quang Than's Tank 843. The street, however, was blocked, and Tank 843 turned left and found itself on Mac Dinh Chi Street. It had lost its way. Tank Leader Than saw two puppet soldiers in camouflage uniforms on the sidewalk.

" 'Where is Doc Lap Palace?' Than asked.

"One didn't answer. The other said:

" 'I know.'

"Than removed their uniform jackets and had them get into the tank, which turned right at the next corner. Than didn't trust them. Seeing a girl on a Honda, he stood up straight in the tank and shouted:

" 'How do we get to Doc Lap Palace, please?'

"The girl stared in astonishment at our fighter. It was surely the first time she'd seen a soldier of the Liberation Forces.

" 'You're on Thong Nhat Avenue. There's the palace, right in front of you,' she answered.

"Tank 843 rolled on to Doc Lap. It was noon."

Colonel Do Viet had heard the tanks approaching, and changing into civilian clothes, he left the Psychological Warfare Command and went toward the cathedral.

"The tanks went by me. First there were three of them, one behind the other. I couldn't believe my eyes. I knew it was over, I knew it would happen like this; but to see the same people of twenty years ago in Hanoi, to see them there with the same uniforms, the same helmets, passing in tanks in front of the cathedral, seemed to me a nightmare, a dream."

Reaching the cathedral, Tank 843 opened fire, shooting into the air as though to announce itself, aiming above the roof where the Republic's yellow flag with its three red stripes still waved. The soldiers of the outside guard had already fled.

From the top of his open turret, Than saw the abandoned uniforms, bulletproof vests, helmets, machine guns, and sacks of grenades on the final stretch of Thong Nhat Avenue. The gate was closed. The tank speeded up, and the iron gate was knocked to the ground like a wooden twig. The tracks rolled rapidly over the grass, turning to the right of the fountain in the middle of the garden, and the tank stopped before the deserted steps of the palace. The other two tanks placed themselves behind and to the sides.

Than, his machine gun in one hand and the NLF flag pulled down from the radio antenna in the other, jumped from the turret. He went leaping in his rubber sandals up the steps to the entrance. Arriving on the big yellow carpet with blue dragons in the hall, Than met Nguyen Huu Hanh, an ARVN general in uniform with a gold star on the collar of his shirt. Behind him were the president, Prime Minister Vu Van Mau, Ly Qui Chung, Nguyen Van Ba, and the rest of the government.

"Where is Mr. Duong Van Minh?" Than shouted.

"Keep calm. We've already surrendered," replied the president, stepping forward.

The crews of the other two tanks were in the hall. A young guerrilla, on reaching the rug, had automatically removed his rubber sandals.

"How do you get to the roof?" Than asked.

"This way," replied Nguyen Huu Thai, the student, showing him the elevator.

A moment later Than was on the roof, and after violently unfurling the flag of the Front with both hands, he raised it on the highest pole in the center of the palace. It was 12:15.

More tanks had arrived from Thong Nhat Avenue. Large trucks unloaded soldiers in front of the palace gate and in front of the steps.

Minh and the other members of the government were taken to the meeting room on the second floor to await the arrival of the Brigade's political commissar. By now the palace was full of Liberation Army soldiers. There was no more shooting.

Other tanks arrived on Cong Ly Avenue. They were the vanguard of the Western Column, coming from Tan Son Nhut, where an ARVN unit that had refused to surrender had put up a stiff resistance. Five T-54s and two hundred Liberation Army soldiers had been put out of action.

Camp Davis, in the middle of Tan Son Nhut airport, where the military delegation of the Provisional Revolutionary Government was stationed, was liberated toward one o'clock in the afternoon.

"When we heard Minh's surrender speech on the radio there were great scenes of rejoicing," Father Chan Tin later recounted. He had spent the night in a bunker with Colonel Giang. "We came up from underground and went to meet General Tuan. The soldiers embraced in the courtyard, they jumped up and down, ran from one hut to another, and Tuan gave the order to kill a chicken and bring some bottles of wine.

"We saw the first tank about noon, but we didn't leave the camp until six in the afternoon because there was still a battle going on around the headquarters of the ARVN General Staff.

"It was wonderful then, after so many years of struggle, to go back into Saigon with the Liberation Army, with people coming to meet us and cheering in the streets. Giang signed our first pass for us. It was dated 30 April 1975."

Some tanks of the Southwest Column had got lost entering Cholon.

"At the beginning of Hong Bang Avenue I saw a Vietcong soldier get out of a tank, read the name of the street, and approach the wall as though he wanted to urinate," a Vietnamese friend told me later. "I went closer and I saw that instead he was checking a compass. He was ashamed to ask where he was."

A tank had entered Le Loi Avenue from the market side, and turned back only at the second crossing, realizing it had passed the thoroughfare leading to the palace.

Tung, the political commissar of Brigade 203, arrived at Doc Lap ten minutes after the first tanks. He entered the meeting room, introduced himself to Minh, and told him and the other eighteen members present to consider themselves free, specifying that they were by no means prisoners. He asked "Brother Minh" to deliver by radio a new order of surrender, to the troops, to help avoid any further needless shedding of Vietnamese blood.

Nguyen Huu Thai's students had already taken over the radio station, but all the technicians had fled and no one knew how to make things work. It took two hours and several attempts before Minh, driven by jeep along with Vu Van Mau to the broadcasting studios in Nguyen Binh Khiem Street, was able to read his last words as president, written for him on a piece of yellow paper by Commissar Bui Van Tung. Radio Saigon, which had been plunged into silence after the first surrender speech in the morning, resumed broadcasting at 2:30 in the afternoon with a simple announcement:

"This is the voice of the Revolutionary Forces of Saigon-

Gia Dinh. I am a representative of the Liberation Forces. Now Duong Van Minh will make an appeal." There was a moment of silence, and then:

"I, General Duong Van Minh, president of the Saigon government, appeal to the armed forces of the Republic of Vietnam to lay down their arms and surrender unconditionally to the forces of the National Liberation Front. Furthermore I declare that the Saigon government is completely dissolved at all levels."

Then Mau spoke:

"In the spirit of harmony and national reconciliation, I, Professor Vu Van Mau, prime minister, appeal to all levels of the population to greet this day of peace for the Vietnamese people with joy. I appeal to all employees of the administration to return to their posts and continue their work."

Minh and Mau were taken back to Doc Lap, where they remained with the other members of the now eclipsed government.

Vice-President Nguyen Van Huyen, who had left the palace half an hour before the arrival of the tanks to go home and rest, came to give himself up at five o'clock in the afternoon. One of his relatives drove him to the palace on a Honda.

The Vietcong up close

The first tanks paraded through an empty, spectral city.

Slowly windows and doors began to open, people leaned out with curiosity, and in a few minutes all Saigon was in the streets.

Pairs of youths on motorcycles followed the march of the armored columns, pointing out the streets to them. Shouting, they urged the undecided to emerge from their homes.

From the sidewalks and balconies groups of women and girls looked astonished, with sudden stupor, at the heads of the Vietcong appearing from the turrets of the tanks; they saw them smile and responded with broad waves of their hands. Tension and fear were melting.

Leaning from the back of the Molotova trucks that were arriving one after another in front of Doc Lap Palace, youthful ranks of Vietcong smiled from amid the palm branches used for camouflage. On the helmet of each was a small strip of white paper with the slogan for the day: "Eat half as much, work twice as hard, to carry Uncle Ho's mission to completion."

Among the Soviet tanks and Chinese trucks, passed an occasional American armored vehicle, its old South Vietnamese insignia covered over by a freshly painted star of the Front. ARVN soldiers still in uniform were happily reentering the city in the midst of the Vietcong, after surrendering.

The garden between the cathedral and Doc Lap Palace had become an immense parking lot for tanks, trucks, antiaircraft batteries, cannons covered with branches and red dust. Thousands of persons mingled with the soldiers, and amid the deafening noise of other tanks arriving in clouds of bluish smoke, I saw nothing but smiles — smiles and waving hands.

Running, jumping on a tank, getting a lift from jeeps, I made a tour of the city.

In working-class neighborhoods the enthusiasm was overwhelming.

On Cong Ly Avenue a priest in a cassock ran up to a tank to climb aboard and embrace the soldiers.

On Le Van Duyet Street, near Chi Hoa Prison, a shouting crowd was tearing down propaganda banners, ripping flags of the Republic, and hanging onto the trucks loaded with soldiers, machine guns, and munitions. In its midst I saw an old woman with a typical conical peasant hat throw her arms around a young guerrilla.

"*Hoa binh, hoa binh!*" (peace, peace), she cried.

Men wept, children unfurled flags of the Front. The red and blue colors were by now on all the houses. Groups of youths with red armbands knocked down signs with the watchwords of the old regime. Everywhere lay piles of abandoned uniforms, helmets, military boots.

Standing before houses still bearing the inscriptions imposed by Thieu, "This Family Will Never Agree to Live Under Communism," groups of people sang "Rise up, Indomitable Saigon."

At the entrance to Chi Hoa Prison, a tank commander stopped to make a brief statement to the crowd:

"The people thank all those who have sacrificed themselves and suffered for the Revolution." The seven thousand prisoners had already been freed. The crowd applauded.

After the tanks, trucks, and armored vehicles, the infantry arrived. They passed, groups of fifteen to twenty in long Indian file, sweaty, in damp muddy uniforms, their shirts twice the size of their narrow chests, in sandals made from rubber tires. Hour after hour came youthful guerrillas with AK-47 rifles slung on their backs, mortars and antitank rockets on their shoulders, the heavier pieces suspended on poles carried by two.

Some carried baskets of water beets, a vegetable Saigon would soon come to know. Together with rice it formed the basic diet of the Vietcong. Sometimes, hanging from the backs of trucks and even on the sides of tanks, you could see small iron cages with chickens inside. The Liberation Army was self-suffiicient.

Fanning out from the palace, the tanks and troops split up and spread out all over the city, into every neighborhood.

There were very few incidents of resistance.

At the City Hall on Le Than Ton Street, an old French mansion with a facade of baroque-style stucco, a group of ARVN soldiers fired on the Vietcong coming to raise their flag over the clock tower. A moment later the guerrillas had slipped into the courtyard and the others surrendered. One threw down his rifle and stood trembling against the wall, facing a soldier with a pointed machine gun. He didn't fire. He looked at him for a moment, smiled, and with the barrel of his weapon motioned for him to leave. He was free.

Some twenty paratroopers had hidden themselves a stone's throw from the palace, behind the Turtle Monument in Chien Si Square. When everything was calm they opened fire—causing a great stampede among the crowd gathered in front of Doc Lap. The Vietcong took shelter behind the tanks and trees, and then, holding their fire, closed in on them. Calm was restored at the end of ten minutes.

At 2:30 the tanks were rolling with muddy tracks along Tu Do Street on their way to take the waterfront and naval base and to reinforce the units that had already entered the Senate and National Bank.

The esplanade in front of the National Assembly filled with people. A local guerrilla in black trousers, blue shirt, and a floppy green cloth hat went to remove Thieu's flag from over the white building and replace it with the Front's. Over the door he stretched a banner with the inscription: "The Spirit of Ho Chi Minh Lives in All of Us."

Two girls with small submachine guns stationed themselves next to the sentry box of the old police station. They were Saigon students. One kept the magazines for her weapon in a Pan Am plastic flight bag.

A young Vietcong entered the lobby of the Continental and asked what was in the building; Joseph and the other waiters were already preparing a banner out of an old sheet and red ink to hoist over the hotel entrance.

Under the Monument to the Unknown Soldier, right where the policeman had killed himself four hours earlier, a dozen young Liberation Army soldiers in green uniforms and red armbands were embraced by women, approached with curiosity and admiration by students, and almost smothered by a crowd of people who craned their necks to see them and reached out their hands to touch them.

The surprise was mutual.

The soldiers, almost all from the North, gazed with astonishment on this corrupt, enslaved, indomitable Saigon they had heard so much about, and were struck by its palaces, avenues, hotels, and its luxury, its Hondas, shops, cinemas, watches, and wealth.

For the people of Saigon, who had feared a bloodbath and expected to be massacred, there was relief.

For years American and Saigon propaganda had projected an inhuman image of this "faceless enemy." Colored posters describing the horrors of life under Communism had been affixed at all street corners. The Vietcong was not a man but a monster with sharpened teeth who murdered peasants, burned down churches, cut the throats of bonzes, and razed pagodas to the ground.

In Saigon, as in all Vietnam, thousands and thousands of families had a brother, a son, a relative on the other side of the seventeenth parallel or in the liberated areas of the South, but people had forgotten or pretended to forget. Everything that happened in North Vietnam was a mystery tinged by fear and terror. "The other Vietnam" was distant, remote, another world: the moon. The only Vietcong many people in Saigon had seen were those swollen, decaying corpses displayed after a battle along country roads by the psychological division of Thieu's army.

Now here they were. The Vietcong. Peasant boys, kind, smiling, brought up in the old ways, who answered any question by calling everyone "brother."

In the first hours after the arrival of the tanks, many families already began to receive visits from old relatives of whom they had heard nothing for years; parents found children they had thought lost.

My friend Cao Giao, returning home about five o'clock, found an unsigned note at his door asking him to go to a certain address. It was his young brother, whom he had left in Hanoi in 1954. He had entered Saigon with a commando sabotage unit on the 27th, and on the morning of the 30th, even before the arrival of the tanks, had gone to see his mother.

At Ho Nai, an outlying neighborhood inhabited exclusively by Catholic refugees from the North, with a church every hundred yards, an old anti-Communist priest received a visit in the afternoon from a high-ranking Vietcong officer who told him:

"I've come to thank you for saving my father's life in 1953 by hiding him from the French police. I owe you an enormous debt."

A tailor in Bien Hoa told me a few days later that he had been at the window watching the first Vietcong go by when he recognized his uncle in the middle of a group. He had never seen him, but the man completely resembled an old photograph of his father, who had died twenty years before in Hanoi.

In a narrow street behind the Ben Thanh market a Vietcong went around with a megaphone asking where a certain woman lived. The neighbors were frightened this might mean trouble, and said they didn't know her. But then two children started shouting:

"Mama, mama, they're looking for you!"

The Vietcong hugged them. He was their father, who had left for the jungle in 1968 at the time of the Tet offensive. Since then the family had had to move to another neighborhood.

Hundreds and hundreds of such episodes took place on the very first day after the arrival of the tanks.

In a few hours the barrier of ignorance, fear, and silence between North and South, between one Vietnam and the other, was shattered. The "faceless Vietcong enemy" had become a person one knew, a neighbor's son, one's own brother, a relative, a Vietnamese like everyone else.

Even the name vanished. From that day on people no longer spoke of the "Vietcong."

The French and other foreigners called them "the little green men." The bar girls and prostitutes, in their elementary American, called them collectively "Ho Chi Minh." And Saigon learned the first word of a new Vietnamese vocabulary that was soon to prevail: "*bo doi.*"

Bo doi meant literally "soldiers," soldiers of the people, but it meant also "revolution," "new order," "new authorities."

From that day on the *bo doi* became the subject of all conversations, of everybody's remarks. You heard nothing but "the *bo doi* said," "the *bo doi* did," "the *bo doi* want that. . . ."

From Saigon to Ho Chi Minh City

By the evening of April 30 Saigon was calm.

Liberation Army soldiers hung out their wash to dry on the iron fence of the presidential palace; tanks, trucks, anti-aircraft batteries, and cannons, covered with reddish mud and camouflaging branches, were massed under the tall tamarind trees on the square between the cathedral and Doc Lap. Thousands of Communist soldiers were camped out in the parks and gardens of the city, in the courtyards of houses. They built their bonfires as though they were still in the jungle they had emerged from only a few hours before to take Saigon.

At six o'clock a curfew was announced, but no one paid much attention. People continued to circulate in the streets and the *bo doi* said nothing. Everywhere you saw little knots of people in discussion, children climbing on tanks, Hanoi soldiers recounting their march to the South and showing their Saigon contemporaries, often ARVN soldiers, how to dismantle and reassemble the Chinese AK-47 rifle, how to aim an anti-aircraft battery.

In the cathedral square the *bo doi* had lit wood fires on tripods improvised from crossed artillery shell cases, and were cooking large pots of rice and water beets, and boiling water for their canteens.

The old Student Center on Duy Tan Street, closed by Thieu, was reopened. Young men and girls, wearing red armbands and with American rifles collected from the surrendered troops, stood guard around the compound. In the rooms inside and on the open terrace groups of students sang revolutionary songs, held meetings, and spoke with comrades who had emerged from the underground and whom they had not seen for months or years.

ARVN barracks and police stations in the outlying quarters were occupied by guerrillas and local political cadres, gradually joined by units of *bo doi*.

After the speeches by Duong Van Minh and Vu Van Mau, Radio Saigon broadcast continuous appeals: first to the employees and technicians of the station itself to come back to work immediately; others to the population to help the Revolutionary Government restore order in the city; to young people to put themselves at the disposal of certain centers whose addresses were given, to receive instructions on tasks that needed carrying out; to public service employees to resume their normal activities.

Students were asked to present themselves at Van Hanh University, which since morning had been the most efficient center for the registration of ARVN soldiers and the consignment of arms. Groups of students, replacing green armbands with a cross worn the morning before with red armbands with the university initials in yellow, had worked all day in the courtyard and classrooms, recording the names and addresses of surrendering officers and soldiers, registering their weapons, and issuing receipts and new identification documents to each.

When the *bo doi* came at six in the afternoon to take over the university—only nominally, since armed students continued to stand guard and guarantee the security of the buildings and I was only able to enter with a pass signed by Nguyen Huu Thai—they found an enormous arsenal in the courtyard and stacked in two large rooms: 1,525 carbines, 2,596 M-16s, 399 M-72s, 174 M-79s, three boxes full of pistols. Fourteen armored vehicles were parked on the street in front of the entrance.

The radio also repeatedly broadcast an appeal to halt thefts in houses, offices, and storerooms abandoned by the Americans and the Vietnamese who had fled with them. Looting had gone on all day.

Passing through Phan Dinh Phung Street at four o'clock I saw about a hundred persons stripping a large abandoned truck loaded with goods, undisturbed in the midst of the tanks that continued to arrive and the *bo doi* marching on foot along the sidewalk. Even in the Brinks, by now reduced to a skeleton, groups of looters milled through the rooms and corridors full of waste paper and broken glass scrounging whatever they still could.

The "thieves' market" around Ton That Dam Street reopened immediately after the arrival of the tanks, and there you could find for almost nothing the most modern stereophonic equipment, movie cameras, radios, and an expanse of whiskey bottles that had just emerged from American storerooms.

Many of the last thefts were committed by individuals who circulated in the confusion with conspicuous red armbands and weapons picked up in the street, pretending to be Front guerrillas. A group of former policemen disguised like this had entered a garage on Le Loi Avenue and "requisitioned" all the cars parked inside.

All afternoon columns of *bo doi* continued to enter the city from the same four directions as the tanks, but especially from the northeast.

Soldiers gazed around from the backs of open trucks passing in front of the National Assembly, the cathedral, and along the river embankment — satisfied, curious, craning their necks like so many tourists before the monuments and other sights they had heard of. Officers in jeeps stopped at certain downtown street crossings and took maps of Saigon out of their brown shoulder bags, trying to orient themselves.

The overwhelming majority of the soldiers who entered the southern capital on April 30 — at least three divisions — came from North Vietnam; many were from Hanoi itself. The Saigonese recognized them by their accent and their height, in general shorter than the southerners. But they did not consider them foreigners.

They couldn't. To the Vietnamese Vietnam had always been a single country. The people of the South and North spoke the same language, had the same habits, the same culture; for centuries they fought against the same enemies. All regimes in the South, Thieu's included, believed in the existence of a single Vietnam, and observed as a "day of shame" the anniversary of the Geneva Accords, which in 1954 had, if only temporarily, cut the country in two along the fictitious border of the seventeenth parallel.

The *bo doi* arriving in Saigon from the North were at home, as were the northern Catholics who came in 1954, and all the military and political leaders like Nguyen Cao Ky who, though originally from the North, had held power in the South. The *bo doi* were countryfolk arriving in the city. That was the extent of their foreignness.

Saigon had been liberated, not conquered. The army of liberators was made up of Vietnamese like the liberated; it was not a foreign occupation force.

"Liberation? Paris in '45 was something else altogether!" said some Frenchmen who were holed up that evening at the Continental, recalling the hysterical enthusiasm with which European crowds had greeted the Allies along their march.

But Vietnam was not Europe, and if in Saigon, especially downtown around the Continental, the reception of the *bo doi* had been cautious and suspicious before becoming an expression of relief and joy, if flowers had not rained down from the windows, this was because of the different history and different roots of this war, and because of the fear and terror Liberation inspired in a great part of the city.

Saigon was a whore of a city that had to learn to survive with all regimes and profit by all wars. This city had shined the shoes of all the expeditionary forces from the French to the Japanese to the American and sold them its women — the war had been its sole industry, an industry that had enriched a few and kept a great many others alive. From a million, the city's population had risen in the last twenty years to two, three, perhaps four million. Census figures had lost count of the refugees.

The American war had not only nourished the Swiss bank accounts of various presidents, generals, police officials, and diplomats; whole Vietnamese families had been able to survive by "renting" their wives to the GIs, and GI dollars had fed the *cyclopousse* drivers, the beggars, the painters of bloody Christs and naked women, the drug pushers, tailors, shoemakers, and bootblacks. Hotels, restaurants, travel agencies, souvenir stores, and forgers of ancient art works had all lived on American dollars.

The arrival of the tanks put an end to war and fear. The dying ended too, but a way of living was also over with. Uncertainty began for a great many Saigonese, as to how they would get their next bowl of rice.

Unlike the Allies in Europe, the *bo doi* did not march in throwing cigarettes and chocolate, they did not bring white bread to people who had been eating black bread, often made with sawdust.

The *bo doi* with their wrinkled, threadbare, badly fitting uniforms, with their Ho Chi Minh sandals cut from old rubber tires, did not bring prosperity "made in the USA"; instead they were the symbol of an austerity, a harshness, to which Saigon was certainly not accustomed and that it would soon have to learn.

But if the liberation of Saigon, unlike that of Paris and other European cities, did not mean flowers, neither did it mean executions.

In Saigon on the day of the Liberation there was no settling of accounts, no hunting down of fascists; the vanquished were not exhibited in public nor humiliated. There were no naked women with shaved heads shoved back and forth between two lines of a crowd, as I saw as a boy during the Liberation in Europe.

In Saigon on April 30 and the days following there was not a single shooting of collaborationists, policemen, or torturers. Strangely, for a city that had always whispered the most false and incredible stories, there was not even a rumor about an execution somewhere.

In the neighborhoods students, before issuing new identity cards to soldiers of the old regime, made them sign declarations in which they professed themselves sorry and ready to obey the directives of the revolutionary authorities. The *bo doi* explained that it was American imperialism that had forced the soldiers and policemen to take up arms against their own people, that they too were victims.

There could be no doubt that Saigon had fallen to tanks, to the divisions of a Liberation Army largely recruited north of the seventeenth parallel. But this, though the most apparent aspect, was also the most incidental.

The Revolution (*Cach Mang* as everyone learned to call it) had not been merely a military fact, much less a question of tanks and divisions. In Saigon as in the rest of Vietnam, as the regular troops advanced, the clandestine political organization that made the advance possible came to light. Out of the shadows emerged a whole formation of fighters who for years had contributed silently from within to the struggle for the country's independence. Cadres emerged from among students, Front representatives from among factory workers, many people at every level of society revealed themselves for what they were: agents of the Front.

In Quang Ngai, the woman who for years had sold sugar cane juice in front of the central police headquarters was a member of the Revolutionary Committee of the city. The "madman" who for years had begged at the bus station, and who every so often would run shouting into the fields, despite the curfew, was actually an officer in the Liberation Army.

In Ban Me Thuot on Liberation Day people discovered

that what they took for a "family" living a short distance
from the Hotel Anh Dao was in fact the NLF group in
charge of the region. The group had chosen the fiction of
posing as father, mother, and sons so as not to be conspicuous.

In Saigon on the morning of the 30th Mr. Binh, a waiter
in the Kim Hoa Restaurant on the corner of Pasteur Street
and Le Loi, a place frequented by high-ranking ARVN officers, diplomats, businessmen, and journalists, asked his
employer for a week off. In the afternoon he returned to
greet his fellow employees with a group of *bo doi*. For ten
years he had been in charge of an intelligence network for
the Front. He spoke French, English, and Chinese. During
the following days he became a security official for the city.

At the Circle Sportif, the exclusive club for diplomats
and foreigners and the last hangout for the old colonial
society, the employees discovered after the Liberation that
a cleaning woman was a high political cadre in the Resistance.

They were scattered everywhere. Father Tran Huu
Thanh, the anti-Communist Catholic priest who had led
the "movement against corruption," discovered that the
young student who accompanied him to every demonstration and acted as his bodyguard was a guerrilla fighter in
the Front. Mme. Ngo Ba Thanh, a leader of the Third
Force, discovered that the secretary general of her movement, a girl by the name of Tran Thi Lan, was a Front
cadre. Even Colonel Do Viet found that two of his fellow
officers in the Psychological Warfare Command were Vietcong agents. It was said in Saigon that even two generals
of the ARVN General Staff had worked for the Front and
that after the Liberation they had been seen at Doc Lap
Palace. One was said to be General Dong Van Khuyen,
who had been in charge of logistics.

Naturally there were some who tried to take advantage
of the situation.

In the offices of the Associated Press on the morning of
the 30th, at the moment of Minh's surrender speech, one
of the Vietnamese photograpers pulled out an armband
with the Front colors on it and said:

"Don't be alarmed. In the name of the Provisional Revolutionary Government, I assure you that nothing will happen to you. I guarantee it myself."

The story of the "Vietcong in the office," written by two
journalists who had stayed behind, made news all over the

world, but it was false. The individual turned out to be one of those last-minute revolutionaries who were quickly identified and put to the side.

The evening of the 30th, the first on which there was no roar of cannons and no fear of rockets, Saigon was already another city.

The radio announced that henceforth it would be called Ho Chi Minh City. But not only the name was new. In a few hours the colors of the flags on every house, building, and vehicle, the soldiers' uniforms, the music broadcast by loudspeakers, the banners strung across the streets had changed as well. The atmosphere, the human landscape of Saigon was also different.

The *bo doi* and guerrillas mingled with the population, and new faces of peasants, workers, and young people kept appearing in the city. Everywhere one had the clear impression of a new class, almost a new race of pale, thin, tough people who had become almost physically different in years of clandestine activity and in the jungle, and who now were coming to power.

Saigon was returning to what it should have been all along: the poor capital of a peasant country.

Soon Saigon no longer existed. It had become Ho Chi Minh City, and slowly, with pain and effort, following the instructions given by the new authorities and repeated on the radio, it learned to be a "civil, clean, healthy, happy and rejoicing revolutionary city, worthy of the great name of Uncle Ho."

III. THE NEXT THREE MONTHS

1: First Steps

Ten thousand years of peace

Saigon had been captured suddenly, easily, with lightning speed.

No one had imagined it would be this way. Least of all the men of the Front and of the Liberation Army. They were prepared for a three-month siege, as they later explained to me in Hanoi: they had taken into account a possible final and devastating blow by the American air force; they had studied ways to retaliate if the southerners were to employ, as they had at Xuan Loc, their CBU asphyxiation bombs; they were organized to take Saigon step by step, street by street. Instead they found themselves at Doc Lap Palace in one jump, with a huge overcrowded city on their hands to feed, administer, and control.

They were not ready for this contingency.

It took a political commissar, arriving ten minutes after Tank 843, to explain to Minh and the members of his government that they were not prisoners of war, as the first *bo doi* had led them to believe.

It took photos by Western journalists to document the historical moments of the Liberation since the guerrilla photographers, though they had infiltrated Saigon in advance for this purpose, arrived in the center of the city when it was all over.

At Loc Ninh they had been preparing new uniforms and helmets for weeks, as well as Front badges and molded rubber and plastic sandals to replace those made by hand from remnants of old tires—to be distributed to the soldiers who would enter Saigon. In the haste of the sudden advance, however, the *bo doi* appeared in the capital with what they had, with their jungle uniforms, and even those in the second wave, who arrived in the afternoon and had been sent to the storerooms, found themselves in Saigon with shirts and helmets of the wrong size and with mismatched sandals.

A great many had forgotten their Front badges, with a yellow star on a red and blue background, which at least in those first days were supposed to confirm the claim that they were all soldiers from the South and not from Hanoi.

Trucks entering the city the evening of the 30th had strips of paper freshly pasted on their sides, bearing the slogan that was to have served for a long campaign:

"Any sacrifice for victory. We are determined to liberate Saigon, the magnificent city of Uncle Ho." Saigon was already liberated.

Political and military leaders entered the city in the course of the afternoon.

General Tran Van Tra—commander in chief of the Liberation Army—is the man who according to French intelligence had directed the urban guerrilla warfare in Saigon in the 1950s and who later, according to the Americans, had been the author and strategist of the Tet offensive in 1968, the man who had spent his life fighting inside and around the capital. He arrived at Doc Lap Palace at 5:30 in the afternoon. With him were Political Commissar Bui Thanh Khiet and the officers of the General Mobile Command who had directed the final phases of the Ho Chi Minh campaign from Bien Hoa.

Also arriving in the course of the afternoon was Pham Hung, the mysterious, legendary member of the Politburo and secretary of the southern section of the Party, who at various times had entered and left Saigon secretly during the war years. Some said he had already been in the capital for days, hiding in the house of friends in the seventh district. He was known to only his closest collaborators. The American and South Vietnamese secret services had never succeeded in gathering much information on him, and the files of the CIA and Saigon's Central Intelligence Organization did not even contain his photograph. He could have strolled quietly along Tu Do Street without being recognized. Perhaps in the past he had done so.

Le Duc Tho arrived on the morning of May 1.

With the Paris negotiations he had become Pham Hung's counterpart on the international stage. Well-known, photographed, interviewed, winner of a Nobel Peace Prize, which he had refused, Le Duc Tho was the negotiator of the Paris Accords along with Henry Kissinger. Actually he had taken over the highest political responsibility for the struggle in the South from Le Duan, who had become Party secretary in Hanoi, and after the signing of the Paris Accords he had spent much of his time in the liberated areas of the South.

At the moment of the Liberation he had probably been in Loc Ninh, or perhaps already in Bien Hoa with Tran Van Tra's advance command post.

Setting foot in the capital for the first time in thirty years, he stopped at Tan Son Nhut and, by means of the military telex of the PRG delegation at Camp Davis, sent his "Politburo comrades" in Hanoi a report on the situation: a poem.

Last night you didn't sleep, I know.
The last battle began at dawn.
You waited
And followed minute by minute, second by second,
Every step of the South, which advances
Boldly and rapidly,
Ready to pour fire on the lackeys' lair.
Around Saigon the circle closes.
Highway 4 is cut, Vung Tau cut off.
Night and day long-range artillery
Bombards Bien Hoa and Tan Son Nhut Airport.
The A-37s and F-5s in flames
No longer take off.
Like rain, torrents, typhoons, a tide,
The armored trucks advance,
And no force can prevent the attack
On the last refuge of the dying enemy.
He raises his hands and surrenders.
On the "Palace of Independence"
The red flag stands forth
To mark the entrance of our heroic and victorious army.
The masses shout, joy overcomes.
The waves of people rise up infinite.
On the tanks the Liberation fighter smiles
And accepts the most beautiful flowers from the populace.
Ah, these tears shed for happiness,
This joy savored
Only once in all one's life.
What do you think of these moments,
You who cannot sleep for joy?
We will resolutely rebuild the future of our country
So that it will be a thousand times richer,
A thousand times more beautiful.
The days of hunger and suffering are over.
North and South are reunited under the same roof.
Uncle Ho's dream has become reality
And he will sleep in peace.
The sky today is splendid and infinitely serene.

Tan Son Nhut, May 1, 1975

It was a spontaneous people's holiday. No one gave orders. May Day was celebrated with no official programs, by hundreds of thousands of men and women who came from all over the city, by automobile, on Hondas, on foot, pouring into the center "to see the Revolution."

Some came with red flags, with the banners of workers' committees, others simply with their whole family, holding their children by the hand or on their shoulders.

All day in front of Doc Lap Palace there was a huge crowd. That was everyone's goal: everyone wanted to stand close and stare wide-eyed for at least a moment at the two sixteen-year-old *bo doi* guarding the demolished gate, to watch the still incredible sight of the Vietcong flag waving over Thieu's roof.

In the afternoon the Liberation Navy also entered the city, but not by ship; it arrived in trucks along the highway from Bien Hoa and proceeded to the waterfront. These were youths from Hanoi, coming to take over the boats that the South Vietnamese had abandoned along the Saigon River when on the 29th the rumor spread that the Vietcong had cut the route to the sea.

That evening, among the very many *bo doi* strolling through the downtown streets, unarmed, often in pairs, and holding hands by linking their little fingers, there were also these sailors in uniforms that might have come from the battleship *Potemkin:* wide blue trousers, and full white jerseys with stars on the collars.

On May 1 the first placard signed by the Saigon-Gia Dinh Military Management Committee, which under the chairmanship of General Tran Van Tra was to govern the capital in the months ahead, appeared on the walls of Saigon. It announced the closing of bars, brothels, dance halls, opium dens, massage parlors, and all places "for American-type activities."

Maxime's, the most fashionable nightclub in Saigon, located at the end of Tu Do Street next to the Hotel Majestic, immediately became a police station, and youngsters from Thieu's old self-defense forces, who had become revolutionaries by virtue of a red armband worn at the elbow, went with their M-16 rifles to occupy it, along with a squad of *bo doi.*

For the first two weeks after the Liberation, numerous groups of these young Saigonese roamed freely through the city, sirens screaming, in jeeps that had once been those of the old regime's police. They directed traffic, guarded public buildings, and turned up everywhere showing off their armbands and their American-made rifles with pieces of red ribbon tied to the barrels.

They were students fourteen or fifteen years old, whom the old regime had armed and organized into paramilitary units charged with the nightly defense of the city's neighborhoods. Their rifles were the symbol of their maturity, and the *bo doi* let them keep them. Psychologically it was the correct thing to do. Thousands of these youngsters felt involved; they had the feeling of participating in the new — of not being pushed aside. You saw them often, boisterous and with a naughty air, standing with outspread legs at a crossing, brandishing their weapons on their hips in a manner picked up from the Americans, directing traffic and watched from a distance by a very modest *bo doi* with his AK-47 slung across his chest.

One morning, right in front of the Continental, one of these kids fired five or six shots in the air to disperse a group of people who had gathered around some quarreling prostitutes. When the incident was settled and the people had gone away, two *bo doi* politely drew the boy aside, took away his gun, and gave him a long talking-to.

By the third week after the Liberation many of these bands had disappeared from the streets. In evening neighborhood meetings the *bo doi*, without making the youngsters lose face, began to withdraw weapons from them and to urge them to "prove their revolutionary spirit in another way."

Some of them duly enlisted in the Liberation Army when the first call for volunteers was issued in June.

On the afternoon of May Day, the first large student assembly was held at the Duy Tan Street center. The auditorium was packed with young people; a great many were unable to get in, and stood outside in the courtyards to hear on the loudspeakers the voice of a student comrade who had come out of hiding:

"We have defeated our most terrible enemies. This is the most beautiful day in our history. Now the Revolution can flourish, now we can build peace that will last ten thousand years. You are the heroes of the Revolution, the future depends on you, on the fire you have within you. The Revolution is not something for one day, one year, or thirty years. It is the task for the rest of our lives."

There was great emotion. Amid girls from good families, elegant in their simple, gleaming white *ao dai,* stood young peasant girls in black pajamas, their hair in long braids down their backs.

At seven in the evening television resumed its broadcasts. The first image to appear on the screen, to the strains of *Giai Phong Vietnam* ("To Liberate the South"), the anthem of the Front, was the portrait of President Ho Chi Minh.

Next came a speech by Huynh Tan Man, the Saigon student who had spent years in prison under Thieu. The Revolution, carried forward almost like an obsession by a generation of old fighters, was not missing the opportunity to confirm its concern for young people, for their involvement.

Another official announcement that day by the Military Management Committee prohibited the printing of newspapers, periodicals, or books without the permission of the new authorities.

A single Vietnam

. It began at the very moment of the Liberation and continued in the days and weeks that followed. Throughout the city, *bo doi* could be seen with papers in their hands, asking for information and seeking someone.

It was as though every soldier of the Liberation Army had arrived in Saigon with the address of a relative or friend in his pocket, or with a letter from someone in the North giving news of himself to a member of his family in the South.

This—like the fact that the *bo doi* from Catholic villages in the North ended up in the neighborhoods of Catholic refugees—was no accident. The success of this operation of psychological guerrilla warfare was enormous.

Human relationships were immediately established between army and population; everywhere people were recognizing one another, talking and picking up ties that had been severed for years. Old people who had left North Vietnam in 1954 so as not to live under the Vietminh regime met the sons of their neighbors, and asked for news of their houses and the tombs of their ancestors.

"I thought my class of people had been destroyed, that my family had been persecuted and dispersed. Instead I now discover that all my nephews have been studying, some in Moscow, some in Peking, and that none of my people or my colleagues were punished," the lawyer Vu Van Huyen told me with great surprise. He had been procurator curator general of Hanoi in the time of the French and had fled to the South after the Geneva Accords for fear of reprisals.

The differences between North and South Vietnam created over the past twenty years of war, and which Western propaganda had found it convenient to magnify, were minimized with the proliferation of these encounters.

The abyss opened in the Vietnamese population by two different political systems that had developed in opposite directions remained; the problems of a differing economic and social structure between North and South could only be resolved with time, but on the psychological level, unification between the two Vietnams was something taken for granted at the moment of the Liberation.

All of a sudden the Vietnamese felt themselves citizens of a single country. Thousands of civilians in Hanoi went to register for work in the South upon the announcement of victory; others set out on the roads toward the seventeenth parallel. And in Saigon one of the most frequent questions put to the *bo doi* was:

"When can we visit Hanoi?"

"Today for the first time we have a clear concept of homeland; there are no longer any differences between South and North Vietnam. I'm proud that we have finally achieved unity. The glory for all this goes to you," Ly Qui Chung, Duong Van Minh's minister of information, declared in Doc Lap Palace to an officer of the Liberation Army.

The pompous arrival in Saigon of "Giap's tanks" and the entry into the city of twenty or perhaps thirty thousand *bo doi* who, even if they wore the emblem of the Provisional Revolutionary Government of the South on their pith helmets, were clearly natives of the North, prompted Western diplomats and observers to say that the Liberation was simply the conquest of the South on the part of Hanoi, and that unification, if it were declared, would be nothing but the annexation of the South by the Communist North.

"The PRG is a convenient screen," they said. "Everywhere those in command are men from Hanoi."

These conclusions were based on the old American assumption according to which the war had been a Communist "aggression" against the democratic South.

And yet, even if it was absurd to link the political significance of April 30th to the name of the city or village written on the birth certificates of the *bo doi* or the political cadres, it was a fact that southern guerrillas had fought side by side with northern army regulars, and that in Saigon itself the administrative structure that emerged after the Liberation was composed largely of southern elements.

The man who took over the Central Post Office and who two months later signed his *nom de guerre*, "Bay Phan," to my authorization to send press dispatches, was a former student from Saigon who had joined the Vietminh in 1945; he had been first in the partisan forces and then in Hanoi, and had returned to his city with the Liberation Army. Was he a northerner?

A fact often forgotten by the Western public is that in 1954, following the Geneva Accords, not only did six to seven hundred thousand Catholics leave the North for the South to escape the "Communist yoke," but a likewise considerable number of partisans, in accordance with the provisions of the Accords, had to move to the North and "regroup."

In the three months I stayed in Saigon, I constantly met men and women from the South in the administration and in the higher ranks of the Liberation Army. They had abandoned their homes and families in 1954 and instead of returning, as they had expected, after the general elections — provided for in the near future by the Geneva Accords but never held — they had had to wait twenty years.

One of these people, who returned to Saigon with the *bo doi* on the afternoon of April 30, was a man I was seeking. His sister, who had left Vietnam to live abroad, married to a Frenchman, had given me his name, Co Tan Chuong, and told me:

"Maybe one day you'll meet him. I think he's now a colonel in the Hanoi army."

Brother number five

"It was as though I were drunk with joy. After listening to Minh's surrender speech, all I could say was: we've won, we've won!" Co Tan Chuong told me when, a month later, I finally succeeded in tracking him down. "I knew it would happen one day, but it seemed to me impossible that that day had arrived and that I was in a jeep on my way to Saigon, to Saigon and home!

"I saw the puppet tanks in flames, the ARVN soldiers throwing away their weapons, taking off their uniforms, fleeing. It was incredible. I was happy.

"I entered Saigon with the Eastern Column, and I knew that once we'd passed Phan Thanh Gian bridge my mother's house wasn't far, but I wasn't able to get my bearings.

"Everything was new, the Bien Hoa highway, the houses. Where once, when I was a boy, there were fields and rice paddies, I now saw nothing but big buildings, concrete blocks, shanties. Everything was changed, and I passed near where my street began without even realizing it. When I had left Saigon in '45 it was still called by its French name, Rue Foucault; I assumed they had changed it but I didn't know to what, and I wasn't even sure my family was still living there.

"I couldn't stop. I had to go all the way to the center with my column, first to Doc Lap Palace and then to the prefecture. There I knew where I was. I recognized the monuments, the cathedral. The Lycée Chasse Loup Laubat—where I had studied—was right there, a stone's throw from Doc Lap.

"It was in that lycée that I first came in contact with the Revolution. I was a Vietnamese but I had to learn the great events of *nos ancêtres, les Gaulois*—'our ancestors, the Gauls.' I understood that I belonged to a people that had lost its history, and when the occasion arose, in the August Revolution of '45, I took up arms against the French.

"It was a hard life with the partisans, and my brother, who was number seven and had come with me, died. He was too young and weak, and the jungle was too much for him."

In talking about his brothers and sisters, Co Tan Chuong did not call them by their names but, as happens in every Vietnamese family, by their number in order of birth, beginning with two. There is no brother number one.

In Chuong's family there had been nine children. In their stories and their various destinies lay the entire history of Vietnam.

The firstborn, brother number two, had been a cadet in the French army. He became a pilot in the Saigon air force and was killed in 1968, shot down by Communist anti-aircraft.

Brother number three was a high school teacher; he had participated in the August Revolution and was later a clandestine activist in the Resistance. He had spent two years in prison under Diem.

Sister number four had died of illness at the age of eighteen.

Co Tan Chuong was brother number five.

Brother number six had been drafted into the South Vietnamese army in 1953. He had made a career of it and become a colonel in the ARVN, assistant to the military commandant of Saigon.

Number seven died in the Vietminh in 1945.

Then came Christine whom everyone, ever since her departure, called by her French baptismal name. She was the friend who had spoken to me of Chuong.

Sister number nine lived in Saigon, married to an ARVN officer.

Last came brother number ten, a painter, who had left as a guerrilla in 1962 and returned to Saigon after the Liberation as a member of the New School of Fine Arts.

"In all the years I spent with the partisans and later in Hanoi," Chuong went on, "I had only one thought: to see my mother again. I wasn't sure that I'd be in time. My father had died while I was away. But once you set out on a path, you must follow it to the end, and for me it would only be possible to return after the complete liberation of the South.

"The only direct contact I had had with my family in Saigon had been a note written to me in '46 by brother number three to tell me that my two-week-old son had arrived home safe and sound.

"He had been born at a difficult moment. The colonialists had broken through our lines at Bien Hoa, many comrades had been killed, and others had lost heart and gone back to Saigon. My wife gave birth in the jungle while the French were conducting continual mopping-up operations.

We couldn't keep him there, and a woman we trusted took him to my mother. That was the last I saw of him.

"I stayed for eight years fighting in zone 'D,' a few kilometers from Saigon, but I was never able to come to the city. Not even in '54. By the terms of the Geneva Accords, we had to abandon our entrenchments and regroup in North Vietnam. They gave us ninety days, and my unit and I were among the first to go to Vung Tau and from there embark for Haiphong.

"In '66 I met my sister Christine in Phnom Penh and learned that my son was growing up with the family and going to school. Later I tried several times to have him approached by comrades working in the South and brought to me, to get him to join the Revolution, but I never had an answer."

No one had dared tell Chuong the truth: his son had enlisted in Thieu's army, trained in the United States, and had become a pilot in the South Vietnamese air force. He knew that he had a father on the other side, since brother number three had once told him, but the subject was never mentioned again.

No one in the family spoke of Chuong; everything that pertained to him had been destroyed, made to disappear. There was not a single photograph of him in the whole house, for fear that one day the police might discover something. But a couple of times brother number six, the colonel, having learned from the ARVN secret service that a prisoner had been captured by the name of Co Tan, had gone to the oldest brother, number three, and asked him how tall Chuong was, how he wore his hair, and both of them, without mentioning it to the others, had rejoiced to discover that the description of the prisoner did not correspond to brother number five.

"I set out to look for my mother the evening of the 30th, as soon as I could get away from my unit," Chuong went on. "I came to my neighborhood and asked for Rue Foucault. They told me the name had been changed to Nguyen Phi Khanh, but that the numbers were still the same as before."

The street is in a middle-class quarter behind Mac Dinh Chi cemetery. The house is a modest one with an iron gate and a small courtyard, from which one enters a large room that serves as living room and kitchen. In one corner, a divan and two plastic-covered armchairs; on a small altar,

photographs of the father and of the dead sister and
brothers; a marble statuette; a single neon light; and, as in
all Vietnamese houses, next to the armchairs, bicycles and
Hondas propped against the wall.

When Chuong arrived in his green uniform and pith
helmet, with his pistol and shoulder bag, and escorted by
two very young *bo doi*, the neighbors crowded in the doorways and peered out the open windows into the courtyard.
Brother number three recognized him immediately.

"For days I'd been saying, 'He's coming, he's coming,' "
he recounted later. "We embraced. We had so many things
to say to each other that for a long time we couldn't
speak."

The mother was in the bedroom upstairs. Since the day
before, when brother number six, the colonel, had come to
say good-bye to her, explaining that he was leaving for
America because he would be killed if he stayed she had
refused to come down.

Chuong lept up the stairs. He opened the door and his
mother began screaming with fear. She saw a Vietcong,
and thought that he had come to take the colonel and
would kill her as well. She was eighty-two years old and
had not recognized him.

A short time later, from the group of relatives and
grandchildren standing in the room around the old
mother, seated in a wicker armchair and wearing a long
white *ao dai*, brother number three took a young man of
about thirty by the hand, led him up to Chuong, and said,
"Let me introduce your son." Everyone was silent and
moved.

When I went there to see them, the family had been
reunited and were all living together once again. On May
5, brother number ten, the painter who had fought for
thirteen years with the Front in the Mekong Delta, had
also arrived, bringing a daughter-in-law and two more
grandchildren.

Each told his story with simplicity, as though it were the
most natural thing in the world. The only subject that had
become taboo was that of brother number six, who had
fled to the United States. No one cared to talk about him.
They were ashamed of him and put the blame on his rich
wife who had forced him to leave.

Chuong's son, who had been persuaded by his uncle
number three to throw away his pilot's uniform and stay,
had already signed up for reeducation.

A swarm of grandchildren were playing in the courtyard and the neighbors were peering from the windows.

During those days thousands of other families in Saigon and the rest of South Vietnam were drawing up the balance sheet from thirty years of war. The return of the fighters was not so easy for all as it had been for brother number five.

There were partisans who came back only to find that they had no more family, that their sons and daughters had left the country, or disappeared in Thieu's prisons, or died fighting the guerrillas.

A daughter of Nguyen Huu Tho, president of the National Liberation Front, had become involved with an American and escaped with him. The wife of a minister of the PRG had become the mistress of a police official and had fled in one of the last helicopters.

Driving lesson

It must have happened much more often to the people of Saigon than to me: you looked around, found everything normal, and then all of a sudden realized that you were surrounded by "Vietcong." It took time to become accustomed to their presence.

Except for them, I might have thought that nothing in Saigon had changed when I threw open my hotel window on the morning of May 2. The shops on Tu Do Street had raised their corrugated shutters and the clerks were dousing and sweeping the sidewalk in front of each' entrance. The bakeries had resumed making bread, and boys with baskets of loaves on the backs of their bicycles were going about delivering it.

When I went down to eat breakfast in the garden of the Continental—where for the first time Joseph the waiter did not greet me by mumbling as usual, "Tea or coffee? Butter or jam?" but proudly and happily shook my hand—I found brioches on the table.

The traffic in the streets was once more as chaotic and stinking as ever. The gas stations were closed and were to stay closed for some time, but cars, Hondas, buses, and three-wheeled cyclos circulated by the thousands. Gasoline

cost ten times its normal price but could still be found on
the black market.

In front of the Post Office, at the principal street crossings, and all along the river, long lines of women and boys
crouched in front of bottles full of purple gasoline, supplied by the Americans to the South Vietnamese army and
stolen in the final days before the Liberation.

In the past the United States embassy, hoping to curtail
thefts, had tinted the gasoline intended for military con-
sumption. But the thefts had naturally continued, and the
Saigonese had become so accustomed to thinking of the
violet "American" gasoline as the best that when the first
supplies of pale, yellowish Soviet gasoline arrived in Saigon
weeks after the Liberation, black market distributors were
obliged to add a purple powder to make their customers
believe that it still came from American reserves.

By May 2 the three thousand refugees who had invaded
the French Grall Hospital in search of protection felt reassured enough to return to their homes. A group of policemen who had barricaded themselves in the hospital chapel
left their guns and ammunition and departed.

Families who had moved from the outlying quarters toward the center of the city, where they thought they would
be safer in the event of a battle, returned to their own
dwellings.

In the midst of the military truck traffic, tanks being
relocated and old cars piled high with people, mattresses,
bicycles, electric fans, and bundles, I could see shining
black limousines that had belonged to the American embassy packed with ten or fifteen smiling *bo doi*. They had
the dark glass windows closed and the shades lowered and
were enjoying the air conditioning with mixed amusement
and embarrassment.

The radio that morning had given the order to clean up
the city, and while groups of students swept streets and
squares, South Vietnamese army cranes towed away the
bodies of cars that had been left scattered all over the city
without wheels, seats, engines, or headlights.

Sanitation trucks scooped up the piles of trash, documents, newspapers, uniforms, helmets, and army boots. A
squad of *bo doi* with scrubbing brushes and soap even went
to clean the courtyard of the American embassy and rake
the garden. Saigon was noisily coming back to life.

Tan Son Nhut Airport had become the quietest place
within range of the city. Past the large concrete and corru-

gated iron building of the DAO, blown up by the last American marines before their departure, an Air America helicopter with crushed blades lay on its side in the square in front of the passenger terminal. You could hear flies buzzing among the wreckage on the huge cement expanse of the parking strips of what during the war had been one of the largest and most active airports in the world.

The fuel and ammunition dumps were still burning, and clouds of smoke rose slowly into the sky.

The control tower was intact; the runways were pock-marked with shell holes and strewn with fragments from the wreckage of destroyed planes and helicopters—at least a hundred of them.

The only things that moved in this enormous concrete cemetery were the shapes of a few *bo doi*. There in the noonday sun, in this space open as far as the eye could see, they were learning to drive the Hondas and bicycles they had found in the storerooms. The arrival of my car on one of the runways created a great sensation, and one after another a dozen *bo doi* asked me to teach them to drive it.

I had gone to Tan Son Nhut to look for Colonel Vo Dong Giang of the PRG delegation at Camp Davis.

At 3:30 in the afternoon on Liberation Day the telex machines at the Post Office and in all the press agencies had shut down. They had resumed for half an hour around six o'clock but had been silent from then on (and were to continue to be indefinitely). Foreign telephone lines no longer worked. All communications had been interrupted and the world did not know what had happened in Vietnam after the arrival of the first tanks.

I had written a few lines to cable to my weekly magazine *Der Spiegel,* and I knew that my only chance for sending them out of Saigon to Germany was Giang.

The *bo doi* on guard had stopped me at the entrance to Tan Son Nhut and would not listen to my reasons for being there, but they finally accepted as a pass an old photograph of myself and the colonel, taken at one of the Saturday press conferences and which I always carried on me with the thought that one day it might be useful.

I reached Camp Davis, on the west side of the airport, by driving through the planes and exploded shells on the runways.

A large flag of the Front fluttered over the camp's water tank. In the huts there was an air of great celebration and demobilization. Interpreters, translators, officers, and guardsmen were packing their kits and putting documents in cardboard boxes. Giang's group was being moved to Doc Lap Palace.

There was Major Phuong Nam, gruff but genial, the only Vietcong I had ever met with a bit of paunch, the man who had answered the telephone during the absurd situation created by the Paris Accords, when all you had to do in Saigon to find out what the PRG's position was on any particular subject was call 924-5149. And there was Giang, who had been the official spokesman for the delegation.

It was a meeting between old acquaintances. We had seen each other at intervals on Saturday mornings for two years. Giang was moved, and when he embraced me his new helmet, which he had put on to leave for the city, fell off and rolled on the floor.

For two years they had taken dozens of photographs of every journalist who frequented Saigon and had been to their press conferences. They had collected every article we wrote, filed every news item that concerned us, and before each meeting they looked up our pictures and memorized our names in order to be able to greet each of us with a personal touch.

My article was dispatched by Giang's orders over the military telex. From Hanoi it was retransmitted to East Berlin, from there to Hamburg. *Der Spiegel* had the first report from liberated Saigon, and on May 5 the article, slightly revised, appeared in three Hanoi newspapers, including *Nhan Dan,* the Workers' Party daily.

Leaving Camp Davis, I went back to the airport terminal.

Groups of *bo doi* were quietly cleaning their rifles, and eating canned pineapple they had found in the refrigerators. Some, leaning on the counter of what had once been Pan American, were writing home on ruled stationery with tinted blue borders and red roses. A twenty-year-old boy was writing to his wife in Hanoi:

"Dearest, I'm finally in Saigon. I'm writing to you from Tan Son Nhut, the airport. I fought heroically. Now that the South is liberated, I hope to go home soon. Take care of our son. Be happy, the war is over."

At 12:50 we heard the distant whirring of an approaching helicopter. *Bo doi* came running from all sides, and I ran with them toward a runway.

1. The author.

2. Cao Giao, the author's friend and interpreter.

3. *(top left)* Big Minh in his garden with his Minister of Information, Ly Qui Chung.

4. *(top right)* French Ambassador Merillon, waiting to depart from Tan Son Nhut Airport.

5. *(bottom)* President Ford and one of the babies "saved" from Communism. (Photo by UPI.)

6. Shoeshine boys in Saigon: "Papa you give me money, I go America."

7. *(top left)* Marine at American Embassy points rifle at South Vietnamese trying to join evacuation flights. (Photo by Cuong—UPI.)

8. *(top right)* Helicopter evacuating Americans and others from top of building in downtown Saigon. (UPI photo by Hugh Van Es.)

9. *(bottom)* April 27, 1975: one of the last images of the Republic. Big Minh has just been sworn in as President, deputies and senators are leaving Doc Lap Palace. The author can be seen in the middle of the photograph, behind the Buddhist monk. (Photo by Jens Nauntofte.)

10. *(top left)* The Hotel Continental.

11. *(top right)* The Hotel Caravelle.

12. *(bottom)* U.S. Ambassador Graham Martin on board the USS Blue Ridge after final evacuation by helicopter from Saigon. (Photo by UPI.)

13. The first tanks on Tu Do Street on their way from Doc Lap to Saigon harbor, April 30, 1975. The Café Givral can be seen at the top center of the photograph.

14. *(top left)* The first tanks on Thong Nhat, April 30, 1975.

15. *(top right)* The first *bo doi* seen by the author, on their way to take over the Ministry of Defense.

16. *(bottom)* Liberation Army Tank in front of American Embassy, April 30.

17. *(left)* Guerrillas in front of National Assembly Building on Liberation Day.

18. *(bottom)* Communist soldiers on a Russian-made T-54 tank in front of Doc Lap Palace shortly after the takeover on April 30. (Photo UPI.)

19. Citizens talking to a *bo doi* a few hours after Liberation.

20. The streets of Saigon the day after Liberation.

21. *(right)* Citizens marching in victory parade, May 7, in front of Doc Lap.

22. *(bottom)* Guerrillas from the Delta marching in victory parade, May 7.

23. *(facing page, top) Bo doi* marines in front of the Monument to the Unknown Soldier, which was destroyed after Liberation Day.

24. *(facing page, bottom) Bo doi* at military parade.

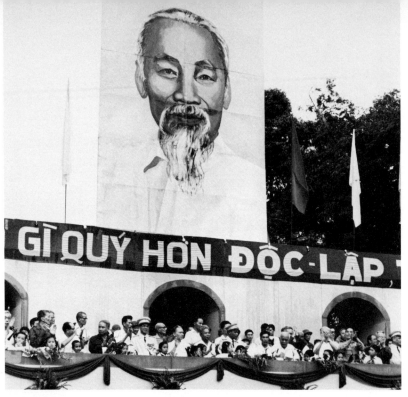

25. In front of Doc Lap on May 15.

26. Looking out from Doc Lap, May 7.

27. *(top) Bo doi* learning to
ride a bicycle on the deserted runways of Tan Son
Nhut.

28. *(left)* Major Phuong
Nam (the "Vietcong with
a paunch") at left, with another Vietcong officer at
Camp Davis.

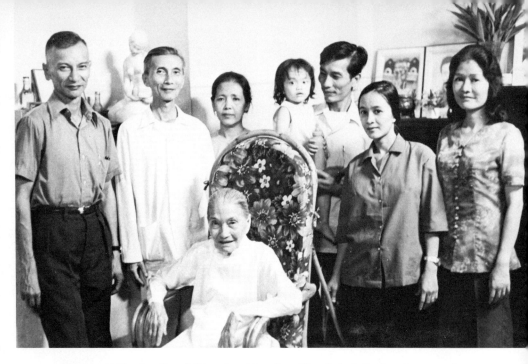

29. *(top)* The family of "Brother Number Five." At left: brother number five, brother number three, the old mother. The son of brother number five is not pictured.

30. *(bottom)* Nguyen Huu Thai, student leader. (See "Autobiography of a fighter.")

31. *(facing page, top left)* Colonel Vo Dong Giang of the PRG delegation at Camp Davis. (See "Come, brothers.")

32. *(facing page, top right)* Joseph, the waiter in the Continental.

33. *(facing page, bottom)* *Bo doi* officer Thanh Cong, who loves Beethoven's music. (See "The *bo doi*.")

34. The Monument to the Unknown Soldier, about to be destroyed.

A large green helicopter with a red star, a Soviet-made Mi-6, alighted on the asphalt. The pilot waved a flag of the Front from the porthole, and as the doors opened a crowd of *bo doi* waved helmets, cheered, danced with joy, and embraced other older *bo doi* who now emerged. Some wept.

It was the first aerial flight from Hanoi to Saigon. Those arriving were political cadres and North Vietnamese air force officers coming to take over the airport installations. There was also a journalist, Le Ba Thuyen, editor of the Hanoi *Illustrated Review.* He was a native of Saigon.

"When I left thirty years ago I knew, I knew that someday I'd be back," he said visibly moved and gazing around.

In the name of the people

On the evening of May 2, the radio and television announced that every sign of the past, every trace of the old regime, was to be erased.

Saigon obeyed without protest. Whatever had not been destroyed or burned in the first hours of the Liberation disappeared for good. The "three-banded" flags painted at the entrance to every dwelling and on the roofs of houses were scraped off. Anti-Communist propaganda posters were so completely eradicated that when a few weeks later officials came from Hanoi to collect documentation for the Museum of the Revolution, they were unable to find a single copy in all of Saigon.

The wall at the entrance to Tan Son Nhut, which for years had borne the inscription in large block letters, THE NOBLE SACRIFICE OF THE ALLIED SOLDIERS WILL NEVER BE FORGOTTEN, was covered with a layer of white paint. On it appeared the sentence by Ho Chi Minh that became the motto of the Revolution: NOTHING IS MORE PRECIOUS THAN INDEPENDENCE AND FREEDOM.

The campaign for the destruction of symbols of the past culminated on May 5 at 10:30 in the morning with the demolition of Thieu's monstrous Monument to the Unknown Soldier in front of the National Assembly. When the head of reinforced concrete rolled onto the ground in a cloud of dust and to a great fluttering of revolutionary banners,

a swarm of bats that had been nesting inside flew away
from it.

Those elements of Saigon society that had been terrified
by the arrival of the *bo doi* in the city accepted this change
of flags with enthusiasm, without understanding that it was
not merely a matter of facade.

After a few days of hesitation many people, having realized that there were to be no firing squads and no hunting
down of collaborationists, thought that the changeover in
power was no different from those in the past, and that by
simply making an about-face they could perhaps go on living as before.

The Rex Bar, the rendezvous of the *jeunesse dorée* of the
capital and the best known center for drug pushers, reopened its doors. Whores and transvestites who on the day
after the Liberation had mingled in modest dress with the
population, some even in peasant clothes, reappeared on
the sidewalks winking and with painted faces, along with
the cripples, the beggars, and the bands of little shoeshine
boys controlled by a gang of former policemen now in civilian clothes.

Downtown Saigon looked surprisingly normal again, under the eyes of the *bo doi* who passed in Indian file as
though from some other planet, their rifles on their shoulders and with the rolling step of people accustomed to hik-
ing in the mountains. Many Saigonese who had not been
able to escape in time and had at first resigned themselves
to staying, now resumed their hope of getting out.

Chinese secret societies in Cholon were guaranteeing
passage by ship to Thailand, Malaysia, or Singapore for
ten thousand dollars a head. Some people left and it was
never learned if they arrived at their destination, but the
price of the dollar on the black market rose again to three
thousand piasters.

"Saigon is like that," said Cao Giao. "On the first day
people are glad to have saved their necks, on the second
they try to get back their Hondas, on the third they organize themselves to go on living by their little business deals."

Saigon, which had learned to sell every sort of thing in
its time, now thought of commercializing the Revolution.

The Chinese in Cholon, who had prepared for the Liberation by replacing the portraits of Chiang Kai-shek in
their shops with ones of Mao, had also fabricated tens of
thousands of Front flags of varying quality and size, of cotton, silk, and even plastic.

On the market stands the imitation American Zippo lighters, adored by the GIs, with the inscription "When I die I'll go to heaven since in Vietnam I've already been in hell" on one side, appeared with a red star engraved on the other.

A fifty-year-old man, aided by his thirteen-year-old son, crouched on the corner of Tu Do Street in front of the Café Givral and began turning out dozens of pairs of "Ho Chi Minh sandals" from old rubber tires. Soon competitors appeared here and there throughout the city.

But the most sought after thing in Saigon became Ho Chi Minh.

Some cunning merchants used the first precious copies of the president's portrait to make thousands of photostats, which they sold at street corners. Others soon succeeded in printing imitations.

On May 5 the first issue of the new daily *Saigon Giai Phong* ("Liberated Saigon") had the smiling photo of Ho covering a quarter of its front page. Other pictures of the president, at work, surrounded by children, meeting fighters of the Front, together with Giap, appeared in the next fifteen issues of the paper.

Ho Chi Minh made his appearance everywhere, a kind of holy image, in homes, framed in offices, in stores, in schools, flapping on the handlebars of bicycles and Hondas, on the windshields of cars and buses.

The *bo doi* reacted to this trade, which was enriching certain businessmen, by going from stand to stand, announcing that "Uncle Ho is not for sale," and that the people's organizations would distribute necessary copies free to every family, factory, and office. But people were in a hurry and the trade continued, with circumspection, under the counter as though it were cocaine: a black-and-white portrait, five hundred piasters; in color, one thousand.

The first *bo doi* arriving in the city had no Saigon money with them, and they began to offer the northern currency, the dong, to buy transistors, watches, and batteries.

The Chinese in Cholon, speculating on the notion that the country would soon be unified, that there would be a monetary reform, and that in any case the dong was worth much more than Thieu's piaster, established an unofficial rate of exchange: two thousand piasters for one dong.

On May 8 the Military Management Committee announced that the dong was not legal tender in the South, that the only valid currency was that of the "puppet regime," and that the exchange would be conducted in due course by the banks. But the banks remained closed and so the black market flourished in this new sector.

On the sidewalks of Han Thuyen Street, a stone's throw from Doc Lap Palace, an exchange which soon came to be called the "People's Bank" was opened: a group of women and men, some recognizable as former policemen and officers in Thieu's army, who traded currency on behalf of the Chinese. Here *bo doi* who were brought in large trucks from the provinces to see the capital and make their purchases could exchange dong for piasters.

"If this keeps up, it won't be the *bo doi* who'll bring order to Saigon but Saigon that will corrupt them," said some inhabitants smugly.

There had been other attempts. Some youths caught stealing in Gia Dinh had tried to get out of it in the old way by offering to share the spoils with the *bo doi*. And when the *bo doi* had come to ask My Linh, madam of the bar and brothel near the Tran Hung Dao monument, what sort of activity went on in her place, she had invited them to sit down and offered the whole squad drinks on the house. In the past she had paid a thousand dollars a month to the local police to protect her business and the thirty-two girls who worked for her and made her rich. The *bo doi* accepted the drinks but returned next day bringing her ten kilos of their rice in payment.

Nguyen Van Ba, a former police informer who had worked on the waterfront, told me his experience:

"One night, talking to a *bo doi* standing guard on the waterfront, I offered to trade him my watch for one of the many cases of whiskey piled in the storerooms. He accepted. Next night I returned with another watch and made the same deal. When I tried a third time, instead of that *bo doi* I found a whole committee. They told me that if I came back again they'd shoot me."

In the days following the Liberation there were at least half a million persons in Saigon, ex-police officers and soldiers disbanded from the old army, all without work and many still armed. They circulated in the streets along with the regular big city gangsters and common criminals released from prison, in search of some way of making quick money.

Rangers and elements of the Special Forces, trained in the past to infiltrate the ranks of the Vietcong and the areas controlled by the Liberation Army, utilized their old disguises, and by pretending to be *bo doi* terrorized the population in some quarters, "confiscated" houses with all their contents, and stole cars and motorcycles.

A dozen *bo doi* were assassinated in back streets at night by people who only wanted their uniforms for criminal purposes.

While political cadres went from quarter to quarter making a census of the population and taking down the names of those who had fled with the Americans, others who pretended to be authorized representatives of the Front followed them, trying to sell favors and influence to the more ingenuous. One of these episodes, which took place in the Vo Tang quarter near Tan Son Nhut, was related to me by a sixty-year-old man who had witnessed it:

"Two days after *Cach mang* (the Revolution), three men came here and assembled the population. They spoke of the war, they told everyone to remain calm and follow the instructions of the *can bo*, the cadres. They told the families of policemen and soldiers not to worry. They should register and nothing would happen to them. They said the policy of the new government was one of clemency and forgiveness. There would be no reprisals against those who had served Thieu and the Americans. The three had the names of the inhabitants of every house and knew the quarter well.

"When they left, a young pseudo-intellectual from the neighborhood spoke up, saying he had been in contact with the Front for some time and would help the population to resolve its problems with the new authorities. Two hours hadn't gone by before the three returned, summoned everyone again, and holding a pistol to the young man's head explained to people that he had no power, that he did not represent the Front, and that if he tried to exploit the situation again they would shoot him."

The military authorities had made repeated radio appeals urging the population to protect both private property and "property of the people" (meaning everything left behind by the Americans and fleeing Vietnamese); notices had been posted announcing "severe penalties" for thieves and looters; but still armed robbery, purse snatching, and breaking and entry into homes and American warehouses continued. An unruly crowd lingered from one day to the next at the large American godown across the Newport bridge, ready to break down the fence and held at bay by a dozen youthful guerrillas. To walk in downtown Saigon with a purse or a simple package in your hand meant taking an enormous risk.

The *bo doi* were then given the order to fire.

Two youths fleeing on a Honda were brought down in Hai Ba Trung Street; three thieves were shot in the central market in Cholon. The corpse of a third was left on view for three days in the Ka Noi quarter with a sign on his chest: "I stole." Another was shot down by machine-gun fire on the Bach Dang embankment, at the end of Tu Do Street.

On Saturday morning, May 17, the *bo doi* announced with megaphones that at nine o'clock there would be a people's tribunal at the corner of Vo Tanh and Truong Tan Buu.

A crowd of about five hundred people attended. In the middle of the street, where traffic had been halted, three *bo doi* brought out two boys, untied and without handcuffs. One was eighteen, the other twenty. A fourth *bo doi* with a megaphone explained to the population that they had been caught stealing a drum of gasoline from a nearby garage. Two witnesses testified to having seen them; the *bo doi* asked the crowd what should be done with them. Someone shouted:

"Kill them!"

The *bo doi* with the megaphone asked again:

"Those who say they should be killed raise their hands." A multitude of open palms were raised in the air. The *bo doi* said:

"In the name of the people." He took his pistol from the holster and fired. Two shots apiece, in the head. And traffic resumed.

Another people's tribunal was held on Nguyen Thien Thuat Street. It was described to me by Trinh Thi Hoa, a girl of twenty-three who had worked as a typist for a commercial firm closed since the Liberation because her Vietnamese employer had left with the Americans:

"I knew him well, the man the *bo doi* shot. He lived near me. He was a drug addict, and with a gang of accomplices he'd become the terror of the neighborhood. He did a lot of harm to many people. He stole and sold drugs, and made young people in the area buy drugs from him. His parents were unable to discipline him. He had been in prison but got out with the Liberation and became even worse than before.

"The other day he went to his mother to ask her for

money; while she pretended to look for it in drawers, his father went to call the *bo doi* to arrest him. It was his parents who asked the Revolutionary Government to do something to free the neighborhood from this menace.

"The tribunal was made up of people who had been this fellow's victims and they voted for the death penalty. The *bo doi* carried it out on the spot. It was violent, but with someone like that what else can you do?"

As the weeks went by, crime diminished in the streets of Saigon. I think that in the three months I stayed in Saigon after the Liberation there were about thirty such summary executions of ordinary criminals, none of a political nature.

Protagonists revisited

I should have been a witness to the release of General Minh and his government, but the young *bo doi* standing guard at the demolished gate to Doc Lap Palace was unyielding. My companion, who had come specially to pick me up at the hotel with a whole escort and a Soviet-made general staff jeep, all enclosed and with a dusty bouquet of plastic flowers beside the wheel, had a hard time explaining in a subdued and persuasive tone:

"Comrade, I am Major Phuong Nam. This journalist has been invited by the Military Management Committee. He must be taken immediately to the Protocol Room. General Tran Van Tra is expecting us. . . ."

It was no use. In the confusion of moving from Camp Davis Phuong Nam, the genial Vietcong with the paunch, had forgotten his identification papers, and the *bo doi*, smiling but firm, refused to let us pass. Thus all I saw, from afar, at 7:30 on the evening of May 2 of the historical last act between the two regimes, the one that had capitulated and the one that had triumphed, were handshakes and the jeeps that took the defeated protagonists home.

Since the afternoon of April 30, General Minh and fifteen of his people, among them Nguyen Van Huyen, Vu Van Mau, Nguyen Van Hao, Ly Qui Chung, Nguyen Van Diep, and Thai Lam Nghiem, had been held in Doc Lap Palace and lodged in the quarters usually reserved for

guests. After the first somewhat painful moments of surprise (Minh had been expecting a PRG delegation to negotiate surrender terms, and instead saw an approaching parade of tanks firing in the air), relations between the old
and new occupants of Doc Lap had been cordial.

Once he was inside the palace, Tran Van Tra had had a
long talk with the group, and Minh, turning to one of his
associates and pointing out the disciplined and efficient *bo
doi* moving around them, had remarked:

"This is the breed of Vietnamese that we thought had
disappeared."

The meeting between these two groups was more than
an encounter between adversaries in what first of all had
been a war against the foreign aggressor and then a civil
war. Among the men in the two camps were some who
had had the same patriotic ideals in the beginning and had
only divided on the way they should be realized.

At the time he was a medical student in Hanoi Minh, a
young nationalist, had been a friend of Huynh Tan Phat,
who later joined the Communist Party and was named
prime minister of the PRG. The August Revolution of
1945 had separated them, but Minh had never felt himself
to be any less of a nationalist than Phat or than his own
brother, who had remained in the North and become a
general in the Liberation Army. Minh had thought it possible to pursue independence without breaking Vietnam's
ties with France and by keeping the country in the Western orbit. He had not been opportunistic; at most he had
been naive. In paying for this historical error, he had
ended up at Doc Lap Palace declaring unconditional
surrender.

Behind him in the Protocol Room sat Thai Lang
Nghiem. Born in Hanoi, he was already a stubborn nationalist and fierce anti-Communist in his university days.
When Ho Chi Minh took power, he went into the jungle
and fought simultaneously against the French and the
Communists. Captured in 1946, he served time in Vietminh prisons; escaping to the South in 1954, he was jailed
by Diem, and later became a supporter of Nguyen Cao Ky
and an angry senator of the Republic. He was imprisoned
once again for his opposition to Thieu. Freed on April 26,
he had put himself at the disposal of the last president.
Minh, Huyen, Nghiem, and many others like them had de-
luded themselves that the liberation of the country could

be accomplished without the discipline, the ideology, the popular base that only the Communist Party had been able to supply. They had been wrong, and in various ways theirs were so many lives wasted in the same manner.

The ceremony for the release of Minh and his followers had been a formal one. On one side of the room were sixteen armchairs with the members of the Minh government, on the other three armchairs with the political commissar Bui Thanh Khiet, the vice-president of the military administration, Cao Van Chiem, and in the center Tran Van Tra. All around were dozens of officers and soldiers of the Liberation Army.

After some general remarks by the political commissar on the capture of Saigon, General Tra had spoken:

"At the end of this very long struggle there are neither victors nor vanquished. It is the Vietnamese people, all the people, who have defeated American imperialism. The Vietnamese people are the only ones in all history to have defeated the Mongols. In 1945 we defeated the Japanese, in 1954 France at Dien Bien Phu, and now we have beaten the United States, which thought itself the strongest country in the world. It is to the Vietnamese people that the glory for all this goes."

General Minh had replied:

"I am happy to be here. I think that by my actions I have helped to avoid a final and useless shedding of blood in Saigon. That has been my positive part in this struggle. I am sixty years old, and today I am proud to be once more a free citizen in an independent country."

The two groups shook hands in front of the palace steps and Minh was escorted to his Tran Quy Cap villa, from which he no longer stirred, refusing to grant interviews or receive visits except from his closest associates of former times.

A week after the Liberation the rumor spread that Minh was to have a role in a future coalition government with the Communists; a month later it was said that the general had been summoned and taken to Hanoi for consultations. But behind all this was nothing more than the aspirations of some of his admirers, and of certain elements in Saigon who were worried at the prospect of a solely Communist government and still hoped to carry some weight through a man like him. As of April 30 Duong Van Minh had ended his role on the political scene. He had done so with dignity, but also certainly without much conviction. Many doubts about the motivations for his rise to power remained, and the place that would be reserved for him in official history was still uncertain.

The men of the Front respected him, and repaid him in their own coin: Minh and all the members of his government were exempted from the reeducation program to which all officials of the old regime were obliged to present themselves. But when the myth began to emerge among the public of Minh as "the savior of Saigon," the Communist press responded with a series of articles that spoke of Minh as "the officer of the French colonialists," Minh "the organizer of the anti-Diem coup inspired by the CIA," and so forth.

Minh was soon forgotten. At the entrance to Tran Quy Cap there was no longer even a guard, and the two telephones in the porter's lodge at the green gate were cut off. A friend who had been to see him told me:

"We always used to imagine the general in his garden, cultivating his orchids and waiting for the nation's call. Now there he is, surrounded by his tropical fish in the aquaria, with the absentminded look of someone trying to decide whether or not to write his memoirs."

After the release I went to see Vice-President Huyen in his house at 181 Hong Tap Tu. Wearing white pajamas, he received me in a modest living room hung with drying laundry, under a large portrait of the pope and a cupboard full of little plastic dolls and plaster statuettes of saints.

A fervent Catholic, with a son a priest and a daughter a nun, he had always been considered one of the most honest men of the old regime. He was a jurist and had resigned as president of the Senate when Thieu had forced through a resolution giving himself full powers.

"It's shameful to have to admit it but Thieu was a puppet of the Americans," Huyen said to me. "When he resigned we understood that there was no other way for us but negotiations. This was the opinion shared by all of us who agreed to work with General Minh. Our position was very different from Huong's. He put up some formal constitutional resistance, but in reality he was a screen for the Americans. If Huong had passed on power to us in time, we would have been able to negotiate, but the Americans didn't want it. It was a very subtle game. They wanted the situation to deteriorate, they wanted a tragedy to justify their departure. Ambassador Martin had decided to leave dramatically, not calmly."

"Then why didn't Minh declare surrender at the moment he was sworn in?" I asked.

"I and the others advised him to. But he refused. The army in Saigon was still intact and there was danger of a coup d'etat—and then the city might really have been in for a massacre! Do you know that two ARVN tanks came with a white flag to Doc Lap at eleven o'clock on the very morning of the surrender? A group of officers went up to Minh's office to ask why, why he had surrendered, but fortunately he succeeded in calming them down."

Among the others released, the economist Nguyen Van Hao declared himself ready to help in the reconstruction of the country in any way that he might be useful. The new authorities soon recalled him to the palace, where together with a group of technocrats of the old regime he worked to prepare an analysis of the southern economy.

Vu Van Mau, the prime minister, repeated to everyone who went to see him that the Third Force no longer existed, since now there was only one force and it had taken power.

Among Minh's young associates, Nguyen Van Ba and Ly Qui Chung were the most enthusiastic over the outcome of events. I found out why later, when their leader Ngo Cong Duc, Catholic deputy from Vinh Binh and former editor of the newspaper *Tin Sang,* who had been sentenced to death by the Central Intelligence Organization, returned from exile. Though not men of the Front, they were members of an informal but well-organized group of persons who, in contact with the Front, had infiltrated various non-Communist organizations in opposition to the regime in order to work toward the solution that had later taken place.

I the undersigned puppet soldier

The brief announcement, published on the last page of the newspaper *Saigon Giai Phong* on May 6 and later posted by the *bo doi* on the walls of the city, was neither a formal or-

der nor an invitation. Signed by Tran Van Tra and addressed to "soldiers, noncommissioned officers, and officers of the puppet army, police, and intelligence," it said
merely that "registration" would be open from the 8th to
the 31st of the month, and gave the addresses at which to
appear: generals at No. 213 Hong Bang Avenue, other officers and soldiers at the neighborhood committee nearest
to their places of residence.

And so Saigon had to familiarize itself with another
word in the new vocabulary introduced by the Revolution:
nguy or "puppet."

"Puppet" did not mean only those who had taken up
arms against the partisans or had worked in one way or
another for the South Vietnamese administration. "Puppet" meant everything that had to do with the old regime,
everything Vietnamese that had been contaminated, de-
based by the foreign — particularly the American — presence.

There were not only "puppet" soldiers, clerks, officials,
ministers, policemen, and magistrates; there was also a
"puppet" culture, a mentality, an art, a way of behavior.
Thus in order to build "a new, fresh, joyous, and revolutionary society," everything designated as "puppet" was to
be excluded, until such time as it had been changed, remodeled, in other words, purified.

To be a "puppet" was a sin, but not an unforgivable one.
There were no punishments by which it could be expiated,
but to confess, to take cognizance of it, was already to re-
deem oneself in part. To be a "puppet" was a sickness, but
not an incurable one. The therapy would come later with
hoc tap, reeducation, the bath in the Revolution.

The registration of military "puppets" was the first step
in this impressive process of purification to which all of
Vietnamese society in the South was to be subjected. Every
man, woman, and child of every social class, every profession, every origin, every educational level was to undergo
hoc tap. For some it would last only a few days, for others
months or perhaps years.

The *bo doi* in their daily conversations with people in the
street and the radio and television in their nightly broadcasts had explained that the policy of the revolutionary authorities was one of forgiveness, that no one would be
punished for crimes committed in the past, that no one
had to fear reprisals. But the "puppets" were not reassured, and on the morning of the 8th, when the registra-

tion centers opened, very few soldiers of the old regime made their appearance. Then the experience of the first ones encouraged others, and day after day one saw long lines of men of different ages—all looking equally re-signed—in civilian clothes, with packets of documents in their hands, standing in the sun and awaiting their turn.

I spent the whole afternoon of May 9 in one of these centers in the town of Bien Hoa, thirty kilometers north of Saigon. With the Liberation the old police barracks, a stone's throw from the market, had become the headquarters of "People's Security."

Along the outer wall at least two hundred persons were lined up in silence, three abreast. At the gate two boy guerrillas, neither more than sixteen years old, stood guard in the black trousers, blue shirts, and soft wide-brimmed hats typical of southern fighters, with their AK-47 rifles resting on their chests. A small crowd of relatives and curious onlookers watched from the other side of the street.

Two or three at a time the "puppets" entered a small room, its walls unplastered and riddled with bullet holes. It had been the waiting room for the former chief of police. They took off their caps, sat down on a wooden bench, and at a sign from another youthful guerrilla presented themselves at a table where two former ARVN officers who had volunteered for the assignment wrote down in a register the name, surname, date and place of birth, residence, enlistment number, and military rank of each.

In one corner of the room, at a makeshift table with a large, dirty teapot from which he offered generous cups of a green and steaming liquid, was a peasant of about fifty. He was a small man, his skin dry and chapped, his hands rough, and he had a forehead full of bumps and a con-stant smile full of gold teeth. He spoke to the "puppets" one by one after they had registered. He asked them where they had fought, under what officers they had served, in what operations they had participated. He made rapid notes of each reply in a square-ruled school note-book. Sometimes he asked for further details.

He was a native of Tu Duc, a village not far from Bien Hoa. He had joined the Revolution in 1959 and from that time on had always fought in the region. He was often fa-miliar with the operations of which the "puppets" spoke, since he had experienced them on the other side of the lines; he and his comrades had been the objectives for the

search-and-destroy missions of the ARVN. It was easy for
him to judge the sincerity of what the men who had come
to register told him.

There were not only ex-soldiers in this scene but officers
as well—officers who had studied, some of them in the
United States, who had held positions of power, and were
now humbly appearing, with respect and even fear, before
a modest peasant dressed in his simple *ao baba*, the black
pajamalike costume of the country people. A reversal of
values, ethics, power, brought about by the Revolution.

At the end of the conversation with the peasant the
"puppets" were sent across the courtyard into another
room with many wooden benches, like a school classroom.
From behind a desk another guerrilla distributed sheets of
yellow paper on which the "puppets" were to write down
what they believed: their experiences under the old regime, their reasons for enlisting, the crimes they had committed, what they thought of the Revolution, and what
they expected of it.

If you forgot for a moment what the relations between
these two groups of people had been up until a few days
before and what lay in the past of many of the "puppets,"
it could be painful to see men thirty to forty years old
packed into school benches too small for their legs, with
their heads bent in worry over the exercise assigned them,
an exercise on which they thought their future in one way
or another would depend.

Some wrote page after page, others only a few lines.
One, after two hours, handed in this sentence: "I the un-
dersigned puppet soldier am sorry for all the evil that on
the orders of the traitor Thieu I did to my people."

All the sheets were returned to the peasant guerrilla,
who at the end signed and handed each of the "puppets" a
piece of mimeographed paper filled out with his name, address, and the date of registration. This was his new identity card. With it he could circulate freely in all of South
Vietnam and could apply to the new authorities to find
work; with it he would later have to appear for reeducation.

All those "puppets" who did not live in the Bien Hoa
area but had come to register at this center, thinking they
would not be recognized and thus be more secure against
eventual reprisals, were given three days in which to appear at the center in the quarter where they actually lived.

One thing that was surprising in the Bien Hoa registration center, and in the others I visited during the following days in Saigon, was the absence of *bo doi,* the regular soldiers of the Liberation Army.

Everywhere the interviews, the gathering of information, and the issuing of new identification documents were carried out by local cadres, Front guerrillas who had often lived and fought in the neighborhood or region.

This was a way of giving credibility to a southern PRG administration, as distinct from the army that came largely from the North, and a means of compensating local cadres with power for their years of struggle. It was also a system, especially in a city like Saigon, for putting local elements to a test.

As some members of the Front explained to me later, the fact that there had been no battle for Saigon had paradoxically created a problem. A situation of crisis which would have tested the clandestine structure of the Front had never come about; in a battle, which could have lasted for weeks, there would have been a natural selection. The population would have chosen its leaders, and there would be no problem of last-minute revolutionaries emerging with red armbands and laying claim to a past as fighters. Many urban cadres, especially among the young, had not proved themselves in battle, and now had to be sifted. The registration of the "puppets" was, in a sense, also a test for some of them.

Among the "puppets" whom I saw appear at the Bien Hoa center was a police major who had worked in the same offices where he was now coming to be registered by his former enemies. As he went through the barracks gate and entered the room with the smiling peasant with the gold teeth, a woman in the crowd standing on the other side of the street shouted something. But no one stirred, the procedure did not change, and everything went forward as with the others. This coolness, this staggering lack of emotions made me think of some simple bureaucratic routine, as though these people were coming for nothing more than an examination for a driver's license.

"We cannot indulge in personal feelings. Our job is to apply correctly the revolutionary government's policy of reconciliation and national harmony," the political commissar of the Bien Hoa center told me in the former police chief's office, still hung with staff diagrams and American-style statistics of captured Vietcong, where he was directing the work of the registration center.

"Here we don't arrest or punish anyone. Those who make sincere and honest statements are forgiven," he said. "And anyway what's so surprising about this policy? We've forgiven the American pilots who bombed our homes and burned our children. Why shouldn't we forgive Vietnamese like ourselves who did what they did on orders from the Americans?"

He too was a peasant. He came from the province of Qui Nhon and had been with the guerrillas since 1945. He had always fought in the South. He had never been to Hanoi. From his green American-made guard belt, on his black cotton trousers, hung a large pistol still bearing the initials "U.S." The weapons of southern guerrillas were often captured ones.

"I'm forty-nine. There's no one left in my family except one brother. All the others were sacrificed in the Revolution." He spoke of himself, after much prompting on my part, but always refusing to give me his name. "This is not the story of a few persons. It's the story of a whole people," he kept repeating.

While he spoke, calm and self-composed behind the desk of the former chief of police, young guerrillas came in with documents or with tiny slips of white tissue paper on which a few words were written in ballpoint. He read them, tore them up, and wrote brief replies on other slips that his men then took away. There was an almost unbearable calm and serenity in the man. His face was continually relaxed in a broad smile and he seemed to be sitting far above everything that surrounded him.

While telling of other episodes of his life in the jungle and of his children, he repeated two or three times the expression "sacrificed in the Revolution." He said it without sadness. It was as though he were speaking of someone who had been touched by grace, someone who he felt certain had ended up in his particular paradise. This was generally the way people in the Front spoke of their war dead.

Phuong Nam, the Vietcong major with the paunch, often spoke of his two nephews, sons of his peasant brother, who had been "sacrificed in the Revolution." It was only two months later, when I went to the Delta, that I found out what had happened. Thieu's police had come with the army to round up the villagers, and had found the two boys hiding with their weapons in a tunnel dug under the wooden bed in their house. There were other sons in the house and all of them would have been killed if the truth had been told.

"We've never seen them. We don't know them," said the mother.

"Then you don't care if we kill them?" asked the police.

The two boys stood before the family with their hands tied behind their backs.

"I've never seen them, I tell you I don't know them," the mother repeated.

An officer took his pistol and shot them dead one after the other. No one moved. No one shed a tear, and the two corpses were left in front of the doorway of the house as though no one were interested in them. It was the neighbors who later buried them in two unmarked graves in the cemetery.

The peasant commissar in Bien Hoa went on with his story: "I lost my wife in 1965. She was captured while on a mission to the city of My Tho and the police tortured her until she died. That's already ten years ago."

Outside in the courtyard, between the room for interviews and the classroom for writing declarations, the "puppet" soldiers, officers, and policemen came and went, timorous, obsequious, with lowered heads, but safe and sound with their papers in their hands. And there he was, with his calm, broad smile, prominent ears and his eyes reddened like those of peasants who have spent too many hours in the sun.

"I understand the reasons for the policy of reconciliation," I said. "But on the personal level, how is it possible to accept reconciliation? How is it possible to forgive those who tortured and killed?"

"It's simple," he replied. "One must understand what lies at the origin of it all. The Americans were the ones who taught the Vietnamese to torture and kill other Vietnamese. The torturers, the police, the puppet soldiers were themselves victims; we have all been oppressed. In every Vietnamese family today there are soldiers of the Front and soldiers of Thieu. One must understand. One must forgive. This is the moment to reunite families, to reunite the people, not to divide them by digging more trenches."

The commissar explained that one of the difficulties was to make the population understand the principles of this policy of reconciliation and national harmony. In Bien Hoa on Liberation Day the families of some police victims had seized two officers and were about to lynch them. The *bo doi* had intervened and the two men had been saved.

Similar incidents had occurred in other places and espe-, cially in the villages, where relations between the population and the oppressors were more personal and people knew each other. The *bo doi* repeatedly had to shut policemen into their own former prisons and keep them under close guard, to protect them from groups of people who wanted to carry out summary justice.

After the registration of military "puppets" came the turn of clerks and officials of the civil administration. Registration for foreign residents of Saigon began on May 10.

Journalists, diplomats—including the French ambassador Merillon and the apostolic nuncio LeMaitre—and representatives of the international and humanitarian organizations had to present themselves at the old Foreign Ministry which, repainted and with a new inscription on the facade, had returned to being such; all others were to appear at the immigration offices.

The announcement regarding foreigners promised that "all those who work honestly, do not oppose the Vietnamese people or the policy of the Revolution, and who respect the laws and customs of the country will be able to continue their normal activities."

There were enough conditions in this simple sentence to make the majority of foreigners, especially the French with their plantations, their factories, their import-export firms, understand that their time in Vietnam was over.

A final point in the announcement specified that no foreigner could leave the Saigon-Gia Dinh area without a special permit from the revolutionary authorities.

On May 25 registration began for Vietnamese in charge of the central organs of the old political parties of the Republic, from Thieu's Dan Chu to those of the opposition.

This was followed by registration for all members of parties and patriotic and parapolitical organizations. Then for Vietnamese who worked or had worked for commercial agencies, banks, firms, or any type of organization controlled by foreigners, or in diplomatic missions.

The procedure was always the same. Each person took his or her identification papers, certificates, and any documents that could prove the truth of his statements. Each told his story, and the reasons for his choices. Each in his way confessed.

2: Prisoners, Leaders, Liberators

The Hung Vuong School

Just how many political prisoners there were in Thieu's jails had never been clear. He and the Americans said none, the Vietcong and their sympathizers said two hundred thousand. No one knew exactly, and in this uncertainty many "objective" observers avoided the subject altogether, while many journalists ended by making it a question of number rather than substance. To me, establishing the exact figure had always seemed irrelevant. It was enough to be convinced, as many Vietnamese were, that the police indiscriminately arrested opponents of the regime or those suspected of being so, that in the interrogation centers people were tortured by every means from electric shocks to soapy water squirted into the lungs, to realize that—be it a thousand prisoners or a hundred thousand—the principle was there. The rest was a matter of details, albeit important ones.

From a tiny office alongside a religious book printer within the enclosure of the Redemptorist church at No. 38 Ky Dong Street, a man had dealt for years with these details: Father Chan Tin. Without enjoying the approval of the Catholic hierarchy, but protected by the fact that as a Catholic priest he belonged to an organization that decisively supported the regime, Chan Tin had kept an up-to-date file on every arrest and every release in the country through his network of personal contacts. For every prisoner he had a card with whatever information or rumor of any kind he was able to get from relatives, friends, policemen, or released prisoners. As a cover, Chan Tin organized and made himself chairman of a committee for "reform of the prison system," which also helped him to receive funds from abroad.

It was Chan Tin who through various calculations ar-

rived at the figure of two hundred thousand, and it was
with his material that Amnesty International prepared its
dossier on political prisoners in Vietnam.

A few days after Liberation Day Chan Tin telephoned
me in the hotel to ask whether I wanted to go to Con Son,
the largest and most important political prison, with the
first ships that were to bring back detainees. If I did I
should apply for a permit next day at seven o'clock at the
former office of the prime minister. He would be there
himself.

Neither one of us obtained a permit. The prisoners were
already en route to Vung Tau and from there would
shortly arrive in Saigon. Perhaps the new authorities preferred to carry out the liberation of political prisoners by
themselves and did not want to enable Chan Tin, the
"Third Force" in which he was active, or even the Catholic
Church of which he was a priest, to gain credit in the eyes
of the prisoners or the Vietnamese public.

I waited in the courtyard of the old building that had
once been Prime Minister Khiem's and was now invaded
by young Vietcong who seemed astonished to see their
own flags fluttering on all the great buildings of the capital. Chan Tin came down the broad staircase looking
vexed. As usual he was wearing his blue-gray shirt, dark
gray trousers, and brown plastic slippers. In recent years I
had seen him in his black cassock, white collar, and tight
black Redemptorist sash only when he took to the streets
with the Third Force to defy Thieu's police. He did not
tell me what reasons the new authorities had given for not
taking us to Con Son or at least letting us go to Vung Tau.
Departing with an irritated look, he blurted out: "It's all
been done, but without us."

The first prisoners from Con Son began arriving in Saigon the second week in May, and I set out to look for a
girl I had known a year before, when she was still locked
up in Tan Hiep Prison north of Saigon.

In February 1974, while collecting material on political
prisoners, I had been taken to a pagoda of Buddhist nuns
outside Saigon by Mme. Ngo Ba Thanh. The mother superior had introduced me to a group of mothers, sisters, and
relatives of prisoners, each with a terrible story to tell. The
police had surrounded the pagoda, and every so often a
plainclothesman with a portable radio came to see what I,
a foreigner, was doing in the midst of all those women and
nuns.

"He's a journalist, my son. Why don't you go and lock up some crook or one of your corrupt generals instead of wasting your time here with us?" the mother superior told him. He smiled in embarrassment, drank the tea he was offered, and went away.

It was February 15, the feast of Buddhist offerings, and somebody suggested that we visit the nearest prison with the pretext of bringing presents. They gave me a large basket of fruit to carry, put me (the only Westerner) in the back of a small truck that filled up with Buddhist nuns, and we drove full speed out through the gateway of the pagoda in the direction of the Bien Hoa highway.

The driver—the only other man in the party—was a skinny old man in his sixties, with a D'Artagnan goatee, sprightly eyes, and a possessed look. I had already seen him shouting and hurling himself at the police during Third Force demonstrations, and after the Liberation I was to meet him again as a block leader in downtown Saigon. Next to him sat Mme. Ngo Ba Thanh and the mother superior, holding the large, five-color Buddhist flag that fluttered from the window of the truck. The police were taken by surprise; only a jeep followed us. The rest remained stationed around the pagoda, where they surely thought I had stayed.

After half an hour we arrived at the gate to the special pavilion of the Bien Hoa hospital reserved for political prisoners from nearby Tan Hiep Prison.

The authoritative waving of the Buddhist flag, the mother superior who solemnly descended from the truck followed by a line of other nuns, all in their beautiful fluttering yellow robes, and I with the large basket of fruit— perhaps all this made the surprised guards think we were an official delegation that certainly must have a permit. Removing the locks and opening the gate without a word, they led us into the building. From outside we had already seen dozens of white hands gripping the bars.

Two doors gave on a small corridor, each door with a slot through which no more than two persons could peer at a time. One door was to a large room for men—some thirty of them—the other to one for women.

I counted fourteen. One lay motionless on a wooden bed with a baby scarcely more than a few days old suckling at her shrunken breast; others approached with surprise and restrained emotion. No one said a word.

The jailers stood rigidly beside us holding bunches of

keys. In the rectangular slot appeared the face of a young girl with a greenish complexion, long black hair, and dry hands with which she continually wiped her forehead as though to remove a cold sweat. A self-contained smile. It was Nguyen Thi Man.

She was twenty-two years old and in prison for the second time. She had been an organizer among liberal arts students and had been arrested one day while transporting leaflets calling for an end to the war. During interrogation they had tortured her with electric shocks, and her left leg had remained semiparalyzed. They had put her in the hospital pavilion because she had been spitting blood.

She had time to write her name and her family's address in Saigon on a piece of paper. We gave her the fruit and slipped a roll of piasters through the door.

On the men's side no one stirred. They looked at us from their beds motionless; many were coughing and spitting into small empty jelly jars.

We stayed a few minutes and left without giving the impression of being in a hurry, before the guards might start asking who we really were. But that stench of cooped-up animals, those frightened faces, those looks that tried to speak without words, and our embarrassing situation as visitors with charitable and useless smiles who would be back in a world of freedom and sunshine in a moment, continued to haunt me.

A hundred or a hundred thousand political prisoners may be arrested and tortured, but as long as they remain anonymous and remote, they are an elusive entity, almost unreal. But the few I had seen there in the stench, with their chests reduced to skin and bone, Thi Man with her smile of decayed teeth, those were real. They were only a few political prisoners, but they were already a lot, too many.

Some time later a girl I didn't know—a friend of friends—picked me up on her Honda at three o'clock one afternoon under the statue of the Madonna in front of the cathedral, and drove me to the address of Thi Man's family. The father was a democratic journalist, out of work and under police surveillance after his daughter's arrest. Amid thanks and tears, holding my hand in his in the Vietnamese way, he told me the story of Thi Man. "A story like others, thousands of others," he kept repeating.

Contrary to the intentions of her father, who insisted on presenting the problem as a general fact and not a personal one, Amnesty International organized a campaign from Sweden to free Thi Man some months later. Tens of thousands of postcards with Thi Man's photo were sent to Thieu. Nevertheless in the middle of 1974 Thi Man was transferred to the prisons of Con Son. She had already been there before in 1969, in the tiger cages.

This is why I went to Bach Dang, a working-class quarter in Gia Dinh, one evening after the Liberation, to the address where I had met Thi Man's father.

NLF and North Vietnamese flags fluttered from every house, and from every doorway dozens of eyes watched this "American" jumping over puddles in an effort to stay out of the mud. There were hovels of wood and sheet iron, and some in bare masonry.

Nothing had disappeared except the barbed-wire fences which Thieu's self-defense forces used to put up at night in working-class neighborhoods to block every alley and little square, to keep the population from moving and Vietcong "agents" from infiltrating.

They embraced me as though I were their son returning from Con Son, but I did not stay long.

A small crowd had gathered outside the door, trying to understand who I was and what was happening. Drunken youths, former soldiers disbanded from Thieu's army, yelled at me while holding one another up, and in the midst of the crowd I also saw some who were still wearing the cloth camouflage trousers of the former special police employed by Thieu against street demonstrations. There was not a single *bo doi*, nor one of the young revolutionaries with a red armband and an AK-47 on his hip, and I did not feel safe. During those days, in neighborhoods like this, Liberation Army soldiers were said to have been beaten and robbed, and four had been found one morning hanging on butchers' hooks with signs on their chests: "Go Back to Hanoi."

I left as soon as I found out what I wanted to learn: Thi Man had returned from Con Son, she had come home for a few hours, and she was lodged, like the other prisoners freed with her, in the Hung Vuong School on Hong Bang Avenue, on the way to Cholon. I went there early the next morning.

The Hung Vuong School is one of those typical former colonial building complexes remodeled with the aid of American dollars: concrete pillars and large simple rooms painted white, in the center a volley-ball court, gardens all

around without grass and full of red dust. The ex-prisoners spoke with the crowd barricaded outside from within,
through the surrounding iron fence. Had it not been for
their smiling faces, and the handshakes I saw them give, I
would have thought they were still prisoners.

Security measures were considerable. Of the four hun-
dred prisoners brought to the school, some were among
the most important political figures to return from Con
Son. There was "the engineer Tinh," who had been the
Party's delegate in the prison, and there was Professor Le
Quang Vinh, a well-known Saigon intellectual who had
been a teacher at the Lycée Petrus Ky and a provincial
Front leader.

At the time of the Japanese occupation the Hung Vuong
School had been transformed into a hospital for those
Vietnamese nationalists who had believed in Tokyo's
promises and had collaborated with the Axis powers
against the French, for a century the colonial masters of
Indochina.

After the Japanese surrender this same school received
the political prisoners of the time after they were freed
from the prisons on the island of Poulo Condor. One of
them had been Le Duc Tho. Vietnamese history is full of
such recurrences. Now, thirty years later at the end of a
new war, other prisoners were being brought to the same
school from prisons on the same island, renamed Con Son
in the meantime.

In front of the barred main gate two young girl guerrillas in black pajamas, strips of red cloth on their arms and
with brand-new AK-47s, held back a throng of people trying to enter, to call out to someone, to pass notes. Relatives
and friends of the prisoners and curious onlookers stood
as though glued to the bars. I was the only Westerner. It
was easy for me to reach one of the guards and explain to
her whom I was looking for. A man in charge of the prisoners came to check my pass, issued by the press office of
the Saigon-Gia Dinh Military Management Committee, and
I was allowed in.

They said my visit was so sudden that they had had no
time to organize a proper meeting. There was still some
confusion in the center, and they weren't yet ready to give
me a due welcome.

I realized that this was a very Asian way of letting me
know that I shouldn't stay long, that my presence was embarrassing. They could not refuse to speak to me, but

without higher authorization they also did not want me to start looking around too much or ask too many questions. Perhaps they also were feeling that typical reserve of simple people who do not want a stranger to see their poverty.

I had to cope frequently with this reticence in my three months of dealings with the new revolutionary authorities in Saigon. They constantly worried about procuring me the sort of comfort in which they themselves, for example, had never lived. For weeks I requested a permit to go to the Delta, and for weeks they asked me to wait, without ever saying no. They said they wanted to give me an escort and organize hotels and meals for me. You might have thought they had things to hide from a journalist, but it wasn't exactly that. And there was no way to convince them that in going to the front lines during the war I had undergone much greater risks, that I had spent more than one night on the floor in some peasant's hut.

"Up until a few months ago," I said jokingly to an official, "I went to see battles and you people on the other side shot at me; now you're worried that something might happen to me if I travel alone in the Delta, which is under your control."

"Yes, that's just it. Now you're our guest. We're responsible for what happens to you," he replied.

When I was finally allowed to make my trip to the Delta I had to change hotels twice in one day in My Tho, until we found one that in my guide's estimate was more suitable for me: air conditioning, European bathroom, spring mattress, and a plastic-covered armchair.

While a young man went to look for Nguyen Thi Man, the man in charge of the prisoner reception center offered me a cup of tea in one of the school classrooms. Everywhere groups of people were chattering. There were prisoners just released from Con Son, political cadres from the city, guerrillas from the security forces responsible for the readjustment program, and nurses. Most wore black pajamas, others brown or wine-red like the ones peasants from the southern Delta wear. Ex-prisoners could be recognized by a red tin star, which they wore pinned to their pajamas over the heart, like a decoration.

Many of them came to speak to me. I met the student who in 1971 had organized terrorist operations against American citizens and installations in Saigon; then a peasant from Cu Chi, a village north of Saigon, who had been sentenced to death as a Vietcong back in 1960, but whose punishment had later been commuted to life imprisonment. I met Le Quang Vinh, the former teacher and Front leader.

When Thi Man arrived, pale and thin as I had seen her the first time, she refused to speak of herself, of her personal case. So I asked her, Vinh, and the others to tell me about the liberation of the Con Son prisons.

The liberation of Con Son

"When I woke up the morning of April 30," Le Quang Vinh began his story, "I realized that something strange was happening. I didn't hear the shouting of the military prisoners in Camp 2, I didn't hear Thieu's three-banded flag being raised. There was an inexplicable silence. Maybe it was still dark. Hardly a breath of air filtered through the peephole at the top of my cell. The light never came in, and it was impossible to know even approximately what time it was. Time went by and the silence remained."

Since the month of January, when he had been put in solitary confinement inside Con Son's special camp, in a cell one and a half by two meters without even a cot, Vinh had scarcely been able to keep track of the time that passed, as he counted in his mind the number of times that the guard opened the hatch to pass him the bowl heaped with rice and stones.

Vinh's jailers had removed the cover from the pail in his cell, in order to make what little damp and heavy air there was even more suffocating. In the constant darkness in which he lived, he was barely able to tell night from day by listening to the few muffled sounds that came from the outside world: at dawn the camp's salute to the flag, and until dusk the shouting and cursing of the military prisoners, the worst thieves and murderers in the "puppet" army — men who kept asking the officers on guard to send them back to the front lines to kill Vietcong, if only to get themselves released.

The soldiers of this kind and ordinary civilian criminals amounted to two thousand prisoners: the other five thousand three hundred were "political" prisoners like Le

Quang Vinh. He was sixty years old, had been a mathematics teacher at the prestigious Lycée Petrus Ky in Saigon and a member of the Resistance since the August Revolution of 1945. Arrested in 1960 for subversive activities, he had been condemned to death. The sentence was later commuted to life imprisonment following a campaign in the international press. Vinh had been at Con Son since 1965.

Con Son Island is located in the middle of an archipelago of fourteen small islands. In the time of the French it was known as Poulo Condor and was the most terrible penal settlement for Vietnamese patriots. Con Son became newly famous in the late 1960s after a journalist accompanying a group of visiting American senators and congressmen had photographed and described the "tiger cages" in which Thieu kept his political opponents.

The "cages" were small pits dug in the earth and covered with iron gratings. The prisoners could not move, and their legs atrophied and became frightful sticks of skin and bone. If a prisoner protested the guards, instead of a handful of rice, threw a shovelful of quicklime down on him through the grating.

The story of the tiger cages went around the world. To hush up the scandal and provide the Thieu regime with an image acceptable to the American voters, who after all had to pay the cost of this war for democracy and freedom in Vietnam, the "tiger cages" were destroyed and an American private firm obtained a contract from USAID to build new concrete cells for prisoners like Le Quang Vinh.

"They wanted to break all contact among ourselves and to isolate us completely from the outside world," said Vinh. "The new cells were extremely functional for the jailers. A system of chains, controlled entirely from outside, held each prisoner by the ankles, in such a way that the guards did not even have to come near us.

"We lived in a vacuum and on the morning of April 30 I couldn't even imagine what might be happening on the outside, what that silence might mean. The last I had heard on the war before I was put in solitary confinement was that Phuoc Binh had been liberated in January.

"In prison it was difficult to receive any news, and only once in a while our 'bases' outside were able to slip in brief messages and some documents. The text of the Paris Accords for instance had come to us on little rolls of paper hidden in the stalks of vegetables. At the end of '74 we

managed also to get three small transistor radios, but they
were soon discovered."

A certain Tua Cua, a jailor's wife with revolutionary
sympathies, had smuggled in the radios in pieces. But
shortly after the liberation of Phuoc Binh some military
detainees informed the guards. Some prisoners were tortured and Vinh, singled out as the head of the internal information and propaganda network, was punished.

Vinh did not know it, but outside his dark and filthy cell
profound changes had taken place in Vietnam and were
also taking place in the small, confined world of the
prison. On April 27 Father Nguyen Gia Thuy, a Redemptorist priest assigned to the parish of Con Son and its prisoners, had returned from Saigon convinced that Minh
would soon become president, that Vietnam would soon
have a coalition government made up of three components, and that he himself could bring about the same
solution on Con Son Island, with its six thousand inhabitants, seventy-three hundred prisoners, three hundred
stationed military men, and two hundred officials and police. The present administration of the island, headed by
Colonel Lam Bui Phuong, governor of the prison and administrative delegate for the district, would constitute the
First Force; the political prisoners, once they were freed
and headed by engineer Tinh, known to be the Party delegate at Con Son, would be the second; and he, Thuy, with
other neutralists, would represent the third, neutralist
component.

Father Thuy spoke of this plan to Colonel Phuong, but
the latter determinedly refused to free the political prisoners. Father Thuy repeated his request in writing on April
28, but still the colonel would not agree. By now he had
his own plan: on the evening of the 29th he summoned his
aides to his office and ordered them to prepare to destroy
with hand grenades Camp 7, where about two thousand of
the most important political prisoners were confined; then,
without telling anyone, he embarked with his family on a
coast guard motor launch and put to sea, hoping to be
picked up by some ship in the American fleet. Running
short of fuel after two days, however, he had to turn back
toward the coast. He landed at Ben Tre and was captured
by Liberation forces.

Seeing themselves abandoned at Con Son, the jailers lost
their heads. On the morning of the 30th the guards
stopped performing their tasks, and many did not even

distribute food to prisoners in the isolation cells. They stayed glued to the radio to follow the news. At the announcement that Saigon had been liberated Ching Kuong, security chief for the island and the highest in rank after the departure of the commandant, summoned the various remaining officials to discuss what measures to take. Many became panic-stricken. Saigon was far away, and news of what had happened there still seemed unreal. Ching Kuong wanted to proceed with the plan for exterminating the prisoners, but had neither enough time nor the forces to act on it. The three hundred soldiers from the regional forces had withdrawn to their barracks—they had assumed a neutral stance and by now would certainly have refused to go and throw hand grenades into the cells of Camp 7. Someone suggested freeing and arming the military prisoners, but the idea was immediately discarded since it was feared they would turn their weapons on their liberators and save the political prisoners instead, in order to better bargain for themselves with the Vietcong. People shouted, some waved pistols, and the meeting broke up in chaos.

As Ching Kuong left the meeting, he realized that many of his police guards had already fled on rowboats to Bamboo Island, ten kilometers from Con Son. He fled too, along with a dozen others.

Now Father Thuy took the situation in hand. Together with the remaining officials—Captain Dau of the regional forces, Hien of the agricultural service, Dong of the welfare service, and a few others—he decided to open the prisoners' cells, starting with Camp 7.

Meanwhile the prisoners, hearing what was happening from some of the jailers, tried to organize themselves in case of attack. Many were still chained, since the guards had fled without opening the doors of the cells, for fear of reprisals.

"It was getting dark when we saw a group of people with a priest and some puppet officers walking toward the camp. They opened the cells, but most of our comrades refused to come out. We didn't trust them," related Nguyen Thi Man, the woman student. "Many Liberation Army officers were locked up in the camp. We were afraid it was a provocation, a trap; surely they just wanted to get us out in the open in order to machine-gun us more easily. I saw a puppet captain go up to Colonel Le Cau, the highest ranking officer of the Liberation forces and a prisoner since 1962. He gave him a military salute and said, 'Colonel, I'm at your orders!' Le Cau, not trusting him, replied, 'My orders are to bring me a radio immediately.'

"Hundreds of us gathered at the exit of Camp 7 to hear the voice of Radio Hanoi saying: 'All of Vietnam is liberated; Saigon, the city of Ho Chi Minh, was liberated this morning. . . .'

"There were great scenes of joy. But even before freeing the other prisoners, Le Cau proceeded immediately to neutralize the soldiers' and police barracks. They put up no resistance. With the weapons we collected we formed two self-defense companies. On one police barracks they hoisted a white flag; an officer came out of another saying, 'I'm ready to go over to the Revolution.'

"Then came a moment of panic. The various camps were far apart, and someone thought of announcing the Liberation to all of them simultaneously through the island's loudspeaker system. In the past it had been used to suppress revolts. When the prisoners in a cell block protested or groups of them started chanting revolutionary slogans, the loudspeakers would blurt out the anthem of the South at full blast. The comrades who went to operate them didn't know how they worked, and when they plugged them in the puppet anthem resounded from all over. We thought the police were organizing a counterattack. But it was only a matter of a few minutes.

"By two in the morning the island was in the hands of the prisoners, but not all the cell blocks had been opened."

Engineer Tinh, Colonel Le Cau, and the others took over the old offices of the prison, where they set up a command post. The liberation of Saigon, the complete rout of the southern army, were elements new to the prisoners. The committee set up to administer the island therefore called itself at first "Con Son Committee of National Reconciliation," a terminology recalling the Paris Accords but by now bypassed by events.

At dawn on May 1 the special camp with its new "tiger cages" was opened. As Le Quang Vinh tells it:

"The silence was frightening and I could not figure out what was happening; then all of a sudden I heard people's footsteps running quickly toward my cell. In the darkness I was afraid. I thought they were coming to torture me again. They stopped in front of my door. I heard a voice: 'Is it you, Vinh, is it you?' I was stunned. I couldn't answer. I knew the voice was familiar, but I didn't recognize it. 'Vinh, answer, are you there?' It sounded like the voice

of Phan Tu, an old comrade who had been with me in the
first tiger cages. But it wasn't possible, Phan Tu was in
Camp 7, how could he be here?

"I heard cursing, someone saying, 'The key, the key,'
and the obsequious voice of the guard: 'I don't have it, sir,
I don't have it. The commandant took it with him when he
ran away.' I couldn't believe it, I didn't understand. I was
afraid it was a trap, that they'd come to beat me, maybe
kill me. I heard them talking about a hammer. Then in
the darkness I heard three loud blows near the door and
the chains fell away from my feet. They had broken the
blocks. The door opened, and in that blinding square of
light I saw the shape of Phan Tu. It was really him, and
on his right hip a pistol was dangling. 'We're free, free, old
friend!' He embraced me. I heard a puppet officer saying,
'Good morning, Professor, I'm with the Revolution too.' It
was Captain Dau. All around were other comrades, all with
weapons in their hands. Then I understood, and laughing
and crying I embraced them all. And then, maybe from
weakness, from emotion, from being struck so suddenly by
the light, I fainted."

Vinh was taken to the office of the revolutionary committee, where he set to work with Le Cau and Tinh.

"In the afternoon who should come to see me but Bay
Dung, a jailer who at the time he was a guard in the tiger
cages had brutally tortured prisoners and killed some comrades with his own hands. 'Esteemed sir, you look pale . . .
I hear you've been ill. . . .' I wanted to hit him, to strangle
him. But I held back. I thought of the policy of the Revolution and said nothing. I went on writing without looking
at him," Vinh recounted.

At a meeting of prisoners it was later decided to arrest
Bay Dung and put him in the tiger cages along with some
twenty other jailers, including the security chief Ching Kuong. When relatives of the police had gone to Bamboo Island to advise him and the others to come back, Ching Kuong had threatened to kill anyone who surrendered. After
a second warning, he himself gave in. On his return to
Con Son he was taken prisoner. Many of the military detainees, freed along with the political ones, also had to be
arrested again and put back in the camps. In the first
hours of their freedom they had started raping the wives
of former administration officials and looting the homes of
the old police.

From all I was able to reconstruct through the various

accounts of people who had been at Con Son during those days, not one political prisoner committed an act of personal revenge. No jailer or guard was killed. Those taken prisoner were handed over to the *bo doi* who arrived on the island on May 4.

"At midnight on May 4 we saw four motor launches appear in the harbor," another former prisoner recounts. "They were flying the flag of the Front, but they weren't making the recognition signals agreed upon in radio contact with the revolutionary committee in Saigon. Were we all in for a counterattack, were the Americans landing to rescue their puppets? Self-defense troops took up positions along the shore, the alarm was sounded. They were about to open fire when, from a lifeboat lowered from a motor launch, someone shouted with a megaphone:

" 'We want to speak with Comrade Le Cau!'

"Someone on the shore yelled: 'They're comrades, they're comrades!'

"We all ran down to the beach.

"It was the end of the prisons of Con Son."

On May 6 the prisoners were taken to Vung Tau and sorted out from there to various assembly centers in Saigon. For them too reeducation was beginning.

From prisoner to *can bo*

The prisoners from Con Son were first examined and sorted out in Vung Tau, where they were held in the old training school for Thieu's "revolutionary" rural cadres. From there many were sent to reception centers set up in their native provinces, others to centers in Saigon like the Hung Vuong School.

The new authorities had various problems to face with this mass of ex-prisoners. First of all, prisoners had to be classified and political prisoners separated from ordinary ones. Second, they had to be readjusted not only psychologically but physically (many were gravely ill) to society. The Revolution, especially in this first phase, needed an enormous number of cadres, of people who could maintain contacts with the population at every level and in every sector, explain revolutionary policy, and help the newly-created organizations manage themselves and take power. The mass of political prisoners constituted a natural reserve of cadres—because of their background and the experience and education most of them had had in the prisons, known for a century in Vietnam as "universities of revolution."

But there was a great variety of prisoners. Some had spent the last fifteen years in one prison or another and had lost touch with the reality of the country. Others had been freed after only a few months of detention. There were young students who had come to the Revolution without any solid ideological foundations, and old militants with a long experience of party and conspiracy. There were dedicated revolutionaries and people who had been arrested for no reason by Thieu's police and taken to politics only since they were in prison.

The process of reeducating each and putting him back into society had to take all this into account.

There was the further problem of singling out, in the midst of authentic prisoners, spies infiltrated by the old police, who could now be expected to try to take advantage of their disguise and protect themselves by joining revolutionary organizations. There were prisoners who had endured torture without yielding or giving the enemy any information on their organization and comrades, and others who had given in or quite simply betrayed.

Since the role of *can bo,* or political cadre, was an extremely delicate and important one, one that had to be an inspiration and example to others, it was necessary to ascertain in every way possible that anyone sent to carry out such work among the people not only had the educational and political equipment to do so, but that he had the proper personal qualities and in no way constituted a risk. And so the prisoners, once freed, were not simply sent back to their villages and families, but placed in reeducation centers where in a certain sense they remained prisoners—prisoners of the Liberation.

"My family understands. The Revolution begins now and I have still to make my contribution," Thi Man replied when I asked her how she reacted to being liberated but not free to go home.

"First of all, we must explain the Revolution's policy of reconciliation to all our freed comrades," the man in charge of the Hung Vuong center told me. "We cannot take a chance on a prisoner returning to his village and

avenging himself on the policeman who denounced him or
on some member of the puppet administration who may
still be there. After years and years of suffering it's a very
human and understandable reaction, but we must help
them to overcome it and to understand the meaning of
reconciliation.

"There may be politically weak prisoners who once
they're out of prison think they have rights over others or
expect privileges. We must fight this attitude, explain that
that's not the way it is, that everyone in his own way has
taken part in the Revolution, and that now there are no
accounts to be settled or debts to be collected. Then we
have a refresher program in which we go over the history
of recent years with the development of the revolutionary
line, for comrades who have been isolated or have not kept
up their contacts with the organization."

Revolutionaries and saints

My visit with the Con Son prisoners had affected me deeply.

As often happened during the three months I spent in
liberated Vietnam, these encounters with certain revolutionaries left me with two emotions that I did not succeed
in reconciling: a great admiration and a subtle fear. I
found in these people who were emerging from prison
and the jungle a strength and a number of qualities that
struck me as difficult to find now in the world from which
I came. People here had an inner fire that made their lives
an extraordinarily complete experience rather than an accidental one. And yet these same qualities, this capacity to
overcome the natural and acceptable inclinations of man,
seemed to me to lead the Revolution itself to the borders
of inhumanity.

In my head I understood it all. I understood what Thi
Man meant when after spending years of her youth in
prison she spoke of having "still to make" her contribution.
I understood how important it was, in order to build a
new and more just society, not to think any longer of
"mine" but of "ours." I understood that it was thanks to
these sacrifices, this discipline, this severity, that the guerrillas had won. It was thanks to this inner certainty of

theirs that the "little green men" who circulated throughout Saigon, and the pale political cadres who slowly were taking power, had been able to avoid both physical and psychological annihilation.

And yet in the pit of my stomach I could not help finding all this simultaneously extraordinary and disturbing.

How could prisoners who had been separated by years of uncertainty and torture from their families agree so easily to a continuing separation, because this was what the Revolution asked of them?

How could Bui Huu Nhan, who had left Saigon with the August Revolution of 1945 and returned with the Liberation as an official in the PRG Foreign Ministry, not rush to his mother whom he had not seen for thirty years and who lived only a hundred kilometers from the capital?

"I can't just now. I have things to do here," he would say, and every day, dressed in his usual shirt full of mended holes, the same pants, and the same plastic slippers, he continued to shuttle back and forth between his new office and a smelly, sunless room that the *bo doi* had requisitioned for him on Nguyen Hue Street.

How could it happen—as it often did—that the tortured asked compassion for their very torturers, from the crowd that quite naturally wanted to lynch them?

These people made me think of the saints I had seen in church paintings as a boy, with their suffering and smiling faces, halos around their heads, and an almost mad light in their eyes. To me they had always seemed unbelievable, so remote from the world.

Sometimes in Vietnam I had the impression of finding them in front of me once again in a modern version, as revolutionaries, with the same features, the same qualities: faith, abnegation, purity. . . . For this too was true: the Revolution was puritanical, but effortlessly so. There was no renunciation, only a natural sublimation of everything in struggle, in revolutionary tension.

One evening after I had been to the Hung Vuong School I received a visit from Nguyen Huu Thai, the student leader who had been at Doc Lap Palace when the Liberation Army tanks rolled in, and who had later been present with a few others in the radio station when General Minh had made his final speech of surrender and abdication.

The historical importance of those moments escaped no one, and in the excitement Thai had been interviewed by some foreign and Vietnamese journalists. He spoke about what he had seen, and in a certain sense he spoke of it in the first person—he spoke of his own role in the last hours of the Republic. As a result he was severely criticized in the course of a student meeting, for an excess of personalism.

Thai found the criticisms just and he accepted them. But his experiences, and the impressions I retained from my meeting with the prisoners of Con Son, kept us up all night discussing the meaning of Revolution, the way that leads one to becoming a revolutionary, and the personal costs and difficulties of participating.

He agreed to tell me his story, not to display his "ego" again, but because it was similar to the story of thousands of other young Vietnamese and it might help others to understand. To understand that the Revolution is a terribly serious affair; that it is a harsh, difficult, at times terrifying experience; that the real Revolution is different from what so many people far away may imagine, though the word revolution is always on their lips.

Autobiography of a fighter

"It was easy for me to arrive at the idea of revolution," Nguyen Huu Thai began. "I wanted my country's independence, and I realized that socialism was the only way to solve the problems of Vietnam. I saw no hope in the lower middle class of the cities, though I myself was a part of it. I sensed all this instinctively but had no way of confirming it. I lived in a closed milieu, my family was bourgeois; my father, who had been educated in France, was an officer in the army of the South. We weren't practicing Catholics, but they sent me to study at a French missionary school. Everything I knew about the 'other side,' about the guerrillas, was indirect, second-hand, out of books. There was an uncle in the family who had gone to Hanoi with the Communists in '54, but I was sixteen at the time and had hardly known him.

"It was prison that changed me. There for the first time I met Communists. They were ordinary cadres, workers and peasants, but they're the ones who impress you the most. The higher cadres, with whom I had contact later, are different. They don't let you get to know them, they don't expose themselves or say anything out of the ordinary, they keep themselves camouflaged. It's a question of style, but also one of caution, of security. You know something? Even today in this period of transition, after the Liberation, there are some very important *can bo* who still remain in the shadows, still keep themselves aloof. The simple cadres instead are open and direct, just like their motivations.

"My discussions with these people were a turning point in my life. I understood that it's one thing to talk about revolution and quite another to make one. The only ones who could really do it were the Communists.

"I'd ended up in prison in '64 after having participated in student demonstrations against Diem's dictatorship. It was the pressure brought by Saigon students, who had elected me their president, that got me out after three months. However, Khanh's secret police—he was president by then—were under orders to eliminate me and I had to go into hiding.

"It was the Americans who protected me. Colonel Wilson kept me in his house; he was an adviser to Cao Ky and a member of the Lansdale gang—you know what I mean, CIA. At that time I was an architecture student. I spoke French and English, and they offered to send me to study in the United States. 'When you come back,' they said, 'you'll have no trouble becoming a minister.' The Americans made no secret of it: they intended to stay in Vietnam for years and so they were making long-range plans. For me it would have been a brilliant solution, and my whole family tried to persuade me to accept. But how could I?

"It was the time of the American intervention in South Vietnam, of the first bombings of the North. I refused. And yet those contacts, though they cost me the suspicion of many comrades then and later, saved me from being tortured when I was arrested again in '66. The police who nabbed me were in doubt as to whether I might not really be a CIA agent, and though they kept me under interrogation for six consecutive months, they never used their usual methods on me. That's how it happened.

"After I'd refused to study in the United States, I made contact with the guerrillas. I visited a liberated area on the outskirts of Que Son, south of Da Nang, and actually stayed in the tunnels with the guerrillas during one of the first 'search-and-destroy missions' by the Americans. I left after a week, having agreed to join the partisans in the region of Binh Duc. There was a liaison man who was supposed to take me there, but at the last moment he was suspected of being a double agent and the plan fell through.

"I then made contact with an urban guerrilla group in Saigon and was part of the unit that instigated the first attacks on American installations and civilians in reprisal for the bombings over Hanoi. The leader was a student like myself; some of the others were little Saigonese gangsters who had been converted to revolution. There was a spy among us and we all got arrested. There wasn't enough proof against me, and so I was never taken into court. But by a simple administrative expedient they kept me in jail for two years.

"I got out a little before the great Tet offensive of 1968. From prison they sent me directly to a recruiting center, and I was forced to enlist in Thieu's army. So I lost a second opportunity to go over to the Front.

"During the attacks that took place in the city in February 1968 almost all my comrades disappeared and joined the partisans. Even my wife's brother crossed over to the other side, and I was left alone. At the end of '68 I was made a second lieutenant in the puppet army. I succeeded in resuming contact with the guerrillas, but they advised me to stay where I was and lie low for a while. To go back and work with the students would have been extremely dangerous for me since the organization, by its nature, was an open one and easily infiltrated by the police. Every six months some network was broken up.

"It was not until two years later, in 1970, that I went back to work. I was admitted to a highly secret organization of young people who carried out armed urban guerrilla operations under the guidance of cadres from the Provisional Revolutionary Government. We called ourselves 'Ban An Men.' My *nom de guerre* was Hai Hoa."

Thai went on with this curriculum vitae the way a young man of his age in Europe might tell of his history with the firms he had worked for after graduation.

"It was tough being an urban guerrilla. Assassination attempts. Reckless acts in broad daylight, in the middle of a crowd. The dangers were considerable, and we had to operate with the greatest secrecy. Not even my wife knew. We worked in cells of three, so that each of us knew only two other comrades. My immediate superior was a student who had deserted from the ARVN and had been in prison from '65 to '70. By exploiting my position as an officer, I was supposed to procure information and weapons for our various coups. Especially hand grenades, explosives, and pistols. I also had the job of keeping track of the Buddhist opposition movement, and in particular the activities of the An Quang pagoda. With the approval of my cell, I appeared as a candidate in the elections of '71.

"It was my cell that organized an attempt on the life of Tran Quoc Buu, the CIA man who controlled the reactionary trade unions on behalf of the regime, but we failed twice. We succeeded, however, in our coup against Nguyen Van Bong, a former Vietminh who had gone over to the CIA when the Party sent him on a mission to Paris.

"Bong was very influential in the leadership of the Administrative Institute, and there was a good possibility that he might become prime minister in place of Khiem. It was important to eliminate him; other groups had already tried, without success.

"As a result of this operation, my cell leader was arrested and I too ended up in prison again since, under torture, he gave names and revealed what he knew about the organization. At the trial I got off with a two-year sentence. The president of the court, who had inflicted very harsh penalties on other patriots, was my cousin and we had been classmates. He left with the Americans just before the Liberation.

"I got out of prison again in 1974, and since I was now under constant police surveillance, the only job the organization gave me was to keep up with Buddhist policy and urge the An Quang pagoda, Senator Vu Van Mau's group, toward a position of reconciliation and national harmony."

It was because of this assignment that Nguyen Huu Thai was present with Minh at Doc Lap Palace the morning of April 30.

"Have you ever considered joining the Party?" I asked Thai.

"In the past I never even thought about it. What counted was to struggle, and to struggle in an organized manner under the leadership of the Front. There were many people like myself who worked without being in the Party, without being a cadre.

"Today I wonder what I ought to do, and I'm uncertain. Anyway it's very difficult to join the Party. You only become a cadre after a meticulous investigation of your character and family background. Once you've been recruited, you join a cell for a trial period, and from time to time are sent to take courses lasting two or three weeks. For my own part, even though I participated in urban guerrilla warfare, I'd have to prove that the natural suspicions some of my comrades harbor toward me are unfounded; I'd have to prove the reasons for every one of my actions in the past.

"In the first days of the Liberation I had many problems getting myself accepted. The Party keeps a file on every militant, and for mine I had to make a very long declaration in which I specified everything, from my family origins to my education, from the names of people I knew to people with whom I've been in contact, from the operations in which I've participated to whatever contribution I've made to each, and so on.

"Now it's necessary for the head of the underground network to which my cell belonged to vouch for me, confirm the authenticity of my statements. But he was in prison at Con Son, and now that he's out, they've sent him away for reeducation. It's up to him to get back in touch with me. That's how it works.

"My student activities are known. But what counts, especially in becoming a Communist cadre, is the experience of armed struggle. To have taken part in guerrilla warfare is highly esteemed—it gives you seniority—since it was very risky and shows dedication to the revolutionary cause.

"It's hard to get yourself accepted," said Thai, as though talking more to himself than to me. "They don't trust anyone. If they have the slightest doubts, they close the door on you. They're right. This is the law of the underground, this is what guarantees the survival of the organization.

"But on the personal level it's sometimes hard, very hard, to accept it. Even the political prisoners returning from Con Son are scrutinized, weeded out, placed under investigation. They look into their past, since there are comrades who behaved incorrectly in prison, others who gave in during interrogation or in the isolation cells.

"Take my cell leader. Despite his great success in carrying out the operation against Bong, later under torture he not only talked, thus getting other comrades arrested, but to escape the death penalty he even agreed to go on television and confess to having organized the assassination plot. And this was a fact about which it was necessary to maintain the most absolute secrecy. Those were the times of struggle between the military and civilian factions within the regime, and it was essential that people go on believing that Bong's elimination had been the work of the military, not ours. He committed an error: if he had had the courage to face death, the Party would have granted him all the honors. Now instead he must make his autocriticism and confess. He'll surely remain a cadre, but not at a high level, and he'll never again be given responsibility over other men.

"It's hard. It's hard to be in the organization. Should I become a *can bo*? My problem, like that of other young men of my social origin, my upbringing, is this: should I become a cadre and sacrifice everything, my personality, my family life, to serve the cause, knowing that one day, under a new name, I could be sent to some part of the world to perform an anonymous task; or should I remain what I am, an architect working in the Revolution?"

Figures and shadows

It was still pitch dark when the delegations from the factories, neighborhoods, schools, and every professional walk of life began to parade in orderly silence through the streets of the city, with flags, banners, and slogans, on the way to their assigned places in the large square with the tamarind trees between the cathedral and Doc Lap Palace.

For the first time in twenty years, Saigon was celebrating the anniversary of the victory at Dien Bien Phu. It was May 7, and the Military Management Committee of the city took the occasion to present itself to the public.

Everything was planned and organized.

Doc Lap had been transformed. A large, smiling, pointillist portrait of Uncle Ho, framed in blue neon, hung in the middle of the facade over the inscription "Nothing Is More Precious than Independence and Freedom." Long flapping colored pennants reached to the ground and all around the confines of the palace; hundreds of little red and blue lights glowed along the fence and between the trees. In what had once been Thieu's garden the *bo doi* had dug latrines, surrounding them with low wooden walls and palm branches.

Unlike the workers' festival on May Day, which had been

improvised and spontaneous, this celebration and all the others that followed in a month full of anniversaries (from the 15th to the 17th celebrations for the Liberation, on the 19th Ho Chi Minh's birthday, on June 6 the sixth anniversary of the founding of the PRG), were government celebrations, organized and regulated in accordance with a Communist liturgy to which Saigon was unaccustomed.

At exactly eight o'clock in the morning, as scheduled in the program, General Tran Van Tra, flanked by members of the Military Management Committee, read his speech from the second-floor balcony of Doc Lap, which had been draped in red. The delegations, arrayed behind a formation of Liberation Army soldiers standing at attention and presenting arms, waved and applauded at every measured pause. From the balcony those being applauded responded with applause. At the end, a group of little schoolchildren in white blouses with red neckerchiefs, made a military salute and ascended to the balcony to present large bouquets of flowers and to be embraced and kissed by the authorities.

On the evening that "Big Minh" had been sworn in I had seen what had been for me the final image of the old regime on the steps of this palace: senators and deputies in dark suits and neckties chatting as they waited for their limousines. Now on the same steps stood rows of men and women of the new Vietnam, their faces in the sun: officers and political commissars; *bo doi* in green uniforms, wrinkled and unmatching, with rubber sandals; middle-aged women in long white *ao dai* and black trousers.

The huge crowd, drawn up beyond the square along Thong Nhat Avenue as far back as the old American embassy, conformed to the new ceremonial rules. Then, in a sudden and spontaneous burst of enthusiasm, they broke ranks, overcame the soldiers barring their way, and rushed toward the palace.

Officers of the Liberation Army were seized by the hands of dozens of youths, tossed in the air, and caught to shouts of "Hurrah, hurrah!" It was a moment of uncontrollable joy. The worried *bo doi* from the security forces tried to check the crowd, but hundreds of simple Saigonese entered the main hall of Doc Lap, trampled the large yellow carpet with its blue dragons, burst through the doors of the reception hall, and helped themselves happily and enthusiastically to tea and coffee from the little cups laid out for what was to have been a small farewell party for the Polish and Hungarian delegations of the International Commission of Control and Supervision, who were leaving Vietnam in the afternoon. It was moving to see Doc Lap—Thieu's old, isolated, fearful lair—suddenly invaded by the people.

In the days that followed the same thing happened with other places connected with the memory of a past that soon became distant and remote.

The exclusive Circle Sportif, rendezvous for old and new colonialists and trading post for high-priced young *cocottes*, became a center for revolutionary art. It opened with an exhibition of paintings and drawings made on the battlefields by guerrillas and *bo doi*. The Circle Hippique, salon of diplomats and rich bourgeois Vietnamese, reopened after the Liberation to play host to an association of political prisoners, who held their first meeting surrounded by colts that grazed, riderless, on the green lawns.

On May 7, after the Dien Bien Phu victory celebration, the Central Post Office reopened and a new stamp, showing Ho Chi Minh dressed in a typical peasant *ao baba* and watering a plant, was put on sale. For the first time since 1954 people in Saigon could mail letters directly to Hanoi.

Communications with foreign countries, interrupted at the moment of the Liberation, were reestablished for the press. Foreign correspondents who had stayed in Vietnam were allowed to send cables. They had to be submitted in duplicate and worded in French or English. Obviously a form of censorship had been set up. Just what the standards and rules were was not specified, not even in the first and last press conference that Tran Van Tra held next morning at Doc Lap.

He received us in the same hall where Minh had made his swearing-in speech. However the position and direction of the armchairs was reversed. Minh had spoken under the panel showing Tran Hung Dao defeating the Chinese; Tran Van Tra spoke from the opposite side of the room.

"You have been witnesses of an historical moment that is the goal of 117 years of struggle for the independence of our people. From now on we will always have freedom and peace, and Vietnam will be a rich and happy country. In these first days we have had difficulties, but they cannot be compared to those of the last thirty years of war."

Tra, short, with a gray crew cut and plastic-rimmed eyeglasses, spoke in Vietnamese with a constant smile on his lips. One of the interpreters who had been at Camp Davis translated his words into English.

Someone asked:

"But does the PRG really exist? If it does, where is it? Why isn't it here yet?"

The general waited for the question to be translated, then answered, still smiling:

"The Provisional Revolutionary Government was established in wartime, without elections. Once elections have been held, it will no longer be provisional. As for its headquarters, at the moment it is in some part of South Vietnam. The military administration of Saigon will last for some time, until we have reestablished order and security."

To Tran Van Tra's right sat an attractive woman in her mid-forties, wearing black trousers and a brown shirt, with a long braid of graying hair down her back. Tra introduced her as "Major Phuong Dung of the Liberation Army."

To his left was Colonel Duong Dinh Thao, former spokesman for the PRG delegation in Paris, who had come back to Saigon as spokesman for the Military Management Committee.

At the end of the press conference someone ventured to ask Tran Van Tra a few personal questions.

"Is your family already in Saigon? How long do you plan on staying here?"

The general smiled scornfully, pretended not to understand, and did not reply.

In the three months I spent in Saigon after the Liberation I had a number of opportunities to go back to Doc Lap and even speak with Tra at length, but I never succeeded in penetrating that polite, warm smile of defense of this modest man, with more the look of a high school teacher than a guerrilla. I was unable to learn any more about him than what the CIA had written years before in a report reserved for American diplomats stationed in Saigon, or what I had gathered from the fascinating but outdated file that the French police had kept on Vietminh leaders in the 1950s and which a military attaché enamored of history had saved from destruction among useless documents at the French embassy in Saigon.

Born January 15, 1918, in a peasant family in central Vietnam (the CIA says born in Quang Ngai), Tran Van Tra (also known by the names Sing Tich, Le Van Thang,

"Brother Tu Chi"), after attending the industrial school in Hue, found work on the Saigon railroads. It is here in the capital of the South that he had his first confrontation with the colonial authorities, according to the characteristic report compiled by the French police: "Arrested in 1939 for subversive activities. Six months in prison."

His freedom did not last long: "Placed in forced domicile in February 1944, the subject escapes in the same year. Arrested again in 1944, he is freed in the course of the insurrection of August 1945."

After a brief period in Tonkin (the northern region of Vietnam), Tran Van Tra returned to the South as deputy commander of all Vietminh forces in the southern region of Nam Bo, under the elusive guerrilla leader Nguyen Binh, who later died under mysterious circumstances in Cambodia.

The political commissar of the Resistance was at that time Le Duan, who later became secretary general of the Workers' Party, the organization of Vietnamese Communists. His successor was to be Le Duc Tho.

According to the French police "the subject was seen in China in February 1949 and in Moscow in December of the same year." Again according to the French, who in those years succeeded in procuring a photograph of Tran Van Tra—young, very thin, in the company of a woman and an unidentified comrade—the "subject" between 1950 and 1952 became commander-in-chief of Special Area 7, which included Saigon and Cholon, then two separate cities. Tran Van Tra would seem to have directed all guerrilla operations in those years against French forces in the South from a post in the jungle near Bien Hoa, where now the neighborhood of Ho Nai has sprung up.

His urban guerrilla squads successfully carried out numerous executions of colonial administration figures condemned to death by the Resistance, among them the head of the French secret police. The French journalist Lucien Bodard, writing of these "squads of assassins terrorizing Saigon," added that "their leader is a certain Tran Van Tra, a true minister of death."

One evening, at the close of a reception at Doc Lap, I asked Tran Van Tra in French (after various conversations through an interpreter he turned out to have a perfect command of the language):

"General, where were you born?"

"I don't remember!"

"The CIA says Quang Ngai."

"Maybe for once the CIA is right."

"Is it true what Bodard writes, that you were the leader of squads of assassins in Saigon in the 1950s?"

He looked at me, took me by the arm, and burst out laughing:

"Ha, ha, ha! Bodard, Bodard, Lucien Bodard!"

"Is it true, General, that just before the Tet offensive you entered Saigon to inspect the targets?"

"I always fought in and out of Saigon."

"General, the CIA writes that you married the most beautiful girl in Nam Bo, a woman named Le Thoa, and that your daughter always stayed in Saigon; that you, General, directed the Tet offensive from the village of An Phu Dong near Thu Duc, a few kilometers from the capital."

Tran Van Tra laughed, amused and embarrassed by this game.

"My wife wasn't the most beautiful girl in Nam Bo, but beautiful, yes, she was beautiful. As for the rest, it's almost all true."

According to information gathered by the Americans, who took over the colonial war from the French first indirectly, then directly, Tran Van Tra went to the North in 1954, and from there to Moscow and Peking for military training.

In 1958 he was a one-star general, in command of the 330th North Vietnamese division. In 1964 Tran Van Tra returned to fight in the South, taking his orders from Nguyen Chi Thanh.

Thanh was the most important rising military star after Giap. When Thanh died suddenly in 1967, not as the Americans claimed under a B-52 bombardment, but from a heart attack in Hanoi, where he had gone for a meeting of the Central Committee of the Party, Tran Van Tra succeeded him as commander-in-chief of all Liberation forces in the South.

The biography of Tran Van Tra compiled by the CIA adds at this point that the general assumed among his various names that of Tran Nam Trung, an alias to which, according to the Americans, no real person corresponded but that was attributed to all the various defense ministers who succeeded each other in this PRG post.

This puzzle was easily resolved at the victory celebrations on May 16 when Tran Nam Trung appeared in the flesh next to Tran Van Tra, among the other members of the Provisional Revolutionary Government.

A riddle that was not resolved was that of Vo Chi Cong, often named by the Front radio as "chairman of the People's Revolutionary Party" (the southern section of the Communist Party), but who has never appeared in public. Some Western intelligence agencies maintained that Vo Chi Cong did not exist, or at most was the alias of Pham Hung. Even after the Liberation he was never seen in Saigon, but a high-ranking Liberation Army officer told me: "The fact that he's invisible doesn't mean he doesn't exist."

Once during a reception at Doc Lap I asked Huynh Tan Phat, prime minister of the PRG, why they went on preserving so much mystery about certain figures now that the war was over.

"It helps, it always helps when our enemies take us for ghosts," he replied. "Look at the Americans. The more they said we didn't exist, the more they were afraid of us."

From 1964 on Tran Van Tra's career was all in the South. In 1968 he planned and directed the Tet offensive, during which his guerrillas succeeded in occupying the American embassy for half a day.

In 1972 he directed the massive spring offensive and took personal command of the troops during the bloody battle for An Loc.

In 1973, after the Paris Accords, by now a two-star general, he arrived in Saigon as head of the PRG delegation at Camp Davis. After two months he was withdrawn and replaced by General Tung and Vo Dong Giang. The Americans said it was because he had fallen into disgrace, but the truth was that the Resistance had realized that the diplomatic solution of the conflict as set forth in the Paris Accords was not going to succeed, and Tran Van Tra was more needed to prepare a new military offensive than to play with words and useless exchanges of notes at the negotiating table.

When on April 30 he reentered Saigon as leader of the victorious Liberation Army, Tran Van Tra was already a myth.

People knew about him, told fantastic anecdotes about his life, but had never seen his picture. Even after the Liberation *Saigon Giai Phong* seldom mentioned him; his photo appeared a couple of times, but never alone, always in a group with other leaders. Even among his associates no one told stories about him or singled out episodes that had happened in his career or during the final days before the Liberation. From one of his officers I succeeded only in learning that "he's a photography enthusiast and the only one Pham Hung has allowed to take his picture."

Pham Hung, who had succeeded Le Duan and Le Duc Tho as political head of the Liberation Army in the South, had refused for years to let himself be photographed. Even when he traveled abroad as Hanoi's deputy prime minister he had kept out of range of the news cameras. An extremely cautious and reserved man, he was one of the members of the Front who more than others had succeeded in keeping the secret of his identity.

"He's an enigma for us too," some of his closest associates later told me.

Pham Hung, appeared for the first time in public before a dozen journalists on the morning of May 15. He was stocky, with broad shoulders, and he had a wide handsome face and straight white hair parted on the right.

Saigon never found out very much about the men who governed the Revolution from Doc Lap Palace. It knew them by reputation, their names entered into people's daily conversation, but their faces, they themselves as individuals, remained elusive. A man like Tra could have walked through downtown Saigon without being recognized. This was a luxury that even Giap allowed himself; when he arrived at the end of the month in the southern capital, where his photo had rarely appeared in the newspapers, he passed almost unseen. The victor at Dien Bien Phu, the man who for thirty years had led the war for the independence of Vietnam, strolled through the city, accompanied merely by two *bo doi*.

This avoidance of exposure as persons, this unwillingness to appear in the first person, this renunciation of the ego even in speech, was typical of all the revolutionaries, but it increased gradually as they rose in the hierarchy.

With the Revolution power passed from the hands of the prima donnas, politicians and generals of the past, into the hands of a vague group of anonymous and faceless men, all alike in their green uniforms, often difficult to identify even by their names.

Saigon was a city that had grown up in the pomp of French-style bureaucracy. A sheet of paper without a pair of signatures and a stamp was not a document. This too was overturned with the Revolution. Important documents and passes, identity cards on which a person's life might depend were written on simple sheets of notebook paper and issued by apparently insignificant figures. They had no titles — not director, secretary, general, or aide to So-and-so. They merely signed with their *noms de guerre:* "Brother Number Three," "Uncle Seven," "Determination and Success," "Man of the South."

A house with two entrances

On the morning of May 15, Saigon was witness to the largest gathering of personalities and legendary figures of the Vietnamese Revolution ever. Tran Van Tra appeared on the reviewing stand erected on Cong Ly Avenue for the victory parade in a clumsy full-dress uniform, a pure Soviet imitation, gray with three stars on the red collar tabs and a gold-braided cap, identical with that of General Van Tien Dung, chief of staff and second only to Giap in the Hanoi military hierarchy.

One could see no difference even among the soldiers. For two hours they paraded past, on freshly painted tanks, amphibious vehicles, polished pieces of artillery, on foot, or at the command posts of Soviet-made SAM missiles drawn by Chinese-made trucks (a small but significant example of Vietnam's equidistance from its two mutually hostile allies). All wore the same uniforms, the same individual weapons, the same insignia.

The diplomatic fiction of two distinct armies, a southern one fighting against Thieu and a northern one confined on the other side of the seventeenth parallel, had ended with the end of the war. Also ended was the fiction of two distinct Communist parties. It was not by chance that the announcement of three days of victory celebrations had been made in Hanoi (on May 5 by the secretariat of the Vietnamese Workers' Party), and that no one spoke any longer about the so-called People's Revolutionary Party, the name given the political organization operating in the South.

"Vietnam is a single country. The Vietnamese people are one. The rivers may dry up, the mountains crumble, but nothing can alter this truth," said Nguyen Huu Tho, president of the National Liberation Front, quoting a famous statement by Ho Chi Minh in his inaugural speech before a crowd of three hundred thousand persons.

The basic unity of Vietnam was forged. The image of unity was there in the single army parading past, in the group of leaders of a single party who smiled from the reviewing stand as from a stage with fake arches and three doors on the backdrop, responding to the salutes of tens of thousands of hands and waving red flags.

There was the eighty-two-year-old Ton Duc Thang, born in the Delta, Ho Chi Minh's successor as president of the Democratic Republic; there was Le Duc Tho, born to a northern family in the South, and who had devoted the last thirty years to leading the Revolution in the South, even during the time he was negotiating with Kissinger in Paris in the name of Hanoi. There was Pham Hung, who had grown up amid guerrilla warfare in the Mekong Delta, gone to the North where he had been deputy prime minister, and later come back as a Party leader in the South.

There were legendary figures from the time of the first resistance against the French like General Chu Van Tan, "the tiger of Bac Son," and others who had become famous with the second resistance against the Americans, like Tran Van Tra or the woman guerrilla Nguyen Thi Dinh, deputy commander of the Liberation Army.

Naturally there remained enormous differences within this framework of rediscovered basic unity—differences between a country that, even with the hardships of war, had been building socialism for twenty years, and one that had emerged scarcely two weeks before from a parasitical situation where a capitalist economy was kept on its feet only by American aid.

There was no total, instantaneous unification. At victory celebrations the governments of North and South presented themselves as two distinct entities mirroring two different situations and with two completely different kinds of problems to face.

Hanoi, for instance, had to raise the living standards of its population, which in the years of wartime communism had necessarily been restricted to the lowest minimum. Saigon had instead to reconvert the whole structure of the South, and to remove from certain well-to-do portions of its population a prosperity that had never been related to the economic reality of the country.

For a period of transition whose duration no one cared to predict, North and South would follow paths that would converge somewhere in the distance. But they would be different paths, especially in the beginning.

The existence of a single party for the two areas would guarantee the unity of general policy, the two separate governments its different application.

Thus the PRG, born in wartime from a coalition of various forces, maintained its facade of a united front even after arriving in Saigon. Its composition remained unchanged and in its public appearance after the victory the southern government reflected this continuity on the reviewing stand: next to old Communist revolutionaries like Prime Minister Huynh Tan Phat, Defense Minister Tran Nam Trung, Presidential Minister Tran Buu Kiem, and the theorist Nguyen Van Hieu, known as the "Lenin of the Front," stood representatives of patriotic groups in the South whose ties with the Party were nonexistent or unconfirmed, like Truong Nhu Tan, minister of justice, Phung Van Cung, minister of the interior, Mme. Nguyen Thi Binh, foreign minister, the woman doctor Duong Quynh Hoa, educated in Paris and who had been named minister of health, and the lawyer Trinh Dinh Thao, born in the North and who had joined the guerrillas only in 1968, to become vice-president of the South.

Now that they had won and had as much time as they wanted, caution and moderation determined the actions of the new authorities.

Nguyen Huu Tho, officially "president of the Advisory Council of the Provisional Revolutionary Government of South Vietnam," but essentially the southern head of state, promised in his speech at the celebrations to build "a new economic system" in the South, and Le Duc Tho referred to the need for an "independent economy." But no one ever once used in public speeches during the first days or in the first three months after the Liberation the word "socialism."

The members of the PRG, conscious of Saigon's deep-rooted anti-Communism had no wish to trifle with it. Rather, they wanted to gain every possible confidence, banish every last fear.

Among the various leaders in shirtsleeves and plastic shoes when the doors of Doc Lap opened for a large informal reception the evening of May 15, were representatives

of the entire non-Communist opposition to Thieu, from
Mme. Ngo Ba Thanh to Catholic priests and progressive
bonzes of the Third Force.

"We want to build in South Vietnam a democratic, progressive, nonaligned regime in which every Vietnamese
who loves his homeland and wishes to serve it, including
the country's bourgeoisie, can have his place," Nguyen
Huu Tho told me in the course of a long interview some
weeks later.

"You always speak of a single Vietnam, but actually
there are still two. What are the juridical relations between
North and South?" I asked him.

"It's certainly not a question of relations between two
states, since North and South are not two different
states. . . . We must find a new formula to define these relations," he said.

Cao Giao had answered my same question by proposing
a formula of his own:

"Vietnam is a house with two entrances. Over one is
written PRG—democratic, nonaligned, and so forth. Over
the other is written Hanoi—socialism, and so forth. You go
inside and you find the same people." I'd say he was right.

Translated into foreign policy terms his comparison
meant that future relations with Western countries might
pass through the PRG door, as might a policy directed toward the countries of the Third World; while old relations
would continue from the Hanoi door, now long committed
to the socialist camp.

The Military Management Committee remained at its
post in Saigon much longer than people had expected in
the days following the Liberation, but this by no means
meant that the military was governing.

Not only were seven of the eleven members of the Military Committee civilians, but the PRG appeared in every
sector of the administration from the first weeks on. The
fact that the Military Management Committee stayed on in
power was due to problems of order and security, and the
men in charge of this task worked side by side with civilian
officials for months.

Despite the PRG's stepping into the limelight, it was
clear to me, especially after visiting Hanoi at the end of
July, that its function was coming to a close. It was provisional, as its very name stated.

The South was to be, for a certain period, an area with a
special regime, Saigon its provisional capital. But general

policy, long-range plans, and the future of the country were being conceived and decided in Hanoi. That was now the real capital of Vietnam.

The relations between the two stumps of the same country were symbolically illustrated by the two flags that, according to instructions given to the population for the three days of celebration, were to be hoisted together outside every door and on every public building. Hanoi's was all red with a yellow star in the middle. The PRG's likewise had a yellow star in the middle, but only the upper part of the flag was red—the lower part was blue. The future was described by these two symbols. The South, still blue, was to become red and then there would no longer be any difference between the two flags.

It was a question of time. At what speed this conversion would be carried out was something unknown to everyone; that it would happen was now a fact about which no one could have any further doubts.

3: The New Life

Reveille at six

The Cong Hoa ("Republic") national cemetery, built with American dollars just outside Saigon to hold the bodies of a hundred thousand South Vietnamese boys who had died fighting "the Communist aggressor," was the only place after the Liberation where you could still see the colors of Thieu's old flag.

At the entrance the monument to the "freedom soldier," in American uniform and leaning on his M-16, had been demolished; but the last ARVN coffins, which had arrived from the northern front the evening of April 28, were still there, lined up next to the open graves and wrapped in yellow palls with three red stripes, waiting to be lowered. No one had done it because at the sight of tanks advancing along the nearby highway the gravediggers had fled.

When I paid a visit to the place the second Sunday in May the rows of white crosses and headstones stretching as far as the eye could see trembled in the scorching air, as though the earth were simmering under the overhead sun. Not a soul could be seen. Formerly on a day like this there would have been thousands of persons walking and praying among the graves. That Sunday the cemetery was empty, deserted. It was as if people were now ashamed of going there to mourn their dead "puppets," fallen on the wrong side in the war.

For many the Revolution had come as something sudden and unexpected. Perspective, the values of life, had been so rapidly overturned that it was not easy for everyone to understand and adapt himself.

"The world was clear to me before. I thought the Communists wanted to take away our homeland and that Thieu was defending it. Now I feel disoriented," said a woman whom I finally found placing a bunch of incense sticks before the fresh grave of her brother. "The *bo doi* came to our house, they asked about our family, about our health, they asked us if we had enough to eat. They were kind. They were Vietnamese like ourselves, and now I don't know who to hate."

The disorientation lasted for weeks, as people's habits and their way of life changed.

Life changed slowly, without orders from above, in an almost natural manner. But each new aspect contained an element of irreversibility that discouraged those who at first had hoped to be able in some way to go back to their old habits or former comfort.

In the first days after the Liberation there was a wave of

The reserves of stolen American gasoline sold on the black market soon ran out, and the Soviet gasoline that began to arrive was rationed, primarily to public vehicles. People had to give up their cars and Hondas and revert to bicycles or walking.

The Saigon of former times, chaotic, noisy, stinking, constantly enveloped in noxious blue clouds of exhaust fumes, became a silent and orderly city like Peking or Hanoi.

The rhythm of daily life changed. People woke up at six in the morning to the clamor of revolutionary music broadcast over loudspeakers set up in the squares and at street crossings. By eight in the evening there was no longer anyone on the street even after the curfew had been shifted to eleven.

Telephones functioned only intermittently; most often private lines were dead. People muttered that the *bo doi* were incapable of repairing the damages caused by the final hours of war, but this was untrue. The telephones of the *bo doi* worked perfectly well. After having cut most urban lines for reasons of security, they had installed their own completely independent communications system, which they maintained with extreme efficiency. One often saw pairs of *bo doi* stringing their brown wires over houses, on trees, and along the sidewalk, unrolling them from crude armatures held together by crossed sticks of wood.

The Liberation left a great many people, and not only "puppet" soldiers and policemen, without work. Private companies and commerical firms whose activities had been linked to the war had closed their doors; factories whose owners had fled with the Americans had been occupied by the workers, but were closed for lack of raw materials or spare parts for the machinery; and the overwhelming majority of civil employees in the state administration, which had absorbed thousands of individuals in this city of services, went to their offices every day to be told by a *can bo*, a Front cadre, to come back tomorrow. Every day it was the same. Salaries for April had not been paid, and the last money pocketed in March had run out for many people.

suicides. The number remained insignificant in comparison to a population of over three million, but it was a symptom of the difficulties that some people experienced in adapting themselves to the new conditions.

Some took place among the military. While twenty-two generals turned up in a single week at the Saigon registration center, others preferred to take their own lives. In addition to General Phu, who killed himself with an overdose of anti-malaria pills, Generals Tran Van Hai, former chief of police, Tran Chanh Thanh, former information minister, Nguyen Khoa Nam, who had been commandant of the Fourth Military Region, and Le Nguyen Vy all committed suicide.

Some of the suicides by political figures in the old regime gave rise to suspicion and unverifiable rumors. After one of Thieu's former ministers killed himself it was said that stones had been buried in his coffin in place of his corpse. He was supposed to be living under an assumed name in a village in the Delta. The same was said of others.

Many of the suicides were young people.

The most dramatic case took place on May 20 on the ruins of the Monument to the Unknown Soldier, in front of the National Assembly. At six in the afternoon a man about twenty-five years old, shabbily dressed, perhaps an ex-soldier, mounted the debris-littered pedestal, doused himself with gasoline and set himself on fire, after having planted a small NLF flag and a North Vietnamese one at his feet. He shouted nothing, he left no message. He could even have been someone protesting against the *bo doi* for their delicate way of handling the old rulers, but Saigon whispered that it had been a gesture of defiance against the new authorities, against Communism.

"He's only the first. There will be many others," you heard people say.

There were no others.

Adapting was a problem for everyone, not only for those who saw their past position decline with the advent of the new.

"It's ridiculous, but in prison I felt more secure. After having been out of it so long, the city frightens me," said Cao Que Huong, a thirty-four-year-old woman who had been active in the peace movement. She had been arrested in 1970 at the funeral for her student husband, who had died under torture at Chi Hoa, and had been able to escape from Tan Hiep Prison only a few days before the Liberation.

"I walk and I always have the feeling I'm being followed. I always feel I should hide myself, that they're looking for me, that I still have to escape."

This factory is ours

Except for Doc Lap Palace, where the windows stayed lighted all night and where jeeploads of Front members and *bo doi* officers entered and left continuously, one of the busiest places in the city after Liberation Day was the building at No. 14 Le Van Duyet Street.

The old headquarters of the reactionary trade union headed by Tran Quoc Buu, the CIA man financed by various organizations of the international Right, had been occupied by a group of workers and students.

Led by Phan Khac Tu, the young Catholic priest better known as "the garbage priest," workers with red flags had entered the abandoned building after the May Day demonstration, torn down the old sign, replaced it with a banner reading "People's Revolutionary Committee," and posted armed guards at the gate.

Since then people had been constantly coming and going, offering help and asking advice. Here more than anywhere else you had the impression that with the Revolution it was the people who had taken power.

The first free workers' assemblies were held in the vast meeting hall, which formerly had served exclusively for demonstrations in support of the regime. Now factory commissions met here, and representatives of the rank-and-file were democratically elected.

The union and all the organizations approved or tolerated by the old regime, like the Third Force movement "for the defense of workers' rights," were dissolved, and the "People's Revolutionary Committee" in Le Van Duyet Street became the sole coordinating center for all action by workers in Saigon.

Employed workers went there to register, the unemployed went there in search of jobs, and worker cadres coming out of hiding went there to make themselves available.

In the hours I spent at the Le Van Duyet center I witnessed some moving encounters between old comrades who had not seen each other for years, who had been separated, often under dramatic circumstances, without one later hearing anything about the other. It was a scene I saw repeated time after time in the first weeks after the Liberation, in the street, during receptions at Doc Lap, at public meetings. In the middle of the crowd two persons would look at each other, recognize each other, remain gazing for long moments from a distance with outspread arms, and then fling themselves into a warm embrace.

The center on Le Van Duyet Street throbbed with activity. In the main hall groups of young people pasted photos of Ho Chi Minh, the battle of Dien Bien Phu, and the Liberation of Saigon on large placards spread out on the floor. Others painted revolutionary slogans in red on white strips of cloth. A group of women from the central markets held a meeting where each told of her experiences under the old regime and spoke of the abuses suffered from Thieu's police. Elsewhere cyclo drivers discussed their problems in renting vehicles from Chinese owners. Everywhere a great hustle and bustle, people rushing back and forth, arriving with new problems, departing with orders, packets of leaflets, signs announcing new meetings.

In the confusion of the first days no one had thought to remove from the walls the photos of the old trade union boss, Tran Quoc Buu, pictured as he shook hands with Thieu or received an honorary award from American Ambassador Bunker. Buu had been one of the staunchest defenders of the old regime, and even after Thieu's departure he had done his utmost to prevent Minh from becoming president. In the end, loaded with money, he had left for the United States.

Around what had been Buu's desk Phan Khac Tu worked with a group of students.

"For the moment we're only the germ of a provisional single trade union. In every liberated city the same work is being carried out, delegates are being named in every factory. Together we will later constitute the Trade Union Federation of Liberation, which will be one of the arms of the people's power. The union's task will be to keep watch over the life of the workers, to forge a bond with all levels of government," Father Tu explained.

He was small, thin as a rail, his hands all bone, with sloping shoulders, an emaciated face, thick glasses for nearsightedness, and two small iron rods forming a cross on his shirt to show he was a priest. Father Tu had worked for two years as a streetcleaner in the Saigon sanitation department, and with the help of another priest, Truong Ba Can, head of the Young Catholic Workers' movement, had organized cells for study and political education that had various contacts with the Front. Many militants in these groups had been jailed by Thieu.

As we spoke, Father Tu's group of students was making photocopies from a worn reproduction of the statute of the Trade Union Federation, which had been in force in the liberated areas of South Vietnam since 1965.

"Many of us haven't even read it," said Father Tu. "Our first job is to train cadres, hold meetings with the workers, and explain the policy of the revolutionary government."

In the first days the situation in the factories of Saigon was still confused. A declaration by the new authorities had assured owners that "manufacturers and dealers will have their goods safeguarded and will be able to continue activities profitable to the national economy and to the life of the population." But in some establishments the workers had announced a takeover, and in some cases had even held the first people's trials against the bosses.

Other factories, like the one that produced "Eagle" batteries and in which Thieu's wife had been a shareholder, had been seized by revolutionary management committees of workers and employees, after the owners had fled with the Americans.

Technically speaking, and in accordance with a formula approved by the military authorities, this meant "taking charge until the return of the legitimate owners." But since the owners would never return, it was an early form of nationalization.

Something similar had also occurred in some small factories operating with mixed Chinese-Vietnamese capital. A manufacturer from Hong Kong told me that on going to a textile plant of which he was co-owner in Cholon, he had found the gate shut and covered with posters. A workers' delegation had barred his way, saying:

"You've exploited us enough. This isn't your home. Go back where you came from."

Even in the large French firms whose owners had stayed in Saigon, relations between management and labor were radically altered by the Liberation.

On the morning of April 30 at the BGI (Brasserie Gen-
erale d'Indochine), which produces among other drinks
the very popular "33" beer, twenty-one hundred workers
disarmed some ARVN soldiers and garrisoned the estab-
lishment to protect it from thieves and saboteurs. They
then elected a revolutionary committee composed of five
employees.

When I went to visit the factory in the first week in May,
I met the chairman of this committee, Huyen Ngoc
Thanh.

"The workers rightly think that everything in Vietnam
belongs to the Vietnamese. Including factories like this
one. For the moment, however, the French can stay. As a
first step we'll simply demand a share of the profits," he
said.

Thanh, aged fifty, had been a welder. In 1958 he was
arrested for subversive activities and spent three years in
prison at Chi Hoa. With the approval of the guerillas he
had signed up as a member of the official trade union,
later controlled by Tran Quoc Buu, and under the guise
of a convert he became the factory delegate. Actually he
maintained his contacts with the underground organization, and every two months took part in discussion meetings held secretly in the city. With the help of a comrade
who worked in the dispensary of the factory, Thanh had
even succeeded in setting up a channel to supply medicines to Liberation fighters. They had never been discovered.

With the Liberation, the revolutionary committee pre-
sided over by the worker Thanh had become the political
voice of the management. The French director was by now
"only technically" in charge.

The problem of maintaining foreign ownership and
keeping foreign technicians in the factories, at least for a
certain period, was felt strongly by the cadres in the center
on Le Van Duyet Street. In their discussions with workers'
committees, which often put forward radical and max-
imalist positions, they advised prudence and caution.

"First of all, it's important to resume production," they
repeated, and this watchword was printed in large capital
letters in *Saigon Giai Phong*.

The *can bo*, the highest-ranking political cadre at the Le
Van Duyet center, was a man of fifty-three, a native of Saigon, who had just come back from the jungle: Nguyen

Nam Loc, member of the executive committee of the Trade Union Federation of Liberation. He had worked in a warehouse at the city's power plant. Arrested in 1956, he had been in prison until 1961, and a few days after his release he had gone into the jungle. He had become a Party member and returned to Saigon with the Liberation Army.

"I still haven't had time to go and see my home," he said.

When a worker in the course of a discussion asked why the bosses shouldn't be expropriated immediately, Loc replied:

"Now's not the moment. Just now it's a question of reeducating the owners. We must make them understand that their profits come from the workers and should be distributed more fairly. We want to encourage enterprise, not discourage it. That's important at this moment so as to consolidate the people's power."

The same problem was debated under the guidance of another *can bo* by a group of cyclo drivers. Their occupation was considered one of the lowest in Saigon. Very few owned the bicycle-taxis by which they made a living. The owners were usually rich Chinese businessmen in Cholon with whole fleets of cyclos, which they rented by the day: five hundred piasters for twelve hours.

The meeting of the *cyclopousses* lasted a whole afternoon. Some of them spoke at length, attacking the "traitor" Thieu, who had suspected them of being Vietcong agents and had forbidden the circulation of cyclos in downtown Saigon in his last three weeks in power. Others thanked the Revolution for "liberating" them. At the end a resolution was passed setting up a committee to reexamine rental charges with the owners.

In another part of the large hall, the market women had finished their "liberation session" and elected a representative who would maintain contact with the Le Van Duyet center. Voting took place in a relaxed atmosphere by a show of hands, amid laughter and joking remarks, almost as though it were a game.

The Revolution inherited a disastrous economic situation, especially in Saigon. The city had always lived by supplying services connected with the war, American dollars paying the bill, and now there were no more.

Thieu had boasted about South Vietnamese industry on the day following the unsuccessful ceasefire of 1973 in order to attract foreign investments, but it existed only in an embryonic state. And even where it had begun to function it involved exclusively manufacturing, and processing of raw or semiprocessed material imported from abroad.

In the opinion of certain Western observers, the faltering economy had contributed more to Thieu's fall than even the attacks of the guerrillas. South Vietnam in Thieu's last year was already a country with its belt tightened; people were dying of starvation, and unemployment was in the hundreds of thousands. The new authorities understood the problem very well and took their time in solving it.

The first thing the *bo doi* did was to take inventory. Toward the last week in May, they began going from factory to factory, workshop to workshop, making an assessment of people, machinery, and supplies. They set out in groups of three, their briefcases bulging with papers. Owners were asked to declare all their operations, and list their machinery, supplies, raw materials, and goods in stock. They were given a warning: anything they did not declare or attempted to hide would be considered "property of the people," once it was discovered.

Then there were questionnaires to be filled out. Among the questions: "Is it possible to import spare parts for your machines and the raw materials you need from socialist countries?"

It would take months to digest all the answers, all the analyses, into a plan that would convert the economy into a healthy and above all "independent" sector.

"This is the new battle we have to fight and win against the remains of imperialism," said Loc, the former warehouseman turned *can bo*.

The new man

No one talked of anything else these days. The *bo doi* said it in their conversations with people in the street, the *can bo* explained it in block meetings, in factories and schools, and it was constantly repeated by radio, television, and the newspaper: Saigon must change. The most common phrases were: "abandon old habits," "make the Revolution," "erase the past." Change. But how?

An editorial in *Saigon Giai Phong* explained it this way:

"Every regime has its own way of life. American neo-colonialism produced, nourished, and left behind a barbarous, American-style way of life in the area occupied by its puppets. This way of life has been the law for several years in the regions controlled by the Americans and puppets, and has destroyed the fine traditions of our culture, particularly in Saigon. This is a very serious obstacle on the road of the People's Revolution. . . .

"Making the Revolution requires first of all the revolutionary man. The revolutionary is a new man; it is he who, besides having a revolutionary spirit, lives a civil, healthy, correct life, in solidarity with the rest of the community. . . .

"The struggle to arrive at this is part of the general revolutionary struggle, a long and painful struggle. To change one small habit in one's daily life is already painful. To change a whole way of life to which one has been accustomed for years will be harder still."

Saigon had no ear for this kind of language and found it difficult to understand.

For many people reading the newspaper had already become a bore. Before the Liberation the Saigonese had had a dozen daily papers to choose from, despite the censorship and press restrictions imposed by the old regime. Some of these regularly published fanciful but juicy stories on the corruption of the generals, Thieu's private life, the intrigues of his wife, and so forth. For the first three months after the Liberation there was only a single newspaper, and all it had to offer was prose of the kind in the editorial, or news relating to production in recently reopened factories.

As time went on *Saigon Giai Phong,* which did not succeed in selling more than a few thousand copies, had to adapt itself a little to the city's taste. In June it began to publish a news section, though keeping to its policy of "political information." In July an interesting series of articles appeared on the old regime; the first was about the involvement of Thieu and his generals in the drug traffic.

Listening to foreign radio broadcasts, something the Saigonese had been in the habit of doing during the war years since they knew that what they read in Thieu's newspapers was far from the truth, was never formally prohibited. It only became one of those activities that the *bo doi* "advised against."

For example, on July 3 *Saigon Giai Phong* published a

letter from a reader, Le Huu T., a resident of the seventh
district:

"Near the Binh Dong market there is a barber, Ba Ket.
Every day Ba Ket listens to Radio Giai Phong and repeats
what he has heard to all customers who go to him for a
haircut. This seems to me an excellent example. On the
other hand, there are still many families in Tran Hung
Dao Street and Luong Van Can who listen to enemy
broadcasts, like the Voice of America, the BBC, Radio Taiwan, and the Voice of Freedom. I suggest that:

"— all those who own radios should obey the laws of the
   Revolution;

"— we must be vigilant and persuade those who listen to
   enemy broadcasts to desist;

"— we must denounce to the revolutionary authorities
   those who persist in listening to and circulating the
   contents of enemy radio broadcasts."

An illustration of the kind of revolutionary life that Saigon had still to experience was provided by the films that
began to be shown.

All movie theaters in the city had closed with the Liberation. The owners, without precise instructions but simply
by sniffing the atmosphere, had removed the old posters
for American and French films, and for the Chinese kung-
fu movies that had become the rage.

When the cinemas reopened in the first week in May
they showed nothing but films brought from Hanoi. One
was about the life of Ho Chi Minh, another about the life
of Nguyen Van Troi, the young worker shot in 1964 by
the Saigon police for having mined a bridge over which
McNamara, then American secretary of defense, was supposed to pass. Another was about peasants in the North
who went into the rice paddies with rifles on their shoulders, prepared to shoot at American planes; and still another, which was excellent, had been filmed on the Ho Chi
Minh trail and showed how soldiers, peasants, and young
people had been able, under American bombs, to keep
that important communication and supply route to the
South open and functioning.

They were all stories of huge personal sacrifices, of lives
dedicated to the Revolution, examples of a simple, austere,
puritan society.

In working-class neighborhoods these films had great
success. The theaters were jammed for weeks. But in

downtown Saigon, after the first days of curiosity, the theaters remained literally empty. Here even films from the Soviet Union and People's China, which began their runs a month later, did not attract much of a public.

I had an example of revolutionary life before my eyes every day at the Hotel Continental. The first *bo doi*, about ten of them, had settled in on May 6. Another group had arrived from Hanoi on the 27th and, sleeping four or five to a room, had occupied almost all the hotel.

They were all in their forties. Some were war cripples, missing a hand or half an arm, and with glaring scars. All wore green uniforms, without rank insignia, and rubber-tire sandals. More than soldiers they were *can bo* — political commissars, economics experts, doctors, engineers.

Every morning when I threw open my shutters, awakened like everybody else in Saigon by the music on the loudspeakers, I saw them in undershirts and white shorts spreading their arms, taking deep breaths, touching their toes, in front of their open windows overlooking the garden.

After fifteen minutes of exercises they descended to the restaurant on the ground floor, ate a bowl of rice and cooked vegetables, drank a cup of tea, and went off to work with their plastic briefcases full of papers. They came home at seven in the evening. Again they ate rice and vegetables, and by nine the lights in all their rooms were out.

For each one's meals (lunch, also basically rice and vegetables, was brought to them in their offices), the military administration paid the hotel three hundred piasters a day. The price of one of my brioches.

There were about a hundred *can bo* like mine in the city. They worked ten to twelve hours a day, behind the tellers' windows of the closed banks examining accounts, in the offices of ministries consulting dossiers, statistics, regulations of the old regime, making notes. Others had gone into the hospitals, into the various university faculties, into the factories. Many lived and slept where they worked.

Where the *can bo* arrived they did not become chiefs or substitutes for the old hierarchy; they took their place beside it.

The man assigned by the PRG to the hospital in Bien Hoa was a fifty-three-year-old doctor from the South, who had gone into the jungle in 1965 and had worked ever since in liberated areas in the Delta.

On arriving at the hospital a few days after the Liberation, he called a meeting of the entire staff, including doctors, nurses, and kitchen help. He introduced himself, told his story in a few words, specified that he had not come to take the director's place, spoke of the general meaning of the Revolution, said that the new values should also be applied in the work of the hospital, and that he was ready to discuss any proposal and examine any innovation with the others. At the end of his remarks he suggested that doctors, nurses, and kitchen help no longer call each other by their titles, but simply "brother" or "sister."

During the three months that I followed the hospital's affairs the old director remained at his post, but his authority progressively diminished. All his instructions and duty regulations were posted on the walls of the wards with the following signature: "Dr. Cao Van Be, puppet director."

Twice a week the entire hospital staff met, in the presence of the *can bo,* to discuss general politics and questions of internal management.

One of the first things done, for instance, was to check all the clinical records of patients in the psychiatric division. After long interviews all the preliminary case histories were rewritten. It was discovered that a great many patients, for fear that what they said might end up in the hands of Thieu's police, had lied about their own past or that of their families.

To avoid reprisals or continual questioning on the part of the police during the war years, many people had claimed that their fathers, brothers, or sons who had gone to fight in the Front were dead. In some cases they had even arranged false funerals.

In the days following the Liberation many of these "dead" started returning. Among the "Seeks Relatives" announcements published daily by *Saigon Giai Phong* you could often read: "So-and-so, given up for dead on such-and-such date, seeks family who lived in Such-and-such Street."

Many orphanages received visits from "dead" parents coming to reclaim their children.

A couple from Quang Tri, declared dead in 1968, went in the middle of June to the "SOS Kinderdorf" in Go Vap, one of the few institutions that had not speculated in children for adoption during the war and had taken no part in the "baby-lift" operation, to look for a little girl whom they themselves had consigned there as an "orphan."

Orphanages, especially those funded by foreign charitable organizations, were one of those institutions the new authorities discouraged by all possible means.

After the Liberation a group of guerrillas went to visit an orphanage in Ben Tre in the Delta and told the Catholic sisters who ran it that the children could very well be taken care of by Vietnamese families. Next day the orphanage was emptied, over the opposition of the nuns, with peasant couples coming to take children to add to their own.

The end of the war, with the reunion of divided families, the release of political prisoners, the return home of the partisans, and a general tendency to settle in the country, resolved the orphan problem in a natural way. Three months after the Liberation, half the orphan population of South Vietnam had already found families.

In the university, revolutionary committees representing students, teachers, and employees had been elected for every faculty. A *can bo* was present on each committee.

The one in the School of Architecture was a native of Ca Mau, the southernmost point in South Vietnam, and in his time had been a student in Saigon. He arrived with his hammock, and for the first months slept and lived with the students. He did not supplant the old dean, who remained at his post.

When he arrived he introduced himself and made what was by then a standard speech on the Revolution and the need to translate what had happened on April 30 into daily life and into the field in which each person worked. The *can bo* said he was the head of "K-7," the section of the Military Management Committee charged with public works.

Unlike the medical school, where many professors had fled with the Americans (half the dentists were gone) only one architecture lecturer had left, and classes were resumed three weeks after the Liberation.

Through the mediation of the *can bo* it was decided that "reeducation" of the teachers and revision of the programs would keep pace with the courses. The *can bo* explained to the students that there was no program of revolutionary architecture to be imported from Hanoi or anywhere else. It was up to them slowly to modify the old through their proposals and experiments. Political reorientation lessons began simultaneously with the specialized courses.

The same thing happened, but more slowly, in the other faculties—except for the School of Social Sciences, which remained closed for good. It had been founded by the Americans, with programs and graduates from universities in the United States. The students who had attended this school were considered "dangerous" by the new authorities and sent for long reeducation courses. Those who were only in their first or second year were absorbed by other faculties.

At the end of July, just as I was about to leave, I met some architecture students for the last time. They told me that they had obtained from the military administration a large piece of land near Bien Hoa, belonging to the provincial chief who had fled with the Americans. They were making plans to build a small city there where they would be able to make new kinds of experiments, including social ones, that might later be used in other parts of the country as well. They were thinking of a large commune. They also told me that another group had made a study of Saigon as well and that the conclusions had been: to reduce Saigon to a million and a half inhabitants, not to build anything new, but to preserve what already existed.

Courses were resumed at Van Hanh University in July, after people's trials in which professors and students who had collaborated in the past with Thieu's police were arraigned. Nothing happened to them and the professors continued to teach.

Aside from a comprehensible class "deafness" on the part of the Saigon bourgeoisie unable to grasp the sense of what was happening, there was also, especially at the beginning, some genuine confusion over what the Revolution wanted, even among those who were interested and were trying to understand. What was the meaning, for instance, of "new man"?

On the other hand, certain forms of revolutionary zeal among young people were criticized and condemned by the new authorities. For example, there was a widespread idea among young students and girls that in the Revolution one did not dress well, that women ought not to use cosmetics, that girls especially should no longer wear beautiful and colorful *ao dai*.

Obviously no one had ever stated this, and it was not enough for Mme. Phuong Dung, assistant to Tran Van Tra and major in the Liberation Army, to appear at a reception at Doc Lap Palace wearing a splendid white *ao dai*. Groups of "ultrarevolutionary" youths continued to ridicule well-dressed girls on the street and some even went so far as to cut up the stylish trousers of some of them with scissors.

One day in the Saigon market the *bo doi* intervened in one of these squabbles. They listened to the youths, then to the girl in question, and decided that the young men should chip in to buy her another pair of trousers to replace the ones that had been torn apart.

The opinion of the authorities on this matter finally came in the form of a reply to a girl's letter. In the first issue of the weekly *Phu Nu* ("The New Woman"), published on May 19, the woman editor wrote:

"A woman ought to be beautiful. The success of the Revolution is a condition that should make women more beautiful. If at the moment we cannot eat well or dress well, it is because our country is poor and we must economize for reconstruction.

"But when this period is over, women will not only be able to dress better: they should do so. In European socialist countries there are specialized organizations for the study of fashions in clothes, in shoes, all working in the interest of beauty.

"Our point of view about beauty is that dressing well, and using cosmetics with moderation, should be done so as to raise the level of woman, and not simply as exhibition."

The question of what "making the Revolution," "becoming new men" meant persisted for many people. But what also persisted, increasingly provocative, increasingly penetrating, was the example of revolutionary life that the *can bo* and *bo doi* provided daily by their very existence.

The *bo doi*

It was difficult, standing there and watching when they arrived hand in hand to buy vegetables in the market, when
a twelve-man patrol passed in single file along the sidewalks, or when they stood their ground at the street corners in sometimes provocatory conversations, surrounded
by a small crowd of persons . . . it was difficult to imagine
soldiers more disciplined, more correct, soldiers so basically unsoldierly.

Had there ever been another case in history like this? A
victorious army entering the city of the vanquished and
not behaving like masters, not boasting of its war, not de-
vising Nuremberg trials in order to hang its defeated enemies?

"It wasn't we, but the Vietnamese people who won. All
the people," they repeated on all occasions.

"If we had taken Hanoi as they took Saigon we would
have turned it into a slaughterhouse," Do Viet, the ARVN
psychological warfare colonel, once told me in all sincerity.

In three months there was not a single serious incident
involving a *bo doi*: not one murder, not one theft, not one
rape.

The great majority of them were boys between sev-
enteen and twenty years old. As soon as they came out of
school they had signed up as volunteers. Many had applied
three times before being accepted. Most came from North
Vietnam, but there were some from the South, since often
it was not entire North Vietnamese divisions that infiltrated the South. Only a few battalions or one or two regi-
ments would depart, and once in the South these units
would be expanded to the fighting strength of an actual
division (usually about ten thousand men) by the addition
of youths recruited on the spot. Every soldier who crossed
the seventeenth parallel automatically became a member of
the Liberation Army, even if he came from the North
Vietnamese army.

Most were country boys, naive, modest, but with no complexes about being peasants coming to town. They were
not ashamed to be different. I once heard one of them
reply to a group of Saigonese curious to know his impressions of the metropolis:

"When I first got here I thought I'd fallen from the
moon. All these lights, the great big houses, and all these
people rushing, rushing around like maniacs."

Often Saigonese youths of the same age would ask *bo doi* to tell about their war adventures, their exploits, but without success. The most common reply was:

"The war is over. Whatever we did doesn't matter any more."

The answers kept recurring. They had one for every question.

The units that had captured Saigon on April 30 had been withdrawn from the city after two or three days, and in the new units that stayed on there was no *bo doi* who had not been given courses on how to behave with the population before entering the city. Each of them knew what attitude to take concerning "puppets" and foreigners, how to respond to people's questions and provocations.

What no course could have prepared them for was Saigon life with its swindles and duplicity, the thousands and thousands of people who knew only one way of living: getting by.

One day on Hai Ba Trung Street, shortly after the Liberation, I saw a *bo doi* who stood for a couple of hours awaiting the return of a little shoeshine boy who had asked to borrow his bicycle "just for a minute." A group of people who had witnessed the scene explained to him that the boy was not coming back, and the flabbergasted *bo doi* kept repeating:

"But this is robbery. It's robbery, isn't it?"

The greatest fun, I must say even for me, was to go and watch the *bo doi* off duty in the square between Doc Lap and the cathedral.

A sort of permanent street fair had been set up there, with little carts selling soup and drinks, and dozens of strolling vendors, often ex-soldiers or Thieu's police, who cheated the poor old *bo doi* in the most indecent fashion. Transistor radios with dead batteries, old watches repolished to look like new, were sold at prices not even a drunken GI would have paid in his time.

To have a watch was the great desire of the *bo doi*. It was the symbol of having been in Saigon. The army issued regulation watches only to the rank of major and up. A watch was a true rarity among the troops. In the jungle the sun had been enough, and the sun was still enough for the *bo doi* on guard at the Foreign Ministry, right in the middle of Saigon, who once pointed at it to inform me that it was noon and the offices were closed to the public.

During the war when their soup was made only with rice

and vegetables and there was no meat in it, the *bo doi* used to say: "We're eating the soup with no pilot." Saigon immediately took up this expression and coined a highly successful (at least with the *bo doi*) advertising slogan: "the watch with twelve lights, two windows, and no pilot." It meant, of course: a watch with twelve numerals, the date, the day, and self-winding.

To show that their watches were also "waterproof," the astute vendors kept within reach a pretty glass and a bottle of water, and it was amusing to see them dip these multicolored contraptions with phosphorescent dials, shimmering as the rainbow, before the dumbfounded eyes of the *bo doi.*

The *bo doi* actually had very little money. Once they were in the South they did not receive a fixed salary, only awards. The one for the Liberation had been a few dong, but they took up collections to buy watches. Each unit taxed itself by a certain sum to buy a watch for one of their number who had distinguished himself in some action. The watch was his to keep. The next month they bought one for someone else.

The other great attraction for the *bo doi* were Polaroid photos. They would place themselves in a group before the fountain in Lam Son Square, smile, and then after the "click" they would flock each time more incredulously around the photographer who, baseball cap tilted on his head, peeled back the paper slowly like a conjurer, revealing the *bo dois'* images in color.

A puzzle that the Saigonese were never able to figure out was how to distinguish *bo doi* officers from simple enlisted men. It wasn't easy. The uniforms and sandals were all the same, and Saigon had to content itself with the assumption that the more ballpoint pens a *bo doi* had in his pocket, the higher he was in rank.

"All we have to do is look each other in the face to know who's an officer," a *bo doi* said to me one day. "If you go to see a family, don't you recognize which one is the father?"

I had met him while he was buying Beethoven cassettes in a music store on Le Loi Avenue. I had heard him pronounce the titles of sonatas in perfect German and asked him if he spoke it. Of course. He had studied chemistry for three years at the University of Leipzig.

I saw him again often during my three months in Saigon. Tran was his family name: peasants in the Red River Delta, not far from Hanoi, born revolutionaries. His grandfather had begun by fighting the French, and one uncle had died at Poulo Condor.

His own father, Tran Huy Lieu, a self-educated member of the Party's central committee who had died in 1969, had been one of the great guerrilla intellectuals of the first resistance against the French.

Once, when Huy Lieu was invited to become a member of the Berlin Academy of Sciences, someone had asked him where he had got his degree, and he had replied:

"In French prisons."

Together with Truong Chin, Huy Lieu was one of the Vietminh leaders who had been able to hold out under the most terrible tortures. He had an amazing memory and in prison acted as a walking library. When one of the prisoners needed a quotation from the Marxist classics to write a document he went to Huy Lieu, who recited it. He knew all of *Das Kapital* more or less by heart.

In 1944 Huy Lieu was taken to a prison camp at Ba Ven in the north of Vietnam. He had not seen his wife for some years, and his comrades succeeded in bringing them together by cutting an opening in the fence and arranging a meeting in a small hut made of branches on the banks of a river called the Cong. It was on this occasion that the *bo doi* I had met was conceived. As a name his father gave him half of his own and the name of the river: Huy Cong.

Shortly after Huy Cong's birth the August Revolution broke out, and his father emerged from prison and became a minister in Ho Chi Minh's first government. The name of my *bo doi* was changed to Thanh Cong, "Success."

After studying in Leipzig, Thanh Cong worked as a chemist in Hanoi, then in 1971 he enlisted in the Liberation Army, and for four years he was a painter-guerrilla. His watercolors were among those exhibited at the former Circle Sportif.

They were scenes of life in bunkers, under bombing by B-52s, or portraits of guerrillas on bicycles along the Ho Chi Minh trail, with tanks in the background.

"This combination of the primitive, the simple, with what is most modern, most sophisticated in the world is the whole secret of our war," he said.

For three consecutive weeks in April Thanh Cong had remained isolated with a comrade in a trench six feet long and three feet wide, on the edge of Highway 13, not far from Lai Khe. His job was to block the ARVN reinforcements trying to reach Xuan Loc.

"We couldn't leave the bunker for even a minute. We even stayed inside when firing the mortar. We used our eating bowls to piss in and just stuck one hand out to empty them. We had enough cooked rice, salt, and water to last two months.

"We got a thousand cannon shots over our heads every day. When a broadside came, we curled up at the bottom of the hole with out ears plugged and our mouths open. But what became more unbearable than the cannon fire was our own stink."

Thanh Cong arrived in Saigon the day after the Liberation.

"Something very funny happened to me. I'll never forget it. For years I'd had to dig trenches to sleep in and to protect myself from the B-52s. It only takes a night to dig a trench but you need the right shovel. Mine was good, but I'd always dreamed of one of those little light ones that the Americans made for the puppets. I was always looking for one but had never found it.

"Just as I got to Saigon I saw one, brand-new, lying on the edge of the road. I stopped the jeep and ran to get it. I was so happy. It took me a minute to realize that I didn't need it any more, that the war was over and I wouldn't have to dig any more holes to hide in like a mole."

I never succeeded in finding out exactly what Thanh Cong did in Saigon, what his function was, but I think he worked as a *can bo* in the political section of the army.

I once asked him if he was a Party member, and he replied:

"It's very, very difficult to join the Party, and still more difficult to stay in. You have to have and maintain a very high political awareness, you have to know how to drag other people along, you have to be like a locomotive pulling railroad cars, and for this you need to have great qualities. You have to fight your egoism . . . it's so easy to be an egoist, it's a difficult attitude to overcome. It's nice to dress and eat well, to hear fine music, but you have to control yourself.

"You know, when you live in the jungle, all you have is a pack on your back, but when you come to a city like Saigon, it's a spontaneous thing to want more. But it's only by winning this inner battle against ourselves that we won the outer ones against our enemies. We must go on. We must be an example to the population. That's the only way they'll follow us.

"For the North, the example was Uncle Ho. But the South, what examples has it had? Thieu? Sure, the population imitated him in his corruption, his greed, and look what it got them. To build a new society it's not talent that's needed, but virtue."

More than an army of soldiers, the *bo doi* were an army of political cadres. In fact instruction in the use of a rifle came after the *bo doi* had undergone a long period of political training.

"They're not courses but discussions," Colonel Tran Cong Man, editor of the *Armed Forces Daily*, later explained to me in Hanoi. "Often the population participates alongside the *bo doi*. The themes that each *bo doi* is confronted with and on which he is instructed are:

" — patriotism;
   — internationalism and working-class solidarity;
   — distinguishing between the friends and enemies of the Revolution, the friends and enemies of the Vietnamese people.

"Political education continues even after he's at the front, since the situation changes, and the *bo doi* discuss with their cadres every new development, whether domestic or international.

"All units that took part in the attack on Saigon discussed the plans for it at length, and even simple soldiers were able to say what they thought. *Bo doi* have the right to discuss the orders of their superiors. The central theme of the courses for *bo doi* who had to remain in Saigon was distinguishing between the beauty of the Revolution and the evils of corrupt life."

I asked Colonel Man how a *bo doi* who did not respect revolutionary discipline was punished.

"There are no prisons in our army. Execution by firing squad is theoretically provided for treason, but its actual application is subject to long discussion. Punishments, if that's what you want to call them, are:

" — criticism in public;
   — warnings;
   — withholding of leave permits.

It's the conscience of the group that punishes, not some written rule."

"Are there any differences in treatment for simple *bo doi* and officers?"

"No. In our army there's no difference. Every soldier

must be prepared to undertake a mission by himself, he must not need officers to guide him. This is the great difference between our army and capitalist ones. In ours, a soldier is a revolutionary; in the others, soldiers are robots.

"Our army is even different from those of other socialist countries. Not even the Chinese and Soviet ones are like this. Ours is the most democratic army. Cadres, officers, and soldiers are united as though in a family. One is equal to another. For us the application of this democratic rule is fundamental."

The *bo doi* entering Saigon knew that they were going to be living in the midst of many people who were materially much better off than they. They knew that most people in Saigon ate "the soup with pilot." But during their preparation courses they had also learned that they would have to go on sacrificing themselves and so allow the population of the city to adjust gradually to a lower standard of living.

The army had a plan to further restrict the already minimal rations of the *bo doi* and resupply Saigon, especially with foodstuffs, so as to achieve a more gentle passage through the period of transistion.

So the army continued to eat soup without meat, and the pairs of *bo doi* returning from the market carrying their large baskets of water beets suspended on poles remained a daily sight on the streets. Saigon could not help but be impressed, at times almost frightened, by so much rigidity, so much austerity.

4: Currents of Revolution

Property of the people

They made their rounds in groups of three. Two with AK-47 rifles slung on their shoulders took up posts at the entrance to a house, a store, a workshop, and one, usually older and perhaps an officer, with a briefcase full of papers, knocked, asked permission to enter, offered polite greetings, and began to ask questions.

They were *bo doi* taking a census. They appeared all over the city, and the questions were always the same:

"Whose house is this? How many are there in your family? Who does the car in the garage belong to? Who owns this television set? And the motorcycle? . . ."

The principle was simple: everything, everything from buildings, factories, apartments, and furniture down to forks and spoons, everything that had belonged to Vietnamese "puppets" who had left the country before the Liberation, was automatically requisitioned and placed at the disposal of the *bo doi*. The same applied to the property of foreigners, particularly the departed Americans.

Many people who escaped had had time to sell their property or to hand it over to relatives staying behind, and the documents of sale were now shown to the *bo doi* in an effort to avoid requisition. It was no use: every contract drawn up after the fall of Ban Me Thuot was declared null and void.

The city was turned upside-down. Families living in houses rented from "puppets," people who had taken over abandoned apartments after Liberation Day had only a few days to find a new place to live. In the streets you saw a great coming and going of carts loaded with the household belongings of people who were moving.

Some were unable to prove that the furnishings in the "puppet" houses were actually their own and had to go away with only a couple of suitcases packed exclusively with clothes.

The *bo doi* moved into every place that was emptied, put up their mosquito nets, arranged their modest belongings

on the floor, and set in place the big aluminum pot in which
each unit cooked its own rice and water beets. On the walls
appeared small pink placards printed with the heading:
"Ten rules for the *bo doi* and his billet":

1) Beware of poisoning. Do not eat food or use medicines left by the enemy.
2) Be careful of the water system.
3) Do not eat raw vegetables.
4) Clean all premises thoroughly before moving in.
5) Learn the use of the bathrooms, W.C., etc.
6) Where there is no W.C., dig latrines.
7) Help the population to develop sanitation services.
8) Get yourself vaccinated.
9) Examine the quarter from the standpoint of health
   and hygiene.
10) Take measures against epidemics.

A whole company of soldiers took over what had been
the British embassy. In the evening when all the lights
were on you could see the *bo doi* lying in their hammocks
and taking the fresh air in front of the open windows.

While they were paying a visit to the building that had
housed the Italian embassy the *bo doi* discovered, right
over the chancellery, a suite of rooms that the CIA had
used to intercept the telephone conversations and radio
transmissions of Italian diplomats. The *bo doi* removed the
electronic devices, weapons, and a file of documents from
the rooms. They also requisitioned all the automobiles
from the embassy itself, but did not take over the
premises.

Everything not immediately occupied by the *bo doi*—such
as stores abandoned by their owners and still full of goods,
and which had to be inspected and inventoried by a special
economics official from the military administration—was
sealed with a simple strip of paper pasted diagonally across
the corrugated shutters and over the locks and bearing the
words: "Property of the people. Do not damage."

In Saigon, at least during the three months I witnessed,
the property of people who had remained on the spot was
not touched. However those who had apartments, houses,
or villas that the *bo doi* judged more than sufficient for a
single family were asked to give up a little of their space.

"It's a very interesting experience," said Cao Giao, who
had eleven young *bo doi* living in his home, along with his
own children. "They're highly educated, they've had a re-

markable political training, and every day we're learning something new about life in the other Vietnam, a place we'd known nothing about for twenty years."

The *bo doi* had entered into the bowels of the city. There was no block of apartments, courtyard, or back street where they had not gone to install themselves. Obviously not everyone was as enthusiastic as my friend over this intrusive, probing, at times alarming presence.

"I knew they wouldn't harm me, but I didn't expect them to arrive with chickens and pigs," a middle-aged woman complained to me. She owned a building with twenty apartments on Pasteur Street, and had been unable to leave because on April 28, as she was on her way to the waterfront, two policemen with drawn pistols had relieved her of a suitcase full of dollars. The *bo doi* had not requisitioned her building, but asked to set up a unit there charged with restocking food supplies, and she found it hard to refuse.

Many of the cars requisitioned by the *bo doi* were placed at the disposal of revolutionary committees or given to offices in the military administration, which removed the old plates and marked them "K-1," "K-2," "K-3," etc. Each sign corresponded to a department: hygiene, security, economy, and so on.

Motorcycles, television sets, electric fans were amassed in government warehouses, and many people claimed to have seen columns of loaded trucks leaving the city on Highway 1 on their way to Hanoi with this booty.

The cost of living diminished in Saigon. In the first days all prices, except for things stolen from the Americans, had risen sharply. Now prices had stabilized, especially for food, and in many cases they fell to below what they were before the Liberation. With all roads open and the connections with the countryside no longer dependent on the vicissitudes of war, the markets were full of vegetables, rice, meat, and fish. The problem was that people had less and less money to spend.

With all state officials and employees remaining without salaries and the banks closed, even upper- and middle-class families were slowly obliged to rid themselves of all signs of their former prosperity in order to scrape up a little cash.

The large square at the entrance to Tan Son Nhut, which surrounded the unfinished American monument to those who had "died for freedom" and which had become a huge stinking garbage dump after the Liberation, was transformed into the largest market for secondhand items that Saigon had ever had: beds, wardrobes, mattresses, sewing machines, motorbikes, statuettes, radios, Hondas, lamps, dishes, bicycles, and watches were piled high in search of buyers.

Families who gave up on the problem of "saving face" ended by displaying the entire contents of their homes on the doorstep or along the sidewalks of the city. Married women who were obviously once well-to-do now stood and waited for someone to come along and inspect their heaps of articles, each tagged with the asking price.

"We're a family of seven. Not one of us has a job any more. All our savings are in the bank, and when I went to the Revolutionary Committee to ask if we could be included in the rice distributions, they said that since we still had a television set, a refrigerator, and a bicycle, we were better off than many people who had nothing and whose need was greater than ours," I was told by a woman who was trying to sell the things she had left in front of her house in Nguyen Du Street.

Who were the buyers? First of all the peasants, who like peasants in all countries distrusted banks and kept what little money they had with them; then officials of the new regime, who received only minimum salaries, but still had fixed incomes.

One had only to walk through Saigon to be struck by this elementary, automatic redistribution of wealth and the elimination, not physical but economic, of an entire class.

The changed conditions in the city and the alterations in daily life had obliged a great many small shops to close down or change their activity. Tailor shops, shoe stores, souvenir sellers, and travel agencies which had done good business with the Americans were left absolutely without customers. Some had cleared their premises and set up tables and chairs to serve simple cups of tea with little cakes. No one, except the few remaining foreigners, ate in restaurants, and these improvised cafes managed to survive.

"Bao Chu" jewelers, at No. 165 Tu Do Street, began offering bowls of soup for 150 piasters instead of the costly bracelets and earrings of former times. Cao Giao and I liked it there and often went, because after the soup of thin noodles and the salad we could drink tea from fine crystal glasses with silver handles engraved "Saigon"—the owner had preferred to put them on the tables rather than leave them unsold in the windows.

If the Thieu regime truly had on its payrolls a million and a half soldiers, policemen, and officials, and each on the average had two or three persons to support, then after Liberation Day there were from three to four and a half million persons in South Vietnam who had lost all sources of income. Many of these were concentrated in Saigon, where it was almost impossible to find other work.

The most natural solution to this problem was to leave the city. A watchword printed several times in red by *Saigon Giai Phong* at the top of its front page said: "To produce is to live. Go back to the country."

The first to depart were the most recent refugees, who had arrived in Saigon fleeing the last battles before the Liberation. Then slowly, as economic conditions progressively worsened in the city, others began setting out.

The authorities did not force anyone to leave, but through the radio, newspapers, and the *bo doi* themselves they kept up an intense propaganda campaign to encourage the "return to one's native village."

Those who wanted to leave but did not have the means to had to appear before neighborhood committees, put their names on a list, and await their turn. Days often went by from the moment of registration to their arrival at their destination, and during this time the *bo doi* furnished half a kilo of rice and two hundred piasters per person a day.

At the three main bus stations, Petrus Ky, Nguyen Tri Phuong, and Nguyen Thai Hoc, endless horn honking announced the departure of vehicles packed to the roof with people, bicycles, and baskets. Hué, Da Nang, Ca Mau, Pleiku . . . were the destinations written in white chalk on the sides and windshield.

The Thieu administration had reckoned that there were about three and a half million hectares (8.4 million acres) of arable land in all of South Vietnam. The new authorities counted on bringing this expanse to 12 million acres as soon as possible, by recovering land that had not been utilized in the past because of the war: contested zones, minefields, areas reserved for military use, and so forth. By a subsequent landclearing program they expected to increase the total of arable land even further.

A high official in Hanoi, speaking of this exodus from the cities and referring critically to what had happened in Cambodia, where the Khmers Rouges had forced the population to evacuate Phnom Penh completely, told me:

"We want the peasants to go back to the country, but we don't want to empty the cities, we don't want to drive away the very workers we need to relaunch and expand industrial production. What we're concerned with is maintaining a sufficient population level for every urban center."

With the war Saigon had become a city of over three and a half million inhabitants. The Revolution's objective was to reduce it to a million and a half.

By the end of the first three months about three hundred thousand people had already left.

Books and bonfires

The task was written into the programs of the National Liberation Front and the PRG: "To eliminate enslaving, decadent, depraved culture that destroys the old and beautiful traditions of the Vietnamese people."

This task had been reaffirmed in the same words in public speeches during the victory celebrations, and the first measure was announced on May 15 in a brief communiqué from the Office of Information and Culture of the Military Management Committee: the circulation, sale, and lending of all publications printed during the American occupation and under the puppet regime must cease within a week.

Publishing houses immediately emptied their warehouses, and the sidewalks of Saigon were engulfed by mountains of books, magazines, illustrated periodicals, love stories, comic books, biographies of Hitler, Mussolini, and Eichmann, and all that anti-Communist literature produced by American and South Vietnamese experts in psychological warfare during the war years.

On Le Loi Avenue, in front of the Café Rex, a great sale at rock-bottom prices was being run by a group of unemployed ex-soldiers of Thieu's army.

One of them was squatting on the pavement behind his pile of books, openly displaying his Ranger tattoo. On his left forearm it said: "Gratitude pays. So does treachery."

From time to time a *bo doi* security patrol passed, gazed silently, and walked on without interfering.

On May 20, two days before the ultimatum's deadline

for the circulation of forbidden publications, the students of Saigon launched their campaign against decadent culture. Their manifesto, appearing first in the student movement headquarters on Duy Tan Street and then posted in the streets, read:

"Saigon is completely liberated. The city, cultural capital of the South, shines today with a new light. We, young people and students, pledge ourselves to provide an example, to be in the vanguard, to contribute to the building of a new way of life, a new society, a new man.

"We are determined to eliminate all that remains of the old regime, and to uproot dangerous sources of poison.

"Young people and students must immediately take to the streets, go into the schools, into the city neighborhoods, and ask the population to join in the campaign to uproot depraved and reactionary culture.

"Young people, students, each of us must be a fighter on the cultural front."

The response was immediate. Processions of young people began to parade through the city streets with signs and banners, stopping to rail against secondhand dealers who still displayed works placed on the "index." Teenaged students from secondary schools and lycées went in groups of seven or eight, first into their own homes and then into their neighbors', to ransack bookshelves and throw out the windows everything that was printed after 1954.

The first street-corner bonfires of books began. The first incidents took place.

On Nguyen Kim Street a "puppet" soldier selling old copies of *Playboy* and *Penthouse* was approached by a group of students who tried to persuade him to burn everything. He released the safety catch of a hand grenade he was holding in his pocket and killed three persons besides himself.

The destruction of the books, records, and musical scores was carried out by these bands of youngsters with no criteria or specific evaluation, and the population began to protest. Some students who appeared with red armbands in the name of the new authorities got thrown out of the homes they intended to search for forbidden publications. The *bo doi* did not intervene.

Young people were the social group on whom the Revolution concentrated more than any other. They were the most susceptible to new ideas, the least resistant to change, and because of their age they had not been involved with the power apparatus of the old regime. The young would be one of the driving forces of the new society, and there was no wish to nip in the bud their revolutionary zeal.

Accelerated two-week courses for the training of cadres began in these days, and boys and girls from the high schools and universities were invited to participate. Those selected were to work at the lower echelons of the city administration.

The campaign against decadent culture was also a way of putting many young people to the test. Natural leaders would slowly emerge, and the students would learn by themselves and at their own expense how to correct their actions and how to resolve their conflicts with the population.

Indeed discussion about the way to carry on the struggle against decadent culture without falling into excesses — which had an immediate counterrevolutionary effect — soon began within the very groups that roamed through the city throwing books to the flames.

At the end of May I sat in on one of these discussions at the student center on Duy Tan Street.

A girl from the steering committee opened the debate by explaining what, in her opinion, the political line to follow ought to be:

"In everything we do we must learn to distinguish. Even among the books published after 1954, there are good ones and bad ones, and we cannot destroy them all indiscriminately just because they were printed at the time of the puppet regime.

"Our struggle should be directed against the production of those publishing houses that have put millions of reactionary volumes in circulation, against books that glorify brute force like kung-fu wrestling, against novels that have imaginary heroes, intoxicating figures, as their central characters. We must struggle against books such as *Love Story* and all its Vietnamese imitations, novels for instance that tell of the amorous adventures between a young student and his woman teacher. These are tearjerkers and they bear no relation to real life, they are not important and don't help to make us good citizens and patriots."

One student asked what should be done with books by famous writers. The girl's answer was:

"It depends. We must get in the habit of analyzing and discussing each case as it comes. Let's take Steinbeck. What he wrote up until 1965 is all right. It's all right to read *The*

Grapes of Wrath but not what came later. After his visit to
Vietnam Steinbeck defended the American role in the war.
Well, we don't need this Steinbeck, just as we don't need
Solzhenitsyn or those Vietnamese authors who used their
talent to divide our people."

The students in subsequent meetings made lists of books
they considered harmful and that they thought should be
removed from circulation. In the case of certain works by
living Vietnamese writers, they decided to invite the authors to discuss their works one by one.

It was later decided that books put on the index should
not be destroyed, but deposited in special collection centers, where they would serve for the study and discussion
of decadent culture.

Despite repeated calls for moderation made by the various student revolutionary committees, the excesses of some
student gangs, especially the very young ones, continued
until the military authorities stepped in and harshly condemned "the attitude of those who call themselves revolutionaries but actually by their actions help the counter-
revolution."

In an attempt to bring a little order into the discussion
of types of lawful and unlawful publications *Saigon Giai
Phong,* using its usual formula of responding to a probably
nonexistent letter from a reader, published on June 6
some general criteria for distinguishing among books:

One can keep:
  — scientific and technical books;
  — novels and works of poetry used for purposes of
    study;
  — books published before 1954 by revolutionary writers
    and poets like Tu Huu, The Lu, Huy Can. . . ;
  — classical and modern French, American, Chinese, and
    Japanese foreign publications that are not counter-
    revolutionary, except publications of an existentialist
    or corrupting nature;
  — history books about our country that do not contain
    falsehoods about the Revolution;
  — foreign dictionaries;
  — translations of novels of world literature, like Tolstoy's
    War and Peace.

Among the books that disappeared from circulation
without much discussion, were all elementary school text-

books. The ones used under the Thieu regime were too
well supplied with anti-Communist notions and references,
too laudatory of the Western world, to find anyone dis-
posed to defend their validity in Saigon's new climate.

Truckloads of textbooks used in the North arrived at the
beginning of July, and Thieu's old government Press Office on Tu Do Street became the central depository from
which books were distributed to the city's schools as they
gradually reopened.

An example of what the new authorities meant by "culture linked to the old and beautiful traditions of the Vietnamese people" had already been provided in the days immediately following the Liberation, when many theaters
reopened and artists, largely from the North, began to
give concerts, plays, ballets, and marionette shows.

Folktales were readapted to contemporary themes with a
political content, old dances were performed with monstrous Americans taking the place of traditional figures
representing evil.

Most important was the rediscovery of folk music, which
Thieu had gone so far as to prohibit since it had become
one of the symbols of resistance. Traditional Vietnamese
instruments were also reintroduced. One evening with Cao
Giao I heard for the first time in a theater in Cholon a
long piece played to the languid, thrilling sound of the
monochord. The audience, a crowd of simple people,
neighborhood women with babies in their arms, youngsters, and local cadres, was spellbound with emotion. Cao
Giao wept:

"It's like rediscovering you're Vietnamese. I'm cured forever of nightclub culture," he said.

Every evening, outside every theater where these performances were given free, there were throngs of people
waiting to enter.

As for the pop singers who had become so rich and famous during the war years, their voices were no longer
heard. Almost all had escaped with the Americans.

Elvis Phuong was said to be dead.

Thai Thanh, who had owned the "Quoc Te" nightclub
and who had given innumerable performances for American and South Vietnamese troops, was last seen on April
28, waiting with twelve suitcases at Tan Son Nhut for an
airplane to take her away. A month after the Liberation
two *bo doi* appeared at her Saigon address to hand over

one of those suitcases, which they said they had found intact on the runway with her name on it, and a rumor spread that she too was dead.

Her records, like those of other singers, disappeared from circulation, and boxes of cassettes and reels of magnetic tape went to fill the trash cans on street corners, while the large stereo sets which had been standard equipment in every Saigon bar ended up unsold in the thieves' market, though offered at laughable prices.

Saigon no longer listened to the music that had once been the obsessive background of every bar, every restaurant, every nightclub.

This is not to say that the Revolution rejected Western music, or Western culture altogether.

When the old opera house, built by the French in downtown Saigon and later transformed into the National Assembly building, reverted to its original function and opened with a concert attended by Nguyen Huu Tho, three fourths of the music played was by European composers.

It was an extraordinary spectacle. The conductor wore tails, the men violinists and drum players wore black jackets and white shirts, the women at the harps pale blue *ao dai*. When the conductor raised his baton this Vietcong orchestra, dressed in the most classical Western fashion, struck up the most typical of Strauss waltzes.

A robust Vietcong tenor then sang, in Russian, the aria "La donna è mobile . . ." from *Rigoletto*, to the applause of a public made up of political cadres, artists, Saigonese intellectuals, and off-duty *bo doi* who called for an encore by waving their pith helmets.

The concerts followed one another, and at night in the silent streets of downtown Saigon you could hear notes of classical music over the hum of bicycles gliding by along the pavement.

Hunting down the obstinate

The registration of "puppets" was proceeding smoothly.
There was a bit of confusion with members of the Dan
Chu, Thieu's single party, because at the time it had been
set up the president's men had swelled the rolls with the
names of all government officials, their families and relatives, and out of the five million "enrolled members" a
great many did not even know they belonged and failed to
show up for registration.

As for soldiers and policemen of the old regime, tens of
thousands had already registered by the middle of May,
but it was difficult for the *bo doi* to calculate how many
were still in hiding, playing "submarine"—as they called
it—in the city. Though they had recovered the lists for the
various units, and knew the names of all ARVN officers, it
was impossible to establish with certainty who had escaped
with the Americans, who had disappeared at sea in helicopters that had run out of fuel or in overloaded boats
wrecked by monsoons, and who had instead stayed in the
country and was stubbornly refusing to present himself to
the new authorities.

"Obstinate" became another of those new terms that Saigon had to learn. "Obstinate" meant anyone who did not
accept the new reality of the country, did not abide by the
new rules of society and persisted on the "path of error."
If "puppet" was an attribute that referred to activities in
the past and was therefore forgivable, "obstinate" referred
to activities in the present. It was the result of a deliberate
choice made after the Liberation and for this reason was a
serious guilt, at times a very serious one. To be "obstinate"
was to be a criminal.

A week before the final date set for registration the "obstinate" received an ultimatum: "appear or suffer the consequences." A long editorial in *Saigon Giai Phong* appealed
to the population to denounce all those who were still in
hiding, and for the first time revealed that some "obstinate" elements had murdered *bo doi*.

Despite what was smugly rumored among Saigonese
society, there was no army of anti-Communist guerrillas
determined to do battle with the new authorities; but there
were some hundreds or perhaps thousands of former soldiers and policemen, still armed, who were refusing to give
themselves up.

Some had organized themselves into actual predatory

gangs, others had left the city in the hope of surviving in the jungle as their Vietcong enemies had done before them. One of these groups had gone to hide in a swampy area around Nha Be, and every so often fired a few mortar shells. Another hung around Lai Thieu, until some unarmed students went out to meet them and persuaded them to surrender.

In some less populated areas of the country "obstinate" groups held out much longer, but since they constituted no danger, the *bo doi* left them alone. They set up security cordons around the area and waited.

"Without the population's help there's no way for them to survive. Sooner or later they'll have to emerge. It's not worth sacrificing a single one of our soldiers to go and flush them out," a Liberation Army officer told me.

The "obstinate" problem was more serious in the city, where they had better opportunities to hide and find support among the population. So after one week which saw the curfew lifted and *bo doi* walking around without weapons in every quarter, the Military Management Committee reimposed the ban on circulating in the streets between eleven p.m. and five a.m. and ordered Liberation Army soldiers not to go out unarmed.

Among the "puppets" who failed to show up for registration were members of Thieu's secret police and many soldiers of the special forces. Paratroopers and Rangers had had their arms and chests tattooed with an anti-Communist oath and feared they would be shot simply for that. "A day is not complete unless I've killed a Vietcong," some inscriptions read. Others had had a cross tattooed for each "VC" they had slaughtered.

Another group with every reason to fear registration were the *chieu hoi*, former Vietcong who had deserted and placed themselves at the service of Thieu's forces and the Americans.

Chieu hoi, literally "open arms," was the program launched by the American psychological warfare command parallel to the Phoenix program. The former was conceived to attract guerrillas to the government side through a promise of clemency and a new life; the purpose of the latter was to "eliminate" (which in most cases meant "murder") the greatest number of persons even only suspected of being agents or political cadres of the Front—at least two thousand a month was the objective.

Thousands of leaflets, printed on one side with the

three-banded flag of the Republic and on the other with a worded pass, were showered on areas controlled by the Vietcong. Any guerrilla who surrendered by presenting one of these slips, instead of being shot or sent to a prisoner-of-war camp, was subjected to a period of questioning and reeducation, and then integrated into the ARVN forces.

The Americans had taken the *chieu hoi* and set up a special corps, the "Kit Carson Scouts," which they used as guides in the more insecure territories of the country. The South Vietnamese used them as bait to attract other guerrillas, or sent them into the front lines to prove the truth of their conversion by fighting against their former comrades.

One of the most famous ex-guerrillas was Colonel Nguyen Be—though the details of his career with the Communists remain murky. On the advice of the Americans, Thieu had appointed him director of the "revolutionary" cadre school in Vung Tau. Be, exploiting his experience in the guerrilla forces, had tried by imitating Vietcong terminology, methods, and even uniforms, to train young men to live among the peasants like the Vietcong, but work for the regime.

In 1974 Colonel Be was replaced at the Vung Tau center and sent to Thieu's social welfare ministry with the task of coordinating all the humanitarian aid provided by foreign governments and organizations. This post involved channeling millions and millions of dollars, often collected in Europe and America in the name of war victims, into a Machiavellian plan: to deploy refugees as a human barrier around the areas controlled by the South Vietnamese government.

In 1954 after the Geneva Accords, Catholic refugees from the North were used to set up a security belt around Saigon—giving rise, for example, to the fervently anti-Communist suburb of Ho Nai, located right at the outer edge of what had previously been the Vietminh-infested forest of Bien Hoa. In the same way the million refugees produced by the 1972 offensive were utilized after the Paris Accords to isolate pockets of territory under PRG administration and protect the lines of communication with Saigon. Whole populations, prevented from returning to their native villages, were blackmailed and forced to settle in contested areas, on arid and untillable soil.

The cost of this program was paid for by humanitarian aid from allied governments and with money collected by such private organizations as "Caritas," "Mani Tese," "Brot für die Welt," and others. The Germans had been among the most generous in this field.

The major portion of private aid was coordinated in Vietnam by an outfit called "Corev," taken in charge by Nguyen Van Thuan, former bishop of Nha Trang, Diem's nephew, and a well-known reactionary. Father Forrest, a Canadian Jesuit in the Apostolic Nunciature, was also involved in this program.

The man who worked for Thieu and the Americans and reputedly controlled this whole circuitous operation was the ex-guerrilla Colonel Nguyen Be. Though he was thought not to have succeeded in escaping, no one had seen him since the Liberation. Certainly a man like him, had he turned up to register, would have had problems reconciliation policy notwithstanding.

Unlike all other "puppets," who were sent home after registration with new identification documents, the *chieu hoi* were sent back to the Liberation Army units from which they had deserted. There, standing before their former comrades, they had to retell the story of their betrayal, recount all the services they had rendered to the enemy to save their skins, and had to listen to the stories of all those who had suffered or died on their account. This at least is what a *bo doi* officer told me happened to the *chieu hoi* after registration. Whatever else may have happened I didn't hear about.

On May 24 the first group of foreign journalists who had stayed in Vietnam after Liberation Day left for Vientiane on board a North Vietnamese Ilyushin airliner. Another group departed on the 26th. Most had been asking to leave for weeks, some had been expelled.

Among the latter was General Vanuxem. During the victory celebrations he had gone to complain to Major Phuong Nam that as correspondent for the magazine *Carrefour,* he had not received an invitation to the reception at Doc Lap. Phuong Nam had thrown him out:

"You killed hundreds of my compatriots, General. You can thank your lucky stars we don't arrest you."

In the middle of April there were about four hundred photographers, cameramen, and correspondents in Vietnam. Before Tan Son Nhut closed down, 150 of them left on the last airliners. One had died, photographer Michel Laurent, killed by crossfire on the road to Xuan Loc. Another hundred or so had left by helicopter with the American evacuation.

At dawn on April 30 there were still 127.

The two Ilyushin flights, and a few other sporadic flights by a United Nations plane, took almost all of them away.

Even journalists who had been brought to Saigon from Hanoi two weeks after the Liberation, members of the Communist press and from socialist countries including China and the Soviet Union, were sent away after a brief stay. At the end of July an office of the American UPI and one of Agence France-Presse were still operating in Saigon, but the PRG had not yet given permission for the opening of the New China News Agency or the Soviet Tass.

Three months after the Liberation not one of the countries that had long recognized the PRG had a resident diplomatic delegation in Saigon. Ambassadors accredited to the PRG, but residing in Peking, had come for the anniversary of the•revolutionary government on June 6, but had departed immediately afterward.

The new Vietnam was entering upon a harsh and more difficult period, and gave the impression of wanting to close in on itself, of wanting to achieve a certain internal order before embarking on relations with the outside world.

The very morning of May 23, while journalists were being taken to Tan Son Nhut to catch a plane that took off only the next day because of bad weather, Tu Do Street was blocked. New "Military Security" *bo doi,* who had appeared in the city for the first time two days before with leather boots, red-and-yellow armbands, and field radios, closed off all the adjacent streets and began a meticulous house-to-house search. For a couple of hours no one could enter or leave the area, and everyone had to show his identification documents. The same operation took place simultaneously in other parts of the city.

The hunt for the "obstinate" was on. The search was a way of persuading hesitant "puppets" to show up for registration in the ten days remaining, but also a way of making it clear that the tolerance of the first three weeks should not be misunderstood.

The first arrests were made. General Do Ke Giai, commander of the Rangers, was taken away by an armed group from the neighborhood revolutionary committee. In the course of a thorough search they found one million piasters in his house. The general was held for two days and was required to make a more precise declaration than the one he had given at the time of his registration.

Each declaration made was thoroughly examined by the security forces, compared with others, and checked with the dossiers retrieved in the various commands. Anyone who had in some way lied was sought out, required to give an explanation, and "warned."

At the end of the month, when the registration period was over, controls were intensified. The *bo doi* set up sudden roadblocks in the middle of the city or on the roads leading out of Saigon, arrested anyone without documents, and requisitioned any motorcycle whose ownership could not be proved and which could be considered stolen.

During one of these lightning street checks the *bo doi* even stopped Jean-Claude Labbé, a lively young French photographer who had been riding around on a Honda given him by a neighborhood revolutionary committee since Liberation Day, with the PRG colors on his arm and a red badge with Ho Chi Minh's picture on his chest.

"Why do you wear all this stuff?" asked a *bo doi*.

"Because I'm a Communist," replied Labbé, who spoke Vietnamese.

"Party card," snapped the *bo doi*.

Labbé took his French Communist Party membership card out of his wallet and handed it to him.

The *bo doi* examined it carefully, raised his right hand to his helmet, gave a military salute, smiled, and said:

"Thanks, Comrade!"

By now the city was clean. The heaps of ammunition, guns, and hand grenades strewn everywhere Liberation Day had been swept up, and private individuals were requested to hand in all weapons in their possession. To acquire even a simple pistol in Saigon had become difficult, and to be found carrying a weapon by the *bo doi* was extremely dangerous.

The expression used by Radio Giai Phong to describe the end of certain "obstinate" elements who had been caught with weapons was: "felled on the spot."

Hoc tap

When they met, people asked as though inquiring about each other's health, and sometimes with a touch of irony:

"Have you done *hoc tap*?"

Hoc tap was reeducation, a bath in the Revolution; it meant erasing the sin of having been in some way a "puppet." A whole society was learning to live in accordance with new standards, new values. It was learning a new behavior; and *hoc tap* was the means for this reconversion. *Hoc tap* meant reforming one's mind, reexamining one's attitude toward life and toward the community—a continuous learning process that took place in various ways and at various levels.

In the schools and universities *hoc tap* was part of the program; you did it by discussing the curriculum in the classrooms, by attending sessions called to arraign teachers and professors who had collaborated with the old regime, by hearing a poet like Cu Huy Can speak in the auditorium of the student center on the role of art in revolutionary society.

In the factories, workers did *hoc tap* by discussing problems of organization, management, and the distribution of profits in almost daily meetings held on the job.

For soldiers, officers, officials, and politicians of the old regime, *hoc tap* was an obligation, a sort of penalty to be served before being reintegrated into society. For the rest of the population it was a necessary experience but one that happened with a certain casualness in the course of each day, though no one could escape it.

Those who did not do *hoc tap* in the offices or factories where they worked ended up doing it in the evening, at the increasingly frequent neighborhood meetings organized by the *bo doi*.

The *bo doi* went from street to street, summoning people with megaphones. The meetings opened with the national anthem of the Liberation Front played on some old phonograph; then a political cadre spoke for an hour, before answering questions from those present. No one was forced to go, but it soon became one of those unwritten duties that everyone learned to perform so as not to incur blame from the neighbors or criticism from the *bo doi*.

Each of these neighborhood meetings had a theme: Vietnam under French colonialism; the struggle for independence; the American intervention; the crimes committed by the United States forces; the Communist Party; the future of the country, and so forth.

They were the same subjects as those written up in the newspaper *Saigon Giai Phong*, talked about on television in a question-and-answer program initiated a month after the Liberation, and discussed in an informal and more immediate way by the *bo doi* with the inhabitants of the houses where they were billeted or with passersby on the street.

The *bo doi*, with their highly developed political awareness, were along with the *can bo* the grass-roots operators of this vast reeducational network through which the entire population was ultimately to pass. Their guidance was not authoritarian, and their "lessons" were offered without arrogance.

One evening, coming out from a horrible Soviet potboiler at the Anh Hue movie theater in Cholon, I overheard some young people speaking among themselves and remarking how boring and unbearable the film had been. They were soon approached by two *bo doi* who urged them to go back into the auditorium with them and see the picture all over again. If they had not understood the meaning of the story, its political value, they would help them, discuss it with them, and answer their objections. The group went back inside.

Reeducation of the same sort—courteous, unobtrusive, sharply insistent but without coercion—was slowly applied to a group of persons who more than any other had characterized wartime Saigon: the prostitutes. In the three months after the Liberation no formal order was ever issued forbidding them to carry on their activities, and some girls continued to appear in the downtown streets in their trousers and close-fitting little sweaters.

The *bo doi* left them alone during the day. Then at curfew time, as the girls returned home through the empty streets, the *bo doi* followed them and explained how they had been victims of the war and the "American imperialists," how the situation had changed, how they ought to go back to their villages and take up some other livelihood before it was too late.

It did not happen in Saigon during the time I was there, but I heard that in the northern provinces some girls who had "obstinately" continued in this trade after repeated warnings had been sent to work in rice paddies or on the construction of irrigation ditches.

In addition to general reeducation, to which the whole population was exposed, every profession had its specific form of *hoc tap*.

Lawyers and judges, for instance, were invited to a series of meetings at which the director of the Juridical Academy and the president of the Supreme Court in Hanoi were present. Both spoke of the new way of conceiving law as a weapon in the defense of the Revolution.

Professors and teachers had to do weeks of *hoc tap* before the schools reopened, reviewing all previous curricula and discussing what the new standards of education should be.

The same happened for various other categories of persons, from doctors to tourist guides to hotel waiters, all of whom had to learn a new mode of behavior toward their clients.

Writers, artists, and Saigon journalists were at first treated by the *can bo* with a certain respect. The political cadre who introduced himself to a gathering of about a thousand intellectuals said:

"I'm not here to give you a lecture, but to submit a report on the situation of the country for your analysis and discussion."

Nevertheless there were other meetings where intellectuals had to listen to lectures delivered by less sophisticated cadres, actual peasants from the guerrilla forces, and this created a certain ill will among those of them who felt belittled and offended at having to take lessons from people they considered "uncultivated." But soon they too realized that it did not pay to refuse to listen to "uncultivated peasants."

Anyone judged not to have been reeducated had to do *hoc tap* all over again.

In the offices of the old administration, the ministries, courts, and post office, reeducation of lower- and middle-ranking clerks and officials took place on the job. Here is how a woman file clerk in the Ministry of Agriculture described her experience to me:

"We were a group of three hundred persons and they divided us into cells of twenty to twenty-five. A *can bo* was put in charge of each cell. Ours was a former graduate from Saigon who had joined the guerrillas in 1968.

"The first day he went over the history of Vietnam under the yoke of French colonialism, then under American imperialism, explaining how the independence of the South Vietnamese Republic had been an illusion.

"On the second day we were given sheets of paper on which to answer these questions:

1) What did you do under the puppet government? Describe your attitudes and actions.
2) What do you want to do to help the Revolution? Be specific in your promises.

"Once we'd handed in our papers, we each had to discuss our answers before the group and reply to questions."

All three hundred persons in this girl's group were judged "reeducated" by the *can bo*.

When I asked her if she really felt reeducated, she was unable to answer and gave an embarrassed smile. Certainly the very way she had told me her story was a result of *hoc tap*. Her vocabulary had already changed.

Aside from these more or less formal courses even a visit to one of the various art and documentary exhibitions that opened in the city and were always crowded with people constituted a form of *hoc tap* for the general public. Young political cadres were always on hand to provide explanations and answer visitors' questions. Every conversation immediately acquired a political undertone, a didactic content, whether it took place in front of the oils and watercolors on view at the Circle Sportif or before the yellowed photographs illustrating the life of Ho Chi Minh and the birth of the Revolution that were exhibited in the halls of the old Bibliothèque Nationale.

One of the most successful exhibitions was the archaeological one that opened on June 8 in the building at the corner of Tu Do Street and Nguyen Du.

For weeks entire classes of schoolchildren and endless lines of ordinary citizens filled the gallery, where artifacts of a Vietnamese civilization that had thrived hundreds of centuries before were shown for the first time in Saigon.

People were curious, surprised, interested, Every tour concluded with the same scene, one that inevitably made visitors smile with satisfaction. After having shown prehistoric necklaces, cooking implements, and knives, the guide, either a *bo doi* or a young cadre, would point out some stone molds used to cast primitive arrowheads, and say:

"These show how the Vietnamese people were capable of making their own weapons by themselves already in very ancient times, and demonstrate the falseness of the theory held by some that these tools were imported from a nearby country." It could hardly escape the most unalert Vietnamese that the polemical reference was directed at China.

The new authorities were so convinced that decades of foreign occupation had infected and destroyed the consciousness of the southerners that they lost no opportunity to reaffirm the tradition of self-sufficiency and independence of the Vietnamese people.

This went not only for the French or American protectors of the past, but also for those whom people naturally saw as their new protectors: the Soviets and Chinese.

In public or in private, every time a PRG leader or simple *can bo* spoke with gratitude of aid received from the "socialist countries," he reaffirmed in the same sentence that the success of the Vietnamese Revolution was due to the determination of the people, to their strength and political beliefs.

To rebuild Vietnamese national consciousness, to inculcate the conviction that all foreign domination of the country was over, were the first objectives of *hoc tap*. The rest, the political education, came later. The guerrilla movement had developed along the same lines: it had been sparked by patriotism, and then strengthened by politicalization. Nationalism had been the deepest motivation, the prime mover of the Resistance; by the same token, uplifting the national spirit became one of the pillars in the reeducation of "puppets."

Emerging from years of prison, Mai Duc Tho, brother of Le Duc Tho, had said to a friend:

"In the worst moments, when you're about to break down, it's not the Party you think of, not abstract ideas like socialism, it's the people, our people."

The Party of course had played a highly important role in the struggle. No one denied it: the Party had given the impetus, provided discipline and an ideology for that spontaneous force, the national sentiment of any people unwilling to be enslaved or dependent on others. Ho Chi

Minh's statement, written on all the walls of Vietnam after the Liberation, was understood by everyone:

"Nothing is more precious than independence and freedom."

It was clear from the first days after the Liberation that the new authorities who were ruling the country would seek to maintain this independence also in the face of their Soviet and Chinese allies.

Saigon was not invaded, as many expected it to be, by "advisors" from Moscow or Peking. Though these allies had paid the material costs of the war, they did not receive special privileges for it.

Nor did the Soviets take possession of the former American naval base at Cam Ran Bay for their Pacific fleet, as a large part of the Western press reported.

"They didn't even ask, since they knew what our answer would be," a high official of the Foreign Ministry said to me in Hanoi.

What the Soviets did ask—and insistently—was to have journalists and diplomats stationed in Saigon, but even this was politely denied them.

As for the Chinese, when their first correspondents came to the South for a brief stay and were taken for a visit to the marble caves of Da Nang, they ended up receiving a nice little statuette of Confucius like everyone else.

The Vietnamese were quite conscious that to maintain their independence they would have to stay aloof from the Sino-Soviet dispute and not allow one to establish itself and have more influence in the country than the other.

During the interview I had with Nguyen Huu Tho—the president of the National Liberation Front and technically new head of the provisional state in the South—at Doc Lap Palace at the end of June, he revealed that in 1965, in response to the massive American intervention in Vietnam, the Chinese and Soviets had proposed to send their "volunteers." The Vietcong had "refused firmly, energetically refused" the offer. The Vietnamese were well aware that beyond a sincere socialist solidarity that obliged them to support the liberation struggle in Vietnam, Moscow and Peking naturally had in view their own national interests as superpowers.

In informal conversations high PRG cadres, as well as a

member of the Party's Central Committee in Hanoi, made
no mystery of the fact that certain neighboring and distant
"friends," for fear of endangering their relations with the
United States, had tried to dissuade the Vietcong from
launching the last offensive that had then led to the liberation of Saigon and the end of the war.

China and the Soviet Union were, as an important member of the Workers' Party told me in Hanoi, "two enemies
with whom we want to be on equally friendly terms."

"It's not an easy thing, but now that we've won the war,
we're stronger and more independent, and it will be possible," he added.

When I asked him what the Vietnamese thought of the
collective security pact that the Soviets have been trying to
sell to the various Asian countries for years, his answer
was:

"We still haven't understood what it's all about."

If Vietnam does not join the Soviet pact, which clearly
has anti-Chinese intentions, this will not mean that the
Vietnamese are pro-Peking.

A few hours after the Chinese in Cholon put up the flag
of People's China alongside those of the Front and Hanoi
during the victory celebrations, groups of *bo doi* and *can bo*
went to tell them to take it down:

"We're in Vietnam and celebrating a Vietnamese victory,
not a Chinese one," they said.

Nothing that happened in the first three months after
Liberation seemed to indicate that the determination with
which the Vietnamese had maintained their independence
and equidistance from their two wartime allies would diminish with peace, or that the new Vietnam would eventually enter into the orbit of one or the other.

On the contrary, there were sufficient indications to suggest that the new Vietnam might develop instead into a
third magnetic pole in the Communist world.

"We have profited by all the revolutionary experiences
of other countries, but we won thanks to our independent
political line," they told me on various occasions in Hanoi.
The same thing was repeated to "puppets" doing *hoc tap.*

In no reeducation course did the *can bo* utter, even par-
enthetically, such phrases as: "in China they do this," "the
Soviets teach us that. . . ." Vietnamese, to be Vietnamese,
was the phrase constantly repeated. The pride of belonging to this people who had defeated the greatest power in

the world was a right to which all, even "puppets," were entitled.

Every *hoc tap* course began more or less with the same words:

"*Giai phong* has been everyone's victory. There are no longer either victors or vanquished among the Vietnamese. The only ones who have been defeated are the Americans."

Such reasoning had a notable psychological effect, encouraged "conversions," and guaranteed the initial success of *hoc tap*.

The first thing reeducation conveyed was that to have found oneself on what had ultimately been the wrong side of the front was not a mortal sin. One was not thereby relegated to the sidelines, excluded. The "guilty" were to be reaccepted by virtue of being Vietnamese, to be retrieved by society. Even those who had taken up arms against the people could be forgiven; the designation of "puppet" disappeared through one's participation in *hoc tap*.

On the same day that the first round of reeducation courses for former enlisted men and noncommissioned officers ended *Saigon Giai Phong* published a three-paneled cartoon that summed up for many people at the time the whole significance of *hoc tap*.

In the first panel a young man with *nguy* ("puppet") written on his shirt smilingly approaches a *bo doi* who rebukes him with the words:

"Sorry, but the people and the Revolution don't allow me to shake your hand."

In the second panel, the youth, contrite, goes for a *hoc tap* course.

In the third, the same young man, happy and no longer with *nguy* on his shirt, is embraced by the *bo doi*, who calls him "brother."

I worked for the Americans

Hoc tap courses for soldiers of the old regime began on June 11.

A bulletin from the Military Management Committee gave a list of addresses to which enlisted men, noncommissioned officers, and officers up to the rank of captain were to report, and issued a final appeal to "obstinate" elements who had not yet appeared for registration and were continuing to play "submarine."

The slogan for the day, printed in red block letters on the front page of *Saigon Giai Phong*, read:

"A policy of humanitarian clemency: to appear and confess will be considered an extenuating circumstance. To continue to hide will be severely punished."

Since the early morning hours, long lines of men had been forming in front of schools, old barracks, and police stations.

The atmosphere was tense. People knew from the bulletin that *hoc tap* would last three days, but they did not know what to expect from these courses of "study and transformation," and the horrible stories of "brainwashing" promulgated by anti-Communist propaganda during the war were surely in the minds of many. Some still thought they would be arrested and perhaps sent to concentration camps that were said to be prepared in the more remote regions of the country.

It took only a few hours to resolve the uncertainty.

At every gathering point in the city pairs of *bo doi* kept order, checked the identification slips issued at the time of registration, and divided the "puppets" to be reeducated into classes of sixty to seventy.

Sitting on the ground in courtyards, or at schoolroom desks, each with a note pad and pencil, the soldiers of the old regime spent the first day listening to political cadres who spoke to them about Ho Chi Minh's life and the various phases of the war of independence.

"They were kind, courteous, and from the first moment we realized that we weren't there to be punished. It was really like going to school," I was told by Loan, an ARVN sergeant who had worked in Thieu's intelligence services and simultaneously for a European news agency.

Loan was a classical product of American and South Vietnamese propaganda. I had known him for years. Everything he said seemed to issue from "psychological warfare"

bulletins; his view of the world was one of obtuse anti-
Communism. He was a "believer," he never had doubts, he
never posed himself any questions about the Vietnamese
on the other side. His position did not change even with
the Liberation, if anything it hardened.

April 30 had been a terrible shock to him. Apart from
his sense of defeat, Loan found himself separated from his
family. He had sent his wife and three children away with
the Americans, fully expecting to rejoin them later after
winding up some final piece of business and withdrawing
the eight million piasters he had saved over the last years
from the bank. But he had not had time.

Through friends he had obtained the address of his
family in the United States: "Arlington Camp, Block 52,
tent 27b." From then on his fixed idea was to find a way to
escape and rejoin them. He had gone for reeducation because he did not want to run any risks with the new authorities.

The second day of *hoc tap* was devoted to confessions.
After speaking about the crimes committed in the country
by Americans, the *can bo* asked the "puppets" to tell what
they had done in the war, what crimes against the people
they had participated in.

In Loan's group there were long moments of silence.
People were afraid to tell the truth. Afraid of the *can bo*.
Afraid of some "obstinate" colleagues who at the beginning
of the courses had urged the others to resist and threatened those who might cooperate.

Then someone began to speak about himself. The ice
was broken. One soldier who had been a helicopter gunner told how while flying over areas designated by the
command as "free-fire zones" he had opened up on peaceful peasants. Another told of having taken part in the interrogation of suspects, a marine of having received a decoration for killing dozens of Vietcong.

"The atmosphere was quite special. The *can bo* was persuasive about inducing each person to tell his story, it was
like suddenly being among friends. I talked about myself
too," Loan said later. "I told about the corruption I'd been
involved in, about the way we falsified war news, about
how I'd been a tool of American propaganda. It was
strange. The more I spoke, the more I felt a burden being
lifted."

After Loan, a soldier told how he had carried out his

commander's orders to "liquidate" some prisoners captured by his unit in the course of an operation.

The *can bo* did not react, did not comment; he took
notes on each story and asked for details of names and
dates.

There were also comic moments. A *can bo* kept asking a
soldier what his faults had been, and the soldier, almost
with embarrassment, repeated that he didn't think he had
any. The *can bo* insisted, his comrades encouraged him,
and finally the soldier said:

"I don't know, I was a bugler . . . the only fault I can
think of is having sounded charge instead of retreat."
There was a general burst of laughter.

In the evening the "puppets" returned home, told about
their experience of *hoc tap,* and any fear of punishment
lingering in the rest of the population began to disappear.

On the third day the subject of the speeches made by
the *can bo* was the policy of the PRG and the need to rebuild
the country from the ruins of war.

Then every group held a session of questions and answers, and finally there was a brief ceremony, like absolu-
tion, during which documents certifying the completion of
the course were handed out.

Someone in each group was required to sum up the general impressions of *hoc tap* and to say, on behalf of the others as well, what he thought of the policy of the new authorities,

Everyone in Loan's group pointed to him as their
spokesman. He was used to speaking in public, had
worked in the intelligence sector and for the press. Loan
demurred, saying there were people older than he in the
group who were entitled to speak. The *can bo* replied:

"Of course the principle of seniority belongs to the Vietnamese tradition and should be respected. But it applies to
the family. In society it's different. Here what counts is not
seniority but personal qualities, a readiness to sacrifice oneself for the people."

Loan let himself be persuaded, and said:

"For years I worked for the Americans. I didn't realize
that what I was doing was against my people. I knew nothing about you, about the other Vietnam. I called you VC
as the Americans had taught me to do and that was
enough.

"Now I know who you are, I know the program of the

Front, and I understand it. I know I have been a tool of
the enemies of Vietnam. But now I feel like another person.
I'm a new man."

The group had applauded. The *can bo* as well. He was
happy.

Loan truly astonished me. At first I thought he was faking; later, as the days went by, I realized that he actually
believed in the things he had said. Perhaps in part he became a prisoner of those words, of the role he was playing,
of the applause, of the approval he received, and was unconsciously trying to adjust his behavior to his declarations.
But something in him had genuinely changed, something
had clicked. Instead of escaping, he now started thinking
about bringing his family back to Vietnam.

Many who emerged from the courses expressed the
change with the words: "I no longer feel a sense of guilt."

Unlike superior officers and higher officials of the old
regime, enlisted men and people like Loan had adhered to
the old regime without any deep-rooted conviction; their
anti-Communist motivations were blunt, superficial, and
fragile.

The overwhelming majority of "puppet" soldiers were
young men born and raised in a country already at war;
they had been formed in the regime's schools and inoculated against everything that came from the other side.

All of a sudden *hoc tap* offered them an alternative way
of seeing the world: the Vietcong were no longer aggressors but patriots, the Americans no longer protectors but
enemies. Everything was turned upside down, but it all fell
into place in a new pattern.

Those who thought they would be excluded, banished
from this new scheme, the new society, realized that *hoc tap*
gave them an opportunity to get back in and be accepted
again. To let such an opportunity slip would have been a
heedless waste.

Hoc tap for the soldiers of Thieu's former army did not
end in those three days. That was only the first step,
though doubtless the most important.

Everyone in Loan's group was classified as "reeducated,"
but in other groups a good ten percent were asked to stay
for another course.

Among those who flunked were many who had so parroted the role of convert that the *can bo* had doubts about their sincerity and suspected them of being "obstinate" holdouts trying to camouflage themselves.

An editorial in *Saigon Giai Phong* on June 16 warned against this attitude: "it is by deeds and not words that one gives proof of one's transformation." What former "puppets" should do was return to their native villages. The slogan for the day was: "Burn your bridges with the past. Go to the country. Produce."

"Bring a sweater"

I went in to have a chat with Georges, the French owner of the Korean restaurant on Tu Do Street, and there I ran into Do Viet, the former ARVN psychological warfare colonel. He was leaving the next day for *hoc tap* and was making the rounds of his friends to say good-bye.

Reeducation did not worry him; in a certain way it even aroused his curiosity. Propaganda and indoctrination had been part of his job and he wanted to see how the *bo doi* would cope with someone like him who was, so to speak, a real pro.

Georges was an old "Indo," as the French called those who had spent a good portion of their lives between Laos, Cambodia, and Vietnam. He was giving Do Viet endless advice, and with a grim sense of humor only he managed to find funny, he insisted:

"Hey, be careful! If the Vietcong send you into the shower without any soap, don't go. It could be a gas chamber!"

The bulletin concerning the reeducation of superior officers, high officials, and important politicians of the old regime was published on June 11.

The timing could not have been better. The fear that *hoc tap* meant psychological torture or some form of punishment or reprisals had just faded, as the first stories about the courses for enlisted men began to circulate in the city. Many officers, still uncertain as to whether to stay in hiding or even go into the jungle, were encouraged by what was happening to their subordinates and preferred to go for *hoc tap* rather than run the risk of playing "submarine."

In the atmosphere of relief created by the opening of the courses for "puppet" troops, Saigon came to read the summons for superior officers with much more optimism than its text—worded with deliberate ambiguity, as was later to be seen—ought to have suggested.

The communiqué read:

Education and reform of officers of the puppet Army, police, espionage services, puppet cadres, and members of reactionary political parties who have already registered.

Places to appear:

— Generals and colonels at No. 230 Minh Mang Street;
— Lieutenant colonels at No. 12 Truong Minh Ky Street and Go Vap;
— Majors at the Petrus Ky, Nguyen Ba Tong, and Tabert schools;
— Police officers, from general to major, at No. 259 Tran Quoc Dung Street;
— Officers and upper and middle cadres of American espionage at the Chu Van An School;
— Puppet officials of the legislative, judicial, and executive branches, from the rank of temporary substitute to president of the Republic, from the rank of office head to minister, senator, and deputy, at the Gia Long School;
— Members of political parties, from the rank of section secretary to secretary general, at the Le Van Duyet Lycée for Girls.

Note: Puppets must appear with clothing, mosquito nets, blankets, articles for personal use, and food for one month.

Date to appear: from 8 to 17 hours on 13, 14, 15 June.

Signed: Gen. Tran Van Tra

At the foot of the communiqué was the following specification:

Advice to officers and officials leaving for the reeducation camp:

1) Food. Food for the first day should be brought prepared. For the next month, 21 kg. of rice will be needed.
2) Personal effects. Bring a change of clothing, a warm sweater, a mosquito net, a mat, a toothbrush, toothpaste, a bowl, chopsticks, note paper, medicines, cigarettes if you smoke, and at most three kilos of additional food.

One conclusion was obvious: these "puppets" were not to remain in Saigon, like their lower-ranking colleagues. They would not do *hoc tap* in the quarter where they lived, and would not be home for supper.

Perhaps the *bo doi* wanted to give their former enemies a taste of the jungle life they themselves had lived for years, people said. The instructions about sweaters and mosquito nets suggested the destination would be in the Highlands.

For how long?

Reading the communique, everyone thought it would be a month, and the authorities did not care to deny it.

The departure of the greatest possible number of upper cadres, civilian and military, of the old administration would also solve an important security problem for the new regime. Any attempt at organized counter-revolutionary resistance would be crushed when all prospective opponents were suddenly uprooted. The most influential persons of the past would be cut off from their social milieu, from their circles of friends and followers.

On the morning of the 13th the scene in front of the Gia Long School, the assembly place of senators and deputies, ministers and magistrates, was almost grotesque.

A young *bo doi* seated at a table in the middle of the sidewalk was absentmindedly dismantling and cleaning a submachine gun. Another went back and forth trying to bring order to a growing mass of elderly gentlemen and distinguished middle-aged personages who were pushing, shoving and quarreling in an attempt to be first at the gate that remained inexplicably closed.

Senator Tran Ngoc Oanh, a Catholic refugee from the North and ex-minister of Public Works, accompanied by his wife carrying his suitcase, shouted that he was entitled to go in first because he was old and ill. The others refused. The group swayed in great confusion. The *bo doi* fired a pistol shot in the air and went back to cleaning his weapon.

On the opposite side of the street two young girl guerrillas in *ao baba,* rubber-tire sandals, and soft green hats over long black braids stood guard at a villa perhaps occupied by some high-ranking officer of the Front.

The group swelled. Ex-parliamentarians, diplomats, judges from the appeals court arrived one by one. Until a few weeks earlier they had been accustomed to travelling pompously in black limousines driven by chauffeur-body-guards. They had been respected, honored, courted, powerful.

Now they arrived shabbily on board a relative's Honda or on foot, accompanied by some member of their family. They were like small children on their first day of school, each with his sack of rice, a bundle of clothing, and the look of someone who does not quite know what he is in for but has to make the best of it.

Some arrived dragging a Samsonite suitcase as though on their way to the airport for a business trip; others with a knapsack as though for a hike.

No one came in jacket and tie. Some had even left their leather shoes at home and almost as if to give an early indication of their good will, put on plastic sandals like those worn by the *can bo*. The only difference was the immaculate and shockingly white feet they revealed.

Very few had the three supplementary kilos of food with them. Many had brought money, thinking they would be able to buy whatever they needed.

A group of curious bystanders stayed all morning to watch this pathetic procession of powerful men stripped of their authority by the Revolution, disoriented by the new things happening around them.

Having read the communique, many expected to witness the arrival of some president of the old "puppet" Republic. But none showed up. Thieu was safely in Taiwan; "Big Minh" had been exempted for having already done *hoc tap* during the two days he had stayed in the palace with Tran Van Tra after the Liberation; and Huong, old, semi-paralytic, and half blind, had obtained a special dispensation to do his reeducation at home in his own villa.

By noon there were already three or four hundred persons in front of the Gia Long School, but no one bothered with them. They stayed there before the closed gate for hours. Then in the early afternoon a *bo doi* came to make lists of those present and divide them into groups. The same thing had happened at the other gathering places.

For three days the high-level "puppets" remained inside their assembly places without being allowed out, listening to lectures similar to those given the ordinary soldiers.

Then they disappeared. Relatives who went to inquire about them were told by the *bo doi* that the "puppets" had left. No one ever found out exactly for where, but a rumor

soon ran through Saigon that long columns of Molotova
trucks, filled with people in civilian clothes, had been seen
a little beyond Xuan Loc and heading northwest.

There was a long month of silence, during which the
most incredible stories were told about the fate of the
"puppets." The *bo doi* were supposed to have poisoned a
whole group of officers in a camp in Tay Ninh; others
were said to have been shot for refusing to cooperate in
the programs.

The authorities, citing "reasons of security," never di-
vulged where or how the courses took place. But Thanh
Cong, the *bo doi* officer I had met buying Beethoven cassettes, said to me once:

"They study and work. That's what we did during the
whole war. You can call it all 'brainwashing': it's a matter
of definition. For us studying is a privilege, not a punishment.

"As for manual work, that's something the country has
an enormous need of. If you discuss it with the puppets,
they all reassure you they want to participate in the reconstruction of the country; they discuss it in the cafés. They
reconstruct everything with words. But if you put a shovel
in their hands and ask them to fill up the craters made by
their own bombs and those of the Americans, then they
tell you they're at forced labor."

Thanh Cong had not picked an idle example.

Earl Martin, a bearded American Mennonite who had
arrived in Saigon from Quang Ngai, where *hoc tap* had begun earlier because the city had already been liberated in
March, said that ARVN superior officers had been set to
work filling bomb craters. Other travelers coming down
Highway 1 from the north told of seeing groups of former
officers in the vicinity of Da Nang, rebuilding the old railroad that had connected Hanoi with Saigon up until 1954.

On the site of the former military base of Khe Sanh,
which the Americans had defended at the cost of hundreds of lives, the "puppets" were building a new city.

The month at the end of which the "puppets" were supposed to come home went by, but none of them turned
up. The "obstinate" seized the opportunity to mount a
protest campaign against the new regime.

At the expiration of the thirty days a rumor was spread
in Saigon that a convoy carrying home the first group of
superior officers home had fallen into an ambush of

counterrevolutionary guerrillas, that many "puppets"—
some said twenty, some two hundred—had been killed,
and that the Military Management Committee had posted
a list of the dead outside the Tabert School.

It was a clever trick. Hundreds of people, especially
women, worried about the fate of their "puppet" menfolk,
appeared at the gates of the school, located in the heart of
the city. When they discovered there was no list, they went
to Doc Lap Palace in search of someone who could explain
what had happened and why the former superior officers,
magistrates, politicians, and parliamentarians were not returning from *hoc tap*.

It was the first forceful demonstration against the new
regime; but contrary to "obstinate" hopes, it remained limited to a few hundred persons who dispersed when a *bo doi*
with a megaphone explained that there had been no ambush, that the "puppets" were well, and that they would
still not be back for some time.

Only then did Saigon realize that *hoc tap* for superior officers did not have a fixed duration like that for enlisted
men. The communiqué spoke of "food for a month," but
it never said that reeducation would last only that long.

Not even the "puppets" going for reeducation had understood this subtle point. When Nguyen Van Y, founder
of the Central Intelligence Organization, chief of police
in the days of Diem and later an advisor to Thieu, went to
the *can bo* at the end of the month to ask if he could leave,
the latter replied:
"You've planted the corn, don't you want to see the ears
sprout?" He had to stay.

After a few more weeks some "puppets" received permission to come to Saigon, either to visit their families or
because they were considered "reeducated," and people
began hearing the first stories about the reeducation
camps.

Almost all of them were in the jungles of the Highlands,
in remote areas far away from villages.

Life in the camps was simple and hard. There were no
fences or guards, and the rules that each "puppet" had to
respect were those they drew up themselves, since it was
up to them to organize their days and life in common.

Reeducation occurred under the guidance of political
cadres who lived in the same camps. Hours of study alter-
nated with hours of work.

When the twenty-one kilos of rice each had brought with

him ran out the *bo doi* supplied more, but the vegetables that the various groups had planted in kitchen gardens after clearing and tilling the soil around the camps had already started ripening.

Anyone who refused to work, such as Tran Van Tuyen, former deputy of the nationalist Right, was not forced to do so, but with such an attitude he would not be considered someone who had done *hoc tap*, and he could hardly expect to return home soon.

As for the stories of executions and poisonings, none of them turned out to be true.

5: The New Society

Once upon a time there was gold in the bank

High-school students were assigned to keep the gardens of Saigon clean and orderly. Divided by classes, led by an old peasant who taught them to handle shovel and rake, boys and girls watered the plants and also succeeded in growing a fine carpet of grass on the large dusty square between the cathedral and Doc Lap Palace.

However they did not succeed in preventing people from secretly tearing off the beautiful reddish bark from the large tamarind trees. This bark was used for cooking instead of charcoal, and the pilfering of it was one more sign of the poverty of the times.

Every week Saigon suffered more. No one died of hunger—free rice distributions saw to that—but more and more people were having to learn to tighten their belts.

Since the month of June clerks and officials of the old administration who still had jobs had been receiving their first "revolutionary" salaries—fourteen, eighteen, and twenty-three thousand piasters, depending on category. But these sums amounted to about half those paid in the past, and they had become the sole source of income since other revenues—bonuses, reimbursements, and "payola"—had disappeared forever.

Soldiers and officers who had done their prescribed period of *hoc tap* returned home "reeducated," but continued to be out of work. There were hundreds of thousands of them—309,000 according to the first count made by the *bo doi* at the end of June. Moving about Saigon, Cao Giao would constantly recognize and point out to me former ARVN lieutenants and captains who had set themselves up as illegal bicycle parking attendants or as cigarette vendors behind a stand.

Some new jobs had been created but they were distributed to those who were both needy and had helped the Revolution. A special office was classifying families who had risked their lives to shelter NLF political cadres and treat wounded guerrillas during the war, or who had consented to hide weapons and propaganda material.

For many who could boast of no revolutionary deeds

this poverty was all the harder. They might still have money, but they could not use it. It was in the banks, frozen in deposit accounts that—so it was thought in Saigon—would never be returned to their holders.

This was not exactly true. Calmly, two months after the Liberation, the new authorities announced an interesting decision: any savings accounts of "the working class" with deposits not exceeding one hundred thousand piasters would be unfrozen. For the occasion "workers, peasants, officials, and clerks" were all considered part of the working class.

Anyone who believed he had the right to withdraw his own savings on the basis of these criteria had to file a special application and explain how he would use the money. Long lines formed at the tellers' windows on the day the banks reopened for the purpose of collecting these requests.

On July 9 Le Minh Chau, the new director of the "Saigon-Gia Dinh National Bank," said in his inaugural speech that unfreezing the accounts of small savers constituted the first step in a new banking policy. The problem of the "more important accounts" would be dealt with later.

Le Minh Chau explained that the bank's goal was "not to make a profit but to stabilize and develop the economy, and aid national production." For this reason applications by firms for the unfreezing of their accounts would also be taken under consideration "in cases of legitimate need."

Le Minh Chau went on to say that the bank would soon begin to grant loans, with priority going to agricultural and industrial production, the production of commodities and export goods.

The offices of the National Bank in downtown Saigon had become the headquarters for dozens of economic and financial experts—many imported from Hanoi, others inherited from the old regime—who together did the basic research for formulating the economic policy of the new administration.

What had happened at the National Bank on Liberation Day and the days immediately preceding remained a mystery on which no one was willing to shed light.

The bank is a huge ugly stone building facing the waterfront and a stone's throw from the Senate. When the *bo doi* arrived there on the morning of April 30 they not only found the bank's governor Le Quang Uyen, his deputy, a

part of their staff and a group of the most important financiers of the old regime—they also found and recovered
the entire gold reserves of the Republic of South Vietnam.

How could this have happened?

"Thieu tried to get away with the gold but the people
prevented it, PRG officials replied if you inquired later
what had happened.

Whether it was "the people" is not so certain. More
likely it was Uyen himself, or someone on his staff, who
had put the gold in safekeeping to hand over later to the
new authorities as ransom for his own political redemp-
tion.

During the last weeks of Thieu's regime incredible intrigues were woven around the gold in the bank. Thieu
himself had tried at least twice to put his hands on the Republic's treasure, without success. When he was preparing
to leave Thieu contacted a Swiss airline, Balair, to inquire
whether they would guarantee the shipment of a quantity
of bullion to Europe. Balair, citing technical and security
problems, refused. Then a few hours before his final departure from Saigon, Thieu sent some of his men over to
Uyen to collect part of the treasure, but Uyen—this at least
is one version of the facts—told them that the gold had already been withdrawn by other emissaries from the president. In the turmoil of flight this hitch was enough to en-
sure that Thieu left without the bullion.

Again according to this version Uyen (some said his deputy) saw to it that all the gold was concealed in the vaults
of the Banque Française d'Asie.

A more fanciful version had it that the gold was buried
in a secret spot somewhere near Tu Duc.

The one sure fact is that the gold remained in Saigon
and that Uyen was found by the *bo doi* in the offices of the
bank, where he had barricaded himself together with his
family and aides, beefing up the special guard and laying
in a whole arsenal of munitions.

Uyen, a young economist not yet forty who was educated in France and had come to power with the Hoang
Duc Nha clique, was summoned to Doc Lap Palace immediately after the Liberation. He declared he had stayed in
Saigon voluntarily.

Malicious voices insinuated however that Uyen had gone
to the bank with his family and staff because the Americans had promised to pick him up there. It was an accident that he did not leave: after waiting for hours in the

sun he had gone to rest for a moment in his office, and once inside the hum of the air conditioners had kept him from hearing the helicopter land. What did leave in his place were all his luggage, his maids, and the guards who found themselves at the right moment on the roof of the building.

Whichever story the *bo doi* chose to believe, Uyen was well treated. Along with the group of young financiers he was invited to work at Doc Lap. Later he too went for his long *hoc tap* in the Highlands, like all other "puppet" officials.

For some time the authorities gave no indications as to their new economic policy, nor was it clear up to what point private firms would be allowed to function as before. *Bo doi* experts in the various industrial sectors went on studying problems and collecting information, but they did not lay down any laws.

As for taxes, no one in Saigon paid them during the first three months. But a rumor circulated that in other regions the *bo doi* had begun demanding arrears from merchants going back to when they had ceased making payments to the Vietminh, in 1954.

For the first three months everyone in business did more or less as he liked, taking care however not to be classified a speculator, since a campaign of denunciation and correction was soon launched against this category of people.

Some businessmen, trying to avoid mistakes, asked the *bo doi* what they should and shouldn't do. But replies were always evasive.

A textile manufacturer who inquired with the economic section of the Saigon-Gia Dinh Military Management Committee about prices for his products was faced with this answer:

"You decide! Just be careful not to anger the people. That could get you in trouble."

Puppet government, phantom government

Many people in Saigon were puzzled. The *bo doi* had now been in power for some weeks, but unlike all previous governments this new one did not seem to know what it wanted. It did not issue orders, or enact new laws or proclaim new instructions. Those who failed to realize to what extent the concept of power had changed with the Revolution had the impression the new authorities were destroying rather than building, disrupting rather than governing.

"There used to be order. You knew how and where to address yourself to obtain information, where to apply for a permit," said the merchants in Tu Do Street. "Now there's chaos. No one knows anything, no one makes any decisions."

With the old regime, every time a government changed or there was a coup d'état that brought a new general to the presidency, the bigshots changed, but otherwise everything continued to function as before. The cop on the beat, the one you had to bribe in order to operate your cigarette stand or run a black market in dollars, was always the same.

This time however the signs on the old offices had been changed, and many had actually been closed. As for the old policemen they had literally vanished, and if new ones existed at all one saw no trace of them. Once in a while groups of four or five students appeared at the principal downtown street crossings, with red armbands and cardboard disks reading "Stop." Each of them made different signals in front of the traffic, which certainly did not profit much from their presence.

"Traffic may suffer, but the self-confidence of these young people gains a lot," a *bo doi* replied to someone who went to him to complain.

The *bo doi* were the first not to respect the normal traffic regulations. As though still in the jungle on the Ho Chi Minh trail, they drove their big trucks loaded with produce or munitions on the wrong side of the road and entered all one-way streets the wrong way, heedless of the imprecations and ironical smiles of ordinary citizens. Traffic lights continued to function for months, automatic and undaunted, as they had in the confused hours of the Liberation; but Saigon quickly learned that there was no harm in going through a red light. There was no penalty and no one was there to collect fines.

Accustomed to the rules and logic of the old administration, people could not understand how the new one functioned. In the past power had been exercised from top to bottom. The president named the provincial chiefs, who in turn named the district chiefs, who named the sector chiefs, who named the neighborhood chiefs, and so on, all the way down to the chief of the family unit that constituted the base for Thieu's administrative and police control.

The new government named no one. But was there actually a new government? Who was the new chief? Who had taken Thieu's place? The new leaders were not seen on television, their photos did not appear in the newspapers, and the only picture that was distributed everywhere was that of President Ho Chi Minh, now dead for six years.

People raised these questions in all honesty and simplicity and the "obstinate," who lost no opportunity to blow on the flames of confusion and discontent, employed the new jargon to spread the joke: "Before we had a puppet government. Now we have a phantom government."

Since Liberation Day the new authorities had issued no broad edicts nor given any outstanding instructions, aside from a few brief communiques announcing the closing of brothels, opium dens, and nightclubs. Through the *bo doi* circulating in the streets, houses, public buildings and schools, the new authorities seemed to be giving advice rather than orders, suggesting correct behavior rather than imposing it by force.

A typical, though marginal, result of this attitude was that for quite a while Saigon never knew exactly what time it was. Revolutionary offices and officials worked and set up appointments according to the Indochinese time zone, also used in Hanoi and by the Vietcong during the war in the liberated areas. But an official announcement abolishing the one-hour daylight saving time of the old regime took forever to come.

So that up until the middle of June, though every symbol, sign, and inscription of the old regime had disappeared from Saigon, all the city's clocks, including the one on the Central Post Office and the one on the pediment of the cathedral, continued to keep what by now everyone was calling "Thieu's time."

The sidewalks of the city had always been encumbered by stalls, beggars, street vendors, lepers, and shoeshine boys. Each had his own reserved space, protected by police-gangster collusion. With the Liberation this small power system fell apart.

The *bo doi* certainly did not ask to see the license of anyone who squatted behind a wooden box selling cigarettes, spirits, newspapers, or simply sweets manufactured in some backstairs closet. As economic conditions worsened a great many people had to begin selling whatever they could to earn a little money wherever they could, and the downtown sidewalks were invaded by stalls.

There was a great blossoming of "sidewalk cafes" at the beginning of July: two or three tiny low tables, a few chairs taken from the living room at home, and a jug of blackish water, heated on a portable charcoal burner. Around the public gardens, in front of the old courthouse, these cafés emerged like mushrooms. On Tu Do Street, where enterprise was in the hands of girls from the old bars, it became impossible to walk on the sidewalks because of all the chairs and stools and the lines of flapping, multicolored parachutes spread between the trees and houses to shelter customers from sun and rain. The various vendors on the square between the post office and the cathedral multiplied daily, and were in constant competition for the most conspicuous places. They sold stamps, soup, and bottles of gasoline and overflowed the sidewalk, invading half the street and making traffic all the more difficult.

The authorities had little to say about it. Every so often a *bo doi* patrol went by with a megaphone and asked everyone to draw back. No one paid any attention, and the *bo doi* would repeatedly say in conversations with the vendors:

"It's your problem. Organize yourselves, form a committee to resolve the question of space. Decide among yourselves who should be where."

This attitude was incomprehensible to most people. Once when I was listening in front of the post office to one of these informal chats between *bo doi* and populace I heard a man in his fifties ask a younger soldier:

"What does the government want from us anyway? What are we supposed to do?" The soldier looked very serious and replied:

"It's up to you to decide."

This impression of a power vacuum that some people had was superficial and false. The new authorities were indeed there, but their way of intervening was discreet, indirect—in a certain sense the chaos was deliberate and meant to be instructive. People had to become aware of their problems, had to learn how to take care of them and resolve them on their own as they had never done in the past.

As for the new power, it was being developed and reorganized day by day in every sector of society, under the umbrella of the Saigon-Gia Dinh military administration, which safeguarded the security of the city and constituted a chain of transmission and command with the highest authorities in the country. This process took place in accordance with new principles and new procedures. Schools, factories, private firms, universities, were the scene of interminable meetings at which members of the various administrative committees, delegates to organizations, and others were elected. The most extensive work was done at the neighborhood level.

One evening I happened to be present at the first meeting of a "solidarity cell" in a middle-class neighborhood of the city.

In the solidarity cell

It was dark and raining heavily. Ever since Liberation Day street lights had been reduced to save energy, and people, hurrying and hopping over puddles, could hardly find their way along the muddy road leading to the school where the meeting had been set for eight o'clock.

"With weather like this I wouldn't have stirred myself even for a banquet. It really took the Revolution to get me out of the house," someone said jokingly, and the others laughed.

The neighborhood, located roughly between Hai Ba Trung Street and Tran Quang Khai, now had a mixed population. Up until a few years ago it had been a residential area for the middle class, those who feared the Revolution, cursed the Vietcong, and boasted of sending their children to study in Paris or the United States. It had been inhabited by the families of lawyers, dentists, government officials, army officers, and large importers. Then little by little as the war drew close to Saigon the poor came, installing themselves behind the stone and brick houses of the rich, along the walls enclosing their backyards: peasants fleeing from the fields, who had built huts of wood and corrugated iron, and who made a living of sorts by small trade or by pedalling cyclos rented by the day. With the prospect of Liberation, the poor had stayed on. As for the rich, some fifty families had preferred to flee with the Americans. But the neighborhood remained one with a strong "obstinate" component.

At ten minutes to eight the main classroom of the school was already full of people. Except for a couple of family heads who had asked their neighbors to make excuses for their absence, all the others were there—about a hundred of them. In addition there were young people, many women, and some political cadres from other neighborhoods, who did not, however, speak or join in the discussion.

Two very young *bo doi* stood at the entrance holding their AK-47 rifles by the barrel, with the butt resting on the ground. They responded to people's nods of greeting but did not check who went inside. On one wall, a portrait in color of Ho Chi Minh and two flags, one for the Front, one for Hanoi. Below, a wooden table and a microphone. In front, many rows of chairs and benches.

The order of business was the election of the chief, assistant chief, and secretary of each of the four solidarity cells represented in the assembly. The preparatory work had already been done.

During the entire previous week groups of two or three *bo doi* had made the rounds of every family in the district, not only to explain the idea of the solidarity cell as a grouping of people who lived as neighbors, but above all to gather detailed information on the personal affairs of each individual, on his economic situation, his connections with the "puppet government," and his behavior "during the American occupation."

This investigation had not been carried out by the *bo doi* who had lived in the neighborhood ever since Liberation Day. Other *bo doi* had come precisely for this purpose from another part of the city, and the ones from here had gone to do the same thing in another quarter where they did not know the people.

After the *bo doi*, representatives of women's groups had come to see each family to talk to the wives about children and schools, and they too had collected information on the life of everyone in the neighborhood.

The reports prepared by these two groups had of course
been read and studied by the *bo doi* who opened the meeting. He was about twenty-five years old, wore a uniform
without insignia of rank, had two pens in his shirt pocket,
and a calm, assured, and persuasive voice. He told me
later that before joining the Liberation Army he had been
a civil engineering student at the University of Hanoi.

"Brothers, sisters, comrades! Power today belongs to the
people," he began. "It is now up to you to decide your destiny. Before you were victims of power; power was exercised from above, and you, the people, did not choose
your representatives. Now this choice is for you to make.
The solidarity cell is the base of the people's power, because it is the cells that will have to elect the revolutionary
committee for the sector, then for the quarter and finally
for the district. It will be a process leading from the bottom to the top, and not the other way around." The *bo doi*
went on to explain that there were no rigid rules, but that
roughly speaking twelve to twenty families constituted a
cell, that twenty-eight to thirty cells made a sector, that ten
sectors constituted a quarter, and so on.

People followed his remarks without great enthusiasm.
Some nodded their heads in a sign of assent.

The cell—the *bo doi* explained—was to concern itself
with the poor people of the neighborhood, it was to find
work for the unemployed and look after young people, the
core of the new society. The cell would examine the work
of political cadres, safeguard the security of the neighborhood, and resolve all its problems.

By now this was already happening in the rest of the
country. Little by little as the Liberation Army advanced
on Saigon, the old administration in every liberated city
and village had been swept away and all "puppet" officials,
from the highest to the most marginal and insignificant,
were removed and stripped of their authority. The Liberation Army guaranteed the regular administration of the
country through its local administrative committees, and its
officers and *can bo* temporarily served as replacements in
some posts left vacant by the "puppets."

Naturally this power structure was one of transition, intended to last only until a new structure, democratically
elected, would first grow up alongside it and then take its
place. "Democratically" should be understood in the sense
explained by the young *bo doi* to the Tran Quang Khai

gathering, just as other *bo doi* and cadres had explained it to the rest of the country.

The process by which the new people's power was gradually leavening to the surface was obviously slow and difficult. It was one thing to name from above a flood of provincial chiefs, district chiefs, neighborhood chiefs and so forth as had happened in the past—that could be done in a day. It was quite another to begin with meetings and discussions in the cells, and then rise step by step through new meetings, discussions, and criticisms to the next level, and on up to the highest level of government, which not accidentally continued to call itself "provisional." In Saigon, with all the procedures at the various levels, it took almost two months to arrive at the election of the first district revolutionary committee. Furthermore once a committee was elected it was not necessarily final, since purges, criticisms, and campaigns might remove officials of the "puppet" administration who had succeeded in infiltrating the new revolutionary structure, and charges of inefficiency might call for new discussions and new elections.

The *bo doi* said that the cell leaders to be elected would stay in office for three months. A vote by the assembly, however, could remove them sooner. To avoid problems, he explained what type of man ought to be chosen as a cell leader.

"He should be a man who has had no connections with the puppet system. He should be a clean, respected person, one who enjoys the trust of the people and who has a correct and nonchauvinistic attitude toward women."

He asked the assembly to discuss the problems he had raised and reply to two fundamental questions: 1) what does the people's power mean? 2) by what standards should the people's representatives be chosen?

"Speak freely. Say whatever you think. It's up to you to express your ideas," the *bo doi* repeated. But the assembly kept silent. Then an almost elegant man in his fifties, with a fine head of white hair, stood up:

"You say we're free, but it's not true. People are afraid to say what they think. You keep talking about the people, the people, the rights of the people, but then you accuse us of being 'puppets,' criminals who have collaborated with the Americans. . . ."

Many people around him nodded. A woman, encouraged by this first opening, spoke up:

"Why do you want to set up a new system? Why do we need a solidarity cell? We already have a system here, the interfamily one; it's always functioned properly in our quarter, and those who've worked in it haven't committed any crime. They could very well go on with their work as before." Later I found out that she was the wife of an ARVN officer. He had been captured at Da Nang and had not yet returned to Saigon; meanwhile she was considered the head of the family. The *bo doi* listened impassively, then replied:

"We must destroy the old system in all its expressions, all its aspects. Even the smallest interfamily chief who has committed no crime against the people has still been part of the puppet system of control and coercion. It must be uprooted, it must be eliminated, so as not to reproduce itself."

After another hour of discussion it came time for the elections. The *bo doi* asked the assembly, which had been divided into four cells, to present candidates, but the names that came up were always those of officials of the old regime, and he kept insisting on the introduction of new candidates. Finally the *bo doi* said:

"Allow me then to nominate a candidate." And he pointed to an elderly professor, a Catholic who had fled from the North in 1954, had never been involved in politics, and had said nothing during the assembly.

The nomination was clearly the result of the investigations carried out before the meeting. The professor was by no means considered a revolutionary, but he was honest and people respected him. He was elected by an overwhelming majority with a show of hands. A clerk in a foreign company was elected deputy leader, the person elected secretary was a former noncommissioned officer who had been discharged from the ARVN five years before and had since been an exporter of handicrafts.

The *bo doi* got up to applaud the results, and so did the assembly. After the elections for the other cells and a brief speech by each elected candidate, who promised the assembly to carry out his duties correctly, the meeting ended. It had lasted three and a half hours.

The work of the cells began immediately next day. Simultaneously a new investigation was begun, more searching than the previous ones, into the character and past of each of the newly elected.

I kept in contact with the professor and followed his activities in the cell. Here are some of the typical problems he found himself facing in the first two weeks.

Case of poverty. There were four clearly indigent families in the neighborhood. By drawing on funds made available by the district military committee, the professor saw to it that they got rice.

A more complicated case was that of a family that had once been rich and lived in one of the best houses in the neighborhood. Four sons, a brother, and a son-in-law were in the reeducation program because they had been ARVN officers; the old father, who was the former chief of the neighborhood interfamily group, had been left penniless since the banks closed, with some twenty people, including daughters, daughters-in-law, and grandchildren, to provide for. The professor understood that he could not simply go to them and offer them rice. It was a question of dignity, of saving face. He spoke about it to the district committee. Next day three girl students knocked at their door with the pretext of having a questionnaire to be filled out. They talked to the family and proposed to go sell a sewing machine and other household appliances on their behalf; then without letting themselves be seen by the neighbors they reentered the house through the back door, depositing twenty-five kilograms of rice in the kitchen.

Case of drunkenness. Knowing that the cell was distributing rice other families came forward saying they needed it. More sacks were distributed, but it was discovered that an old man was selling his share to buy himself alcohol. Some people protested. The professor summoned the heads of families. The matter was discussed and it was decided, in this specific case, that the man was too old to understand. He had lost two sons in the war, and perhaps he drank in order to fall asleep. No measures were taken against him, and they continued to give him his portion.

Case of security. The professor received from the military committee the list of all "puppets" who were supposed to show up for the reeducation course. Among them was an officer who was planning to avoid the course by going into hiding among some of his relatives in the Delta. It was his wife who warned the professor. He went to see him and explained the revolutionary government's policy of reconciliation, reminding him that sooner or later he would be discovered and that it was better to undergo the course now than to be captured and sent away later. The professor also promised to provide material assistance to the family while he was away. The former officer agreed.

"Much of my work is handing out tranquilizers," the professor remarked in telling me this incident. "People want to be told that things will turn out all right, they want to hear over and over again the reasons for every action of the *bo doi*."

Case of sanitation. Every morning at six the *bo doi* swept the streets in front of the houses where they lived. During a meeting the cell leader asked the heads of families if this seemed right to them. They then decided to do the work themselves in place of the *bo doi*.

"Now they even sweep too often. People haven't much to eat and there's very little garbage. Sweeping once a week would be enough, but they all do it once a day," said the professor.

Case of returning to the country. One of the poor families wanted to return to its native village in central Vietnam, but did not have the means. The cell procured the necessary sum for the trip, wrote a letter of introduction to the revolutionary committee at the family's destination, and granted funds for the first three months of resettling. The case was discussed in a meeting of the whole cell. A district political cadre attended and explained that the policy of the revolutionary government was to send as many people as possible back to the country. He asked all those of peasant origin to take this possibility into consideration.

After two weeks the professor was delighted with his work. The cell had no headquarters, and he was obliged to go from house to house in order to deal with all the various problems. Thus he came to know his neighbors well, establishing relationships with them that would have been impossible before. The investigation of his own background had turned out favorably. Relatives questioned in other parts of the country, as well as acquaintances in the city, had confirmed the information he himself had given the *bo doi*, and the people of the quarter had declared themselves satisfied with him as a cell leader.

"The biggest problem is still the barrier that exists between man and man, between family and family," he told me in talking about his activities. "We're used to living each for himself, involved with our own problems, immersed in our own private life, and now it's hard to persuade people to open up, to speak about their concerns, to admit their own troubles or their own mistakes. I try, and

for me it's a completely new experience. I've learned, for
instance, that you can begin by talking about the way a
family cooks a fish, and eventually touch on the things that
really matter to them. Unfortunately, some families in my
neighborhood insist on keeping their front doors shut,
coming and going secretly through the back entrance."

Some of the other cell representatives whose election I
had witnessed in the Tran Quang Khai neighborhood had
problems. One who had been made responsible for the
distribution of gasoline was removed because he had profited by putting aside a few liters for himself. Another met
his downfall when the newly formed revolutionary organizations launched a harsh campaign to uproot elements of
the old regime and he was forced to confess before the
whole cell that he had been a police informer. In the
course of their investigations the *bo doi* found a dossier
bearing his name in the old national security files, anno-
tated with the sums he had been paid each time he
"squealed" on someone.

An editorial entitled "The Immediate Principal Task Is
the Building of a Strong Power at the Base," in the July 3
issue of *Saigon Giai Phong* dwelt on the setting up of the
revolutionary organizations and the difficulties involved. In
the usual heavy, repetitive, and boring language—a language, however, that was precise and effective as well
since, as I realized later, people learned it slowly and began to make increasing use of it—the editorial explains the
problems and priorities of the moment, justifies the reten-
tion of the military administration, and points out that
though "the people's revolutionary action is fundamental,"
the decisions handed down from the power at the top are
"extremely important." The new authorities who had installed themselves in Doc Lap Palace were taking great
pains to see that certain actions at the base did not become
transformed into excesses and often, as in the case of the
campaign against decadent culture, they intervened to call
a halt to certain ultrarevolutionary attitudes. Here is the
text of the editorial.

> The complete victory of the spring offensive and uprising
> has annihilated the oppressive machine of the American
> enemy and its lackeys. Revolutionary power has been estab-
> lished and its effectiveness is shown in the administration of
> our recently liberated country.
>
> Our power is the power of the people. The regime of the

military administration is the first form of this power. Its
mission is to crush all resistance by the last enemy remnants, build the apparatus of new power, reestablish order
and security, and normalize the life of the city in every one
of its sectors.

The Saigon-Gia Dinh Military Management Committee
and the network of people's revolutionary committees at all
levels have successfully carried out these tasks in the past
two months.

The strength of the people's power expresses itself prin-
cipally at the base. The quarter, the subquarter, the solidarity cell are the level at which the people directly exercises
its rights as master of the country, the level at which the
people holds and directly utilizes its power in order to continue the revolutionary struggle in every sphere. The quarter, the subquarter, the cell are at present the places in
which doctrine and policy are transformed into revolutionary action.

The people's power has just begun to establish itself at
the base. Naturally, being in its beginnings, this power is
not yet strong enough, and in some places it is still having
difficulties. This is inevitable. It is for this reason that the
building of a truly strong people's power at the base is today the most important task of the Revolution in Saigon. A
strong power at the base assures the resolution of the most
urgent problems: work, bread, the hunt for obstinate reactionaries, law and order.

Having defeated the enemy power, the Revolution is responsible for all activities of society. This leadership is realized through the power of the people. Each policy is transformed into an order, into a decision of authority, and
becomes the starting point for every revolutionary action by
the great mass, especially at the base.

At present our formula for carrying out the Revolution is
the coordination of decisions of power from top to bottom
with mass revolutionary action from bottom to top. Though
the people's revolutionary action is fundamental, the decisions of the authorities are extremely important and constitute the support for revolutionary action by the people.

The population of Saigon is acting promptly to establish
the people's power through popular assemblies. In a great
many localities these meetings have achieved good results
from the standpoint of building and strengthening the revolutionary power of the people. The people are rising up
to denounce the crimes of the American imperialists and

35. General Tran Van Tra, head of the Saigon-Gia Dinh Military Management Committee. Behind Tra is Government Minister Tran Buu Kiem.

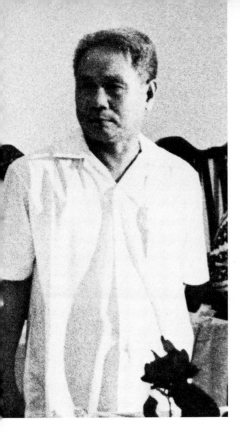

36. *(facing page, top left)* NLF President Nguyen Huu Tho.

37. *(facing page, top right)* Communist Party secretary for the South, the mysterious Pham Hung.

38. *(left)* Defense Minister Tran Nam Trung.

39. *(facing page, bottom)* Minister of Foreign Affairs Mme. Nguyen Thi Binh with Defense Minister Tran Nam Trung.

40. *(bottom)* Prime Minister of the PRG, Huynh Tan Phat. (Photo by Nayan Chanda.)

41. Members of the Saigon-Gia Dinh Military Management Committee and Vietcong officials posing on the front steps of Doc Lap a few days after the Liberation. Compare with the photograph taken a few days earlier (Figure #9).

42. From the left: NLF President Nguyen Huu Tho, PRG Prime Minister Huynh Tan Phat, Vice President Trinh Dinh Thao.

43. *Bo doi* on the streets of Saigon.

44. *Bo doi* making purchases at the thieves' market.

45. "Puppet" officers at *hoc tap* session.

46. The "Circle Sportif" transformed into a gallery for revolutionary art.
(Photo by Nayan Chanda.)

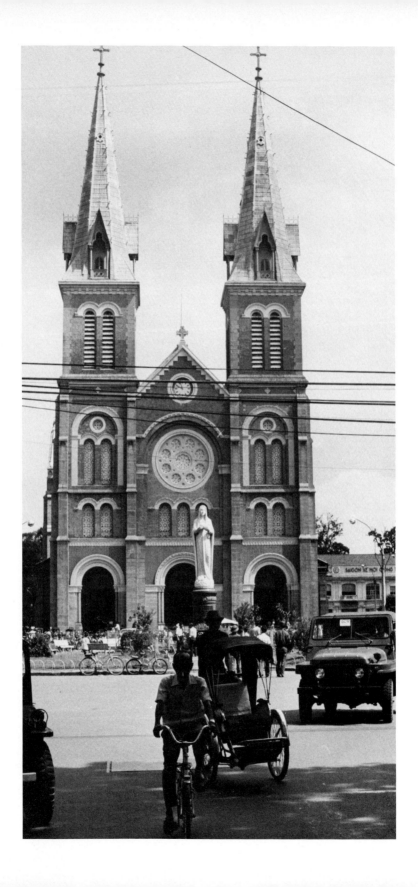

47. *(facing page)* The Cathedral.

48. *(top)* Father Tran Huu Thanh at his redemptorist church. (See "Vietnamese first, Catholics second.")

49. *(bottom)* Redemptorist Father Chan Tin. (See "Come, brothers" and "The Hung Vuong School.")

50. A *cyclopousse* reading *Saigon Giai Phong* in front of the Hotel Continental.

51. Relics of war in the Delta. In the middle of ricefields, an ARVN heli-copter, abandoned without fuel by its crew on the day of the Liberation of Saigon.

52. "Puppets" at *hoc tap* session in a village in the Delta.

53. Vietcong guerrilla
leader in the Delta.

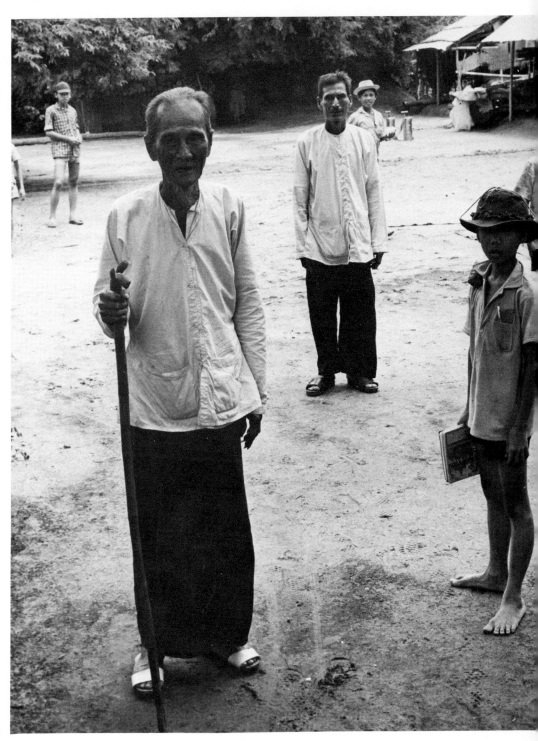

54. Three generations of peasants in the Delta.

VIET NAM
HOA BINH
THONG NHAT
ĐỘC LẬP
DAN CHỦ
VÀ GIÀU MẠNH
MUÔN NĂM

KHÔNG CÓ GÌ QUÝ HƠN
ĐỘC LẬP TỰ DO

55. Downtown Hanoi, with the poster showing a united Vietnam.

56. A helmet maker in Hanoi.

57. Hanoi: a couple relaxing in the park surrounding the Lake of the Recovered Sword.

58. Air raid shelter being dismantled in downtown Hanoi.

their puppets, to reeducate the unfortunate victims of domination and exploitation. The people are denouncing the obstinate. All this goes to show our determination to build and consolidate our power. The people continue to rise up to combat and destroy everything that remains of the imperialists and their puppets. In some localities the people have eliminated reactionaries and bad elements that had infiltrated the mechanism of revolutionary power, and have chosen the most loyal, most revolutionary elements of the population to administer power at the base.

The substance of the Revolution is power. The poor and working population, those who were most oppressed under the old regime, are permeated with this principle more than any other. Thus it is that for the working population, which constitutes the majority in the solidarity cells and in the quarters, to have a strong people's power at the base is to have everything: order and security, bread, joy and prosperity. To build a new life, a good and beautiful new society, we must begin with the building of a truly strong people's power at the base.

Vietnamese first, Catholics second

The only building in Saigon over which the flags of Hanoi or the Front never waved was the cathedral. There had not even been an attempt to hoist it. This was a sign of respect on the part of the new authorities.

The first Sunday after the Liberation, when the city's churches filled up as usual, many young *bo doi* in uniform came to hear mass with the other faithful.

The Revolution had long promised to leave the population their freedom of religion, and when it took power it kept this pledge.

Catholics in South Vietnam had certainly not distinguished themselves for their progressive attitudes during the war years. On the contrary they had been one of the most solid pillars of all past "puppet" regimes. But they also represented ten percent of the population, they were organized and influential in the society of the South, and the new authorities preferred to gain their sympathies rather than alienating them further in a direct clash.

The Catholic Church grew up in the days of the French, when missionaries landed in the wake of occupation troops, and thanks to their relationship of trust with the colonial power Catholics became a privileged class in Vietnam. To be Catholic meant to have access to the best schools, to get the best posts in the state administration. From one generation to the next the majority of doctors, lawyers, magistrates, and officials had been Catholics.

With the Geneva Accords and the regrouping in the South of all pro-French elements this Catholic elite concentrated in Saigon, and since 1954 it had dominated the South Vietnamese political scene with its staunchly anti-Communist position.

In the weeks preceding the Liberation the rapid Communist advance had sowed among Catholics an understandable fear that they, more than any other social group, might suffer under the new regime. This did not happen.

After April 30 no Catholic was arrested, persecuted, or discriminated against as such. The Church was not considered an organization whose members had to register. Only military chaplains had to do so, but in their capacity as ARVN officers, not as priests.

Of course this was not enough to banish from people's minds the deeply-rooted conviction that Communists were sworn enemies of religion, that Marxism and Catholicism were mutually exclusive.

"In a church in the diocese of Bac Tien, a woman embraces a *bo doi* and says to him: 'Thank heaven you've come in time to liberate us, otherwise we'd have fallen into the hands of the Communists and suffered the fate of martyrs!' The *bo doi* looks at her in surprise and answers: 'But, my good woman, I am a Communist and a Catholic as well!' "

This story, printed in the first issue of the Catholic weekly *Cong Giao van dan Toc,* published on July 10, is perhaps apocryphal, but it illustrates well the problem that a group of progressive Catholics who had decided to cooperate with the new regime had set for themselves: to persuade the bulk of the faithful not to remain outside the flow of Vietnamese history and to enter actively into the Revolution.

The new authorities looked favorably on this initiative, and it was no accident that *Cong Giao van dan Toc* (literally "Catholics and People") was the first publication by a nongovernment organization to be authorized by the Military Management Committee.

The editor was Nguyen Dinh Thi, a young priest who had worked for years in exile in Paris and had returned to Saigon by way of Hanoi on May 31, on a special plane with other Third Force figures such as the lawyer Nguyen Long and the writer Thieu Son.

"We must keep the Church from retreating into its shell, from becoming a Church of silence, from laying the foundations for a Catholic resistance movement in socialist Vietnam," said Father Thi. "We have no intention of setting up a church parallel to the official one, only of fighting the church of purple cinctures and red skullcaps: we want to reinvigorate it.

"The Catholic Church in this country is an authentic, original fact, and it is the only social body whose old power has not been swept away by the Revolution.

"By tradition Catholics in Vietnam have always set themselves against the people. The complete liberation of the country is an opportunity for Catholics to rediscover that they are part of the people."

In a way this too was a form of *hoc tap*, and as in the re-education of the "puppets," nationalism was expected to be the catalyst for this process of change.

"In the past we had Catholics who were also Vietnamese," Father Thi told me. "Now what we ought to have is Vietnamese who are also Catholics."

Significantly, the title of the lead editorial in the new weekly publication was "Vietnamese and Catholic."

For years a small group of priests like Thi had operated on the edges of the underground. Kept on the sidelines by the hierarchy and persecuted by Thieu's police, who had guessed what they were up to but did not dare to touch them since they were Catholics, they had been active in various sectors. They presented themselves as exponents of the Third Force, but in reality they were part of an operation whose purpose was to back up the struggle of the National Liberation Front:

Chan Tin, at the head of a "Committee for the Reform of the Prison System," concerned himself with political prisoners;

Truong Ba Can and Huynh Cong Minh, and their "Young Catholic Workers Movement," took care of the relations between students and the world of labor;

Phan Khac Tu, the "garbage priest," interested himself in the workers;

Nguyen Dinh Thi and Tran Tam Tinh worked abroad as anti-Thieu propagandists;

Nguyen Ngoc Lan kept up contacts with the Front.

"The Gospels should have pushed us right into the Revolution but theology, which after all is the history of the Church, kept us away from it," said Father Chan Tin. "Up until '68 we all more or less held positions of pacifism and nonviolence. The Tet offensive was a turning point for us as well. We actually realized that ever since 1930 the innovating force in our national history had been the Communist Party and that it was impossible to deny its existence.

"Today this fact is clearer than ever: only the Party can take credit for the independence struggle and for victory. The Party has a right to rule, since it's the only genuine mass organization with a popular base.

"The fear Catholics have of the Communists is unjustified. Of course we don't agree with them on matters of faith, but faith is a problem of the heart, and the Communists cannot interfere. As for the rest, if we are true Christians we must share the social goals of the Communists.

"How can we serve Christ if we don't see Man standing before us? The Communists indicate Christ's path to us without knowing it, and their cadres, the ones who fought for years in the jungle for the dignity of man, what are they if not Christians who are unaware of being so?"

The group of young Catholic progressives emerged informally in 1969 around a Catholic monthly whose first editor was Chan Tin and which was called, significantly, *Doi Dien* ("The Dialogue"). The first issue came out in July. Thieu's agents immediately began dogging them, but not wanting to alienate the Church, they did not touch the priests or the magazine. They confined themselves to arresting its readers. To fool the police the magazine, while keeping a double "D" in its title, repeatedly changed its name. First it was called *Dong Dao* ("The Song of the Fields"), then *Dung Day* ("Arise"). Ultimately, under the editorship of Father Lan, it went back to the old *Doi Dien*.

"In '68 I had my first contacts with the Front. It was Professor Chau Tam Luan who took me to Ben Luc, in a liberated area near My Tho," Father Lan told me after the Liberation. "Our religious brothers and lay friends had decided to cooperate with the Marxists, and we were ready to take orders from the guerrillas.

"But there were no orders for us. The political cadre I met told me I had been invited only for discussions and that it was up to us to establish our own course of action.

"The Front never expected the Church to go over to its side; all it wished was for the Church to keep out of the conflict. So this became our task."

Father Lan explained to me that one of his group's major concerns was to prevent the Third Force from being manipulated.

"Ever since the Second World War France and the United States have used the same tactics: every time the first force was defeated a new force was discovered and inflated to contest the rightful power of the Communists.

"It is reminiscent of the fable of the frog who wants to become an ox.

"The first frog was Bao Dai, who swelled and swelled until he burst at Dien Bien Phu; then came the turn of Catholics from the North and of Diem. That blew up in '63. The An Quang Buddhists were the third frog. The Americans tried to sell them as the personification of patriotism, freedom, and the national spirit. They blew up too, in '66. Then it was Thieu's turn, and Ky's, and whatever was left from previous 'explosions.' That frog blew up on April 30 with the Liberation. Another attempt put forward by the French but surely with American support, was to make the Third Force a new frog; but this we were able to prevent."

Fathers Lan, Thi, Chan Tin, and the others were only a minority. Their position was certainly not shared by the Vietnamese clergy and the obtuse, bigoted, reactionary Church, headed by the apostolic nuncio Monseigneur Le-Maitre.

A Belgian aristocrat, LeMaitre had been in Saigon for years and had warmly supported the Thieu regime and the American war effort. He had wanted to leave with the evacuation, but the Vatican ordered him to stay on. Along with his second in command, a Polish priest recently arrived to replace Monseigneur De Castro (a reactionary young Portuguese transferred to Canberra), LeMaitre hoisted the yellow and white papal flag and barricaded himself in the Nunciature on Hai Ba Trung Street to await the arrival of the Vietcong.

When I went to try to speak with him three days after the Liberation he was still shut up in his residence, and no one on his staff had ventured to stick his nose out.

"We spent the whole time in prayer," Father Forrest told me. "Some Vietcong soldiers came to station themselves in our garden, but we were able to convince them that their presence would be a serious embarrassment to us."

The war between these two factions in the Church began immediately after the Liberation, and it was LeMaitre who fired the first shot.

Right after the Liberation LeMaitre named Monseigneur Thuan as coadjutor to the archbishop of Saigon, with the right to succeed the archbishop. Monseigneur Thuan, Diem's nephew, was a conservative traditionalist who had been the former bishop of Nha Trang, as well as president of "Corev," the organization that had channeled humanitarian donations from all over the world into the service of the regime.

The appointment was a provocation, or at least that was how progressive Catholics saw it. In the new climate created by the Liberation they had asked the archbishop of Saigon, Nguyen Van Binh, to inject fresh blood into the hierarchy, urging him to send old advisors to the Curia off to country parishes and replace them with younger ones more open to the ideas of the new Vietnam. But LeMaitre was placing at Binh's side the very symbol of the past, and moreover designating him as the archbishop's successor.

Groups of Catholic students began to picket the Apostolic Nunciature. "LeMaitre must go!" their signs read. At night the demonstrators paraded silently with torches before LeMaitre's locked gate: "to illuminate his conscience."

The *bo doi* did not interfere.

Then, on June 3, there was a counterdemonstration. About five hundred persons, led by old-guard parish priests, marched along Trung Minh Gian Street to the cry of "Down with the dissident anti-Rome Catholics!" Their objective: to "free LeMaitre" from "the siege" of the rebels. At the corner of Truong Tan Buu Street they found their path blocked by *bo doi*. There were shots, two or three people were wounded, some were arrested, and the counterdemonstration dispersed.

The incident provided an excellent opportunity for the new authorities. They had already let it be known that all diplomats accredited to the "puppet" regime would have to leave the country. In LeMaitre's case they added that his presence was causing disorders, and he was asked to depart.

While the *bo doi* in customs meticulously inspected his luggage at Tan Son Nhut, a "Giai Phong" television crew kept their lights and cameras constantly trained on him.

With LeMaitre gone, relations improved between the new authorities and the Church, even the official one. Archbishop Nguyen Van Binh gave his support to Father Thi's group and to the magazine *Cong Giao van dan Toc* ("Catholics and People"), and participated along with 250 other prelates in a meeting organized at Doc Lap where members of the PRG explained their policy and reassured the Catholics.

Binh tried to bring Monseigneur Thuan along to the meeting, but the palace told him that his presence was not needed. When I left Saigon Thuan was rumored to be negotiating his resignation in exchange for permission to leave Vietnam.

As a first concession to the new authorities the Church agreed to participate on a joint committee that quietly began studying the possibility of changing the wording of prayers.

"I don't see what there is to change. Thousands of Vietnamese have gone to heaven with those prayers," Father Tran Huu Thanh said acidly.

Father Thanh had stayed in Saigon. He had not placed himself at the head of an armed band of Catholic resisters and he had not been imprisoned by the *bo doi,* as it was rumored after the Liberation. Even he, one of the symbols of the most deepseated Catholic anti-Communism, was able to carry on with his life in the Redemptorist church on Ky Dong Street.

When I went to see him one Sunday in June he had just finished saying mass. The sacristy was full of people coming to confess or to ask advice, and in front of the gaudy Madonna there was the usual crowd of women praying and beggars holding out their hands.

Of all the parish priests who had fled from the North in 1954, he had been one of the most influential. An ideologue and adviser to Diem, it was he who designed the "three-banded" flag that flew over Saigon until the Liberation.

"The three red stripes represent the three regions of Vietnam—Tonkin, Annam, and Cochin China—but also the Trinity," he once explained to me.

After the fall of Diem he had still remained in close touch with the circles of power. For seven years he had held what he himself called "the chair in anti-Communist psychology" at the Military Academy of Dalat, through which all ARVN superior officers passed.

He set himself apart from Thieu only in the middle of 1974, when he started the "Movement against Corruption," a right-wing opposition group to the regime, and began to campaign for a healthier, more honest, more efficient government, one better equipped to fight the Communists.

Father Thanh did not easily relinquish his hopes of continuing the anti-Communist crusade, even when three-quarters of the country was already lost and the Vietcong were at the gates of Saigon. Together with Marshal Nguyen Cao Ky, he drew up a list of officers ready to fight on, sketched out the outlines of a new government, and prepared a generals' proclamation. It was to be a mini-coup d'etat to take place around April 10, with the object of removing Thieu and replacing him with a directorate that would declare war to the bitter end.

"Everything was ready," Father Thanh told me with his usual naive and infatuated air. "It was the Americans who blocked it. An American journalist came to see Marshal Ky and myself, and on behalf of Ambassador Martin he told us to wait—three more days and the Americans would remove Thieu and give the presidency to Ky. When we realized we'd been deceived it was already too late."

The Liberation surprised Father Thanh in various ways. A few hours after the tanks rolled into the city he received a visit from a group of *"chieu hoi."* A few months earlier he had helped them to find work in Saigon and now they turned out to be infiltrated guerrillas. Then he was surprised to be invited to Doc Lap, where the vice-president of the Republic, Trinh Dinh Thao, leader of the non-Communist component of the Front, asked him to cooperate with the new regime. He could help by reassuring the Catholics and promoting their confidence in the new authorities, he was told.

In his own way Father Thanh did just that. Using the old "God and Fatherland" motto he preached to his faithful what he had always preached, obedience to the government and respect for the laws, as though they were the will of God. It was the same language as in the past, only the government and laws had changed.

"I'm still an anti-Communist, but at another level," he kept saying.

To keep pace with the times, he had fired his cook, and he now washed his cassock himself. He had still not been able to stop chainsmoking.

However much Father Thanh may have changed with the times, it was certainly not to the likes of him that the Vietnamese Church could turn for its own survival and renewal after the Liberation.

Instead it was the young progressive priests who indicated the path and who were already bridging the gap between Catholics and the regime. They were the ones to gain gradually more power and influence in the Curia, and they were the ones to whom the new authorities paid greater attention.

Chan Tin, Truong Ba Can, Phan Khac Tu, and Nguyen Ngoc Lan were invited to all official receptions at the palace, alongside representatives of the Front and other non-Communist forces that had participated in the Liberation struggle.

At the reception on June 6 for the sixth anniversary of the founding of the PRG, another well-known Catholic figure made his appearance at Doc Lap, at the arm of President Nguyen Huu Tho. He was Ngo Cong Duc, perhaps the most important pawn in the game of restoring relations between the Catholic bourgeoisie and the Communists in the new Vietnam.

The last time I had seen Duc he was in exile in Bangkok, where he was trying to meet anyone coming from Vietnam who might have something to tell him about the country Thieu had forced him to leave. A month after the Liberation he returned to Saigon by way of Hanoi, where he had had a meeting with Pham Van Dong, prime minister of North Vietnam.

Duc, cousin of the archbishop of Saigon, was born in 1936 into a wealthy family in the Delta. His father, a large Catholic landowner, had been killed in an ambush by Vietminh guerrillas.

By origin, upbringing, wealth and connections Duc was destined to become a defender of the South Vietnamese Catholic, anti-Communist cause. He began his career in the pro-Diem youth movement, later becoming a deputy, and publisher and editor of the newspaper *Tin Sang*

("Morning News"). He was famous, respected, powerful, and on the way up, but the massive military intervention by the United States in Vietnam made him take another path.

Duc realized that the American presence was not saving the country, but debasing and destroying it. His famous editorial "Yankee Go Home" created a sensation; he spoke in it as a pure nationalist, and his argument convinced many.

From a supporter of the regime he became an influential opponent. Thieu saw the danger, but Duc had ties to the Church (in 1970 he was received in audience by the pope), was related to the archbishop, and could not be silenced as easily as others. In two years *Tin Sang* was confiscated 282 times. Then, in February 1972 it was shut down. Duc, heeding the "warning" of two attempts on his life, left the country.

He traveled from country to country on a Swedish passport, giving lectures and writing against the regime. But most of all he held together the strings of a network of friends and associates he had organized and left behind in Saigon. Duc presented himself as an exponent of the Third Force, while he was actually working for the Front, not in it but alongside it. In July 1973, during a trip to Eastern Europe, Duc had a long conversation with Pham Van Dong.

Duc's men in Saigon included Ly Qui Chung, Ho Ngoc Nhuan, and his own brother-in-law, Nguyen Van Binh. When he left Duc gave them precise instructions: to infiltrate any group or movement in opposition to the regime with the objective of overthrowing Thieu and helping the Front to take power.

Binh, married to Duc's sister and president of the press association, was to concern himself with the right-wing opposition and the moderates: among other things he became an adviser to Father Thanh.

Ly Qui Chung was to join the reconciliation forces and keep track of the Buddhists: he became a minister to "Big Minh."

Nhuan was to stay with the more progressive forces: he was, for a few hours, the last mayor of Saigon.

"We weren't revolutionaries, but the Front taught us the techniques of infiltration and sabotage, and we applied them on a political plane," Duc told me when I went to see him in the modest house near the Thi Nghe bridge that had become his headquarters.

From abroad Duc kept in touch with his group by letter and telephone, and through unsuspected emissaries of the regime who could enter and leave Vietnam. His work had borne fruit, and the PRG had recognized Duc's contribution: his men were among the twenty-nine persons who did not have to go for reeducation.

"I'm not a Communist, but who knows? I might become one," said Duc, smiling. "You change as you go along, you learn many things. When I left Saigon I had a car with air conditioning. Now I'm back and I ride a bicycle that I bought in Vientiane."

There it was, propped against the wall, next to the couch on which we were sitting. It was very much like Duc—a bicycle, to be sure, but a racing model, all chrome and flaming yellow.

Duc was a subtle politician, intelligent, warm, and charismatic, but not a revolutionary like those in the Front, nor a "saint" like the guerrillas. He was a bourgeois with a profoundly nationalist soul who felt his country changing and wanted to stay with it. He was a genuine man, even in his contradictions. A large portion of the Saigonese Catholic intelligentsia who had not fled with the Americans and who had listened to, worshipped, and followed him when he was Thieu's critic, identified with him and felt reassured by his presence. His return to Saigon calmed many. It was like a guarantee. Duc was well aware of his role:

"I want to go back to being a journalist. I want to work to convince people that the country belongs to everyone, that even those who collaborated with the old regime have the right and duty to help with reconstruction. The future lies not in division but in national reconciliation."

Before leaving I met him once again, at Givral. He had just obtained permission from the Military Management Committee to resume publication of his newspaper, *Tin Sang*. It was to be the first privately-owned Catholic daily to reappear after the Liberation, the second paper after *Saigon Giai Phong*.

6: Criminals and Relics

People's trials

Le Trinh, remember when you beat me the whole day long? Remember?"

"Look here Le Trinh, look what you did to me! Remember when you tortured me with electricity? I begged you to stop, to give me a breathing spell, but you kept right on going. Remember?"

Le Trinh, former policeman on the special squad in Quang Ngai, stood on a wooden platform erected in a corner of the soccer field, head bowed, hands tied behind his back. Behind him was a table with three people's judges, the NLF and North Vietnamese flags, and in the middle the smiling portrait of Ho Chi Minh. At least a thousand persons were watching him; many had been his victims in the "interrogation room" of the police station during the war years.

"It was him! It was him!" a young woman yelled, mounting the platform and turning to the crowd. "Remember, Le Trinh, when you put a snake in my vagina, remember!"

The trial began in the early afternoon and lasted for three hours, until it was dark. From the height of the platform one witness after another told the crowd what he or she had suffered.

Le Trinh wept and trembled. Every time he raised his eyes from the ground he could see on the other side of the soccer field, next to the bell tower of the Catholic church, the old police station fronting on Phan Boi Chau Street, where for years he had done the job of interrogating the people his men arrested, trying to discover the lines of the Vietcong network operating in the city.

At the end one of the people's judges rose and asked:

"Le Trinh, have you nothing to say?" He was not even able to answer; terrified, he went on trembling.

"In your opinion, should this man be sentenced to death?" the judge asked the crowd. A hundred, a thousand hands were raised with the cry:

"Yes! Yes!"

Two *bo doi* took Le Trinh by the elbows and dragged him away.

The trial took place in Quang Ngai in central Vietnam on April 17. When I was told about it at the end of May by a friend who was present and had come to Saigon, Le Trinh had not yet been executed.

While "puppets" in Saigon were still going through registration and reeducation without difficulties, reports from other parts of the country that had been liberated earlier told with increasing frequency of people's trials like the one against Le Trinh. People in the capital believed that soon they would also take place there.

They did.

On June 19 Le Van Hoi, block leader in the fourteenth district of Binh Hoa, was taken before a crowd of at least four thousand persons in Le Van Duyet Stadium. The scenario was the same: a platform, a table, three judges, the flags, anyone who had something to say about him coming forward to testify.

It began with a seventy-seven-year-old woman. Le Van Hoi had stabbed her son to death before her eyes, then ordered her to throw the corpse into the canal in front of the house or suffer the same fate herself.

Then came parents who told how for years they had had to pay Le Van Hoi ten thousand piasters a month not to arrest their sons and send them to the front.

One man told how Le Van Hoi had extorted all his savings by threatening to arrest him as a Communist, and how at the end, when he had no more money, he had tortured him for a month.

The crowd called for Le Van Hoi's death, but then the sentence was not carried out. One of the judges explained that the policy of the Revolutionary Government was forgiveness, that the rule was: "first reeducation, then punishment." Le Van Hoi would go for a long period of *hoc tap*, and only if he were not "transformed" would he be punished.

On July 4 in Tan Quy Dong, near Nha Be, came the turn of five "torturers." The chief defendant was a certain Tuy, who had been village leader and was later in charge of the Phoenix program for the area. In 1968 he had killed eleven NLF fighters with his own hands, and exposed their corpses with the ears and noses cut off, to terrorize the population. After the Liberation he had taken to the jungle along with his co-defendants. Again the sentence was "a long *hoc tap*."

Some of those tried were persons the new authorities defined as owing "debts of blood to the people." Many had not turned up for registration for fear of reprisals, and therefore were forced to confess their crimes in these "people's accusation assemblies," as *Saigon Giai Phong* called the trials.

Others had registered but had been recognized by the population as "criminals," and were required to undergo a treatment harsher than the normal *hoc tap*.

It was said in Saigon that these special cases were being reeducated in a camp near Vung Tau, where the *bo doi* had also confined officers and soldiers caught trying to leave the country after the Liberation.

There were of course no written laws or precise standards by which to establish the degree of the crime or the extent of punishment. But in general only those who "owed debts of blood to the people" and had also committed "counterrevolutionary acts" after April 30 suffered the more serious consequences.

The authorities made no secret of these cases. And certainly one of the reasons that *Saigon Giai Phong* regularly published news items like the following from July 12 was to discourage other "obstinate" elements:

> The tribunal of the Military Management Committee of Chau Doc has tried and sentenced to death Le Nhat Thanh, former puppet lieutenant, who had committed many crimes against the people, hidden himself after the Liberation, and committed more acts of sabotage against the Revolution.
>
> Denounced by the population and arrested by the security forces, he was found in possession of six pistols. The revolutionary authorities tried to reeducate him, but since he remained obstinate, the tribunal in the presence of ten thousand persons sentenced him to death and confiscated all his property.

In fact these trials were meant not only to do justice, but to educate the population. Their purpose was not just to punish guilty "puppets," but to cure their victims. The "people's accusation assemblies" introduced the second state of *hoc tap* for the population.

People were meant to understand that the Revolution was a clean break with the past, that it was impossible to turn back. Everyone had to rid himself of his fear, rage, and respect for the persons, things, and rituals of "puppet" times.

It was not enough to explain and repeat it in neighborhood meetings. Each person alone had to free himself of everything the past had put in his bones, everything it embodied for him.

The trials provided this opportunity. The defendant was not an abstract criminal, someone anonymous and unknown: he was someone one had lived with, whose arrogance one had personally suffered. Facing the former block leader, chief of police, or informer, people spoke out, told of the past, shouted, vented themselves, and accused. Each person discovered that he had an unsuspected power over the authorities he had once respected, feared, hated, or admired—a power even of life or death.

Opportunities for these trials were not lacking.

Since the deadline had already passed for the presentation of all "puppets" for *hoc tap*, there was in almost every neighborhood some "torturer to be unmasked," or some superior officer to be sent back for reeducation because he had pretended to be an enlisted man in the hope of doing only three days of *hoc tap*.

Then as time went by and the Revolution, embarking on a harsher course, began to launch various campaigns of denunciation, more "puppets" were there to be tried—infiltrators of revolutionary organizations, speculators, and those who did not respect the unwritten rules of a new morality.

One day, crossing the Cholon market just at the end of one of these improvised trials, I saw in the midst of a crowd a woman who was covering her face, asking people's pardon. On her chest was a sign reading *con di* ("whore"). The man standing beside her carried a sign which read *khach dam* ("lecherous customer"). They had been found together in a brothel that had continued to operate despite the ban.

Apart from these trials of "criminals" there were "people's accusation assemblies" in factories, workshops, and offices, where absent owners or former chiefs still on the job were attacked for having exploited their employees and unjustly enriched themselves.

Often these sessions concluded with no penalty for the "defendant" other than the fact itself of having been accused.

For the accusers this was an opportunity to vent old resentments, to throw past injustices in the teeth of their former superiors. In the course of these assemblies the old hierarchical relationship disintegrated and new relations were established within the various groups.

One trial of this kind took place before my eyes. Both accusers and defendant were people I knew.

The Continental

When Joseph the old outdoor waiter got up to speak — small, dressed as usual in his threadbare white uniform with the initials "C.P." (Continental Palace) embroidered in blue on the front and wearing the huge, black pointed shoes he had been given by some foreign guest along with the name "Joseph" (his real name was too hard to pronounce) — everyone fell silent: the staff employees, the cooks, the two switchboard girls, the porters, the waiters and the floor "boys."

Since Liberation Day Joseph had been one of the most active members in the group of Vietcong sympathizers that had surfaced in the hotel. He was the one who wrote the first victory banner. He was the one who came to invite me for what was surely the only event of its kind in the history of the Continental: a reception for the hotel guests, organized and offered by the staff to celebrate Ho Chi Minh's birthday.

"We have to have compensation," said Joseph, "and he's the one who has to pay it. He's got the money. He's rich and we're poor. Just look at him. Thirty years ago he was one of us, he was the ice-cream boy. And now? Now he's big and fat. He's twice my size. And he's rich, rich as they come. At home he has air conditioning in all the rooms. He has a car with white upholstery, and even there he's put in air conditioning. He's made all his money on our backs. And that's why he has to pay compensation."

Thuc, a "boy" on my floor, the one who made up my room every day, spoke next:

"Yes, yes, the comrade is right. He's made his money by taking a percentage from the suppliers and pinching on our wages. For years he's been paying us eight to ten thousand piasters a month. What's that for a month's work? It's what a guest pays for a meal. We've been able to get along because we got tips, but now that there are no more tips what are we supposed to do? He has to pay compensation. It's true what the comrade said, when he started working he was one of us, and now he puts on airs: Mr. Manager here, Mr. Manager there. Okay, Mr. Manager, now it's time for you to cough up."

The manager, "Monsieur Loi" as everyone called him, was a man in his sixties, genial, able, with the broad face of a smiling Buddha. He stood there incredulous, getting angrier and redder by the minute before the accusations of his employees.

Always impeccably dressed in white and with his paunch extended, Monsieur Loi used to accost his guests in the lobby of the hotel every morning, to shake hands in the French manner and ask: "Sleep well? Did you sleep well, Monsieur?" He would spend the rest of the day sitting amid papers in his office next to the concierge's desk, under a large portrait of the old *patron,* Mathieu Franchini. Because he actually was fat, hearty, and elegant, Monsieur Loi seemed cut out from the start to play the role of defendant in the new situation.

The assembly took place on the ground floor of the hotel, in the salon opening on the garden, where dances, diplomatic receptions, and wedding parties had been held in the past.

At the table, under the portrait of Ho Chi Minh, the two flags and banners extolling the Revolution, were two *bo doi,* a woman *can bo* representing the trade unions, and Thao, the second-floor "boy" who had been elected chairman of the hotel's revolutionary committee. In front, in rows of ten, sat all the employees.

Like the rest of Saigon, the Continental too was changing. Located in the center of the old city with its gleaming white facade, its plate glass windows facing the Assembly square, its high-ceilinged rooms, its "boys" who slept stretched out in the hallways, its large fans, old-fashioned furniture, huge beds, and with a jar of water always ready in the bathroom in case the faucets did not work, the Continental had been the symbol of colonial Indochina.

A vast collection had passed through its rooms: generations of war correspondents, planters coming to town for a spree, adventurers, and odd characters who lodged for months without anyone ever knowing for sure whom they were working for.

Warriors from all the battles of Indochina had rested themselves on the terrace of the "Conti": men from the Foreign Legion, French, Japanese, and British conscripts, and finally the American GIs.

For old "Indos" the Continental was linked to memories of the heroic and romantic era: the child prostitutes, the intrigues, the opium, the traffic in piasters, the adventures.

With the death of Mathieu Franchini the hotel had passed to his son Philippe; but the latter lived in France and was more interested in painting than in business, and he had given Monsieur Loi a free hand in the management of the Continental.

Seeing the end approaching for Saigon, Philippe had come to Vietnam to sell the hotel, and had promised the employees that with part of the proceeds he would pay some compensation for all the years they had served his father and himself. But he had found no one crazy enough to invest money in Vietnam in 1975, and so he had quietly departed again a month before the Liberation, without resolving a thing.

"It's not my hotel," said Monsieur Loi, trying to defend himself against the accusations. "I'm an employee like yourselves. I can't pay compensation; but if you don't want me any more, all right, I'll leave and the *bo doi* can run the hotel."

Here was one more reason to accuse him.

"That's too easy!" shouted Hoang, another waiter in the restaurant. "Loi can't get out of it like that."

Monsieur Loi could no longer cope with them. He began to stammer, to falter, and his son-in-law, who worked as head bookkeeper in the hotel, came to his rescue:

"You people accusing Loi are all disloyal and ungrateful. You're taking advantage of the situation, and the ones doing the most talking are the worst employees. . . ." And he began listing each one's faults.

The woman *can bo* representing the Liberation trade unions interrupted him:

"That's enough. You have committed a very serious error. You've insulted the working class." The son-in-law had to withdraw his remarks and apologize to everyone.

The "boys" were not satisfied yet. They said that the appointment of his son-in-law as head bookkeeper was one more example of Loi's favoritism, his filthy tactics in running the hotel.

"He made his son-in-law head bookkeeper so that together they could steal what they wanted and cover it up by falsifying the accounts," said the waiter Ba.

After long discussion the assembly voted to start an investigation of the son-in-law and his ledgers.

The meeting condemned Loi to stay on as manager. He had to come to the office each day to make himself available, but he had actually lost all authority.

"Loi's not against the Revolution," Thuc told me later when he came to do my room. "We're not after him as a person, we're only after his social role. Loi's a comprador, he's been a middleman between the colonialists and the people."

In the span of a few weeks Loi became a broken man. He fell ill, lost weight, and the last time I saw him he had to walk with a cane.

The Continental was taken over by the *bo doi*. They checked the whole building room-by-room, taking stock of every chair, every towel, and counting the forks and spoons.

Then one day in mid-June, when a young British writer named James Fenton and I were the only paying guests left (the new ones were all *bo doi*), a very polite *can bo* came to tell me that I had to give up my room. I put up a little resistance, but he said smilingly that the "hotel is no longer a hotel."

Certainly it was no longer the hotel I had once known. Every time I rang the bell at five in the afternoon to order a tea with lemon I would receive—after an hour if I was lucky—a lemon soda, and I had already been poisoned once in the restaurant by "pre-Liberation" meat.

The "boys" were now spending hours curled up in the corridors, holding group meetings, listening to one of them reading *Saigon Giai Phong* aloud, preparing posters and arguing about the compensation they no longer hoped to obtain from the government.

When I descended the stairs with my suitcases on my way to a stinking room on Tu Do Street, not one of the "boys" who came to say good-bye held out his hand for a tip.

Givral

During the American occupation the ownership changed. The family of French half-castes retired to the pastry shop next door and gave up the bar to some Chinese from Cholon. Even the name had changed. "Garden" had been inscribed in large letters on the corner windows, but everyone continued to call it by its old French name, "Givral."

For years it was the nucleus of a certain Saigon. Located right at the corner of Tu Do and Le Loi in front of the National Assembly and between the Continental and Caravelle hotels, Givral had become the customary point of encounter for deputies, journalists, spies, secret agents, whores, lawyers, and foreign correspondents.

In thirty years of war, conspiracies, maneuvers, and assassinations, Saigon had always been a city filled with rumors, gossip, indiscretions. Givral was at the heart of all this whispering. It was the center where every kind of news, true or false, was collected and spread around. At Givral you always met someone who had an exceptional story to tell, one that must not be repeated, that was supposed to be verified in a few days' time. There was no coup d'état that was not announced in advance on the "Givral grapevine," except those that actually took place. Even one of these, it is said, was more or less hatched at Givral, but there is no reason to believe it: the customers were always wooers of those in power, clients of this or that political clique, agents or provocateurs from this or that secret service, more than men of real power. Hoang Duc Nha, Mme. Thieu's mediocre and conceited nephew, used to go there in his student days, but when he later became a special adviser at the palace and an *éminence grise* of the regime, he gave up frequenting Givral and sent his minions instead.

However Givral was a place where you could easily feel the pulse of the political and business world of the city. Around its yellow plastic tables gathered members of the wealthy middle class, officials from the various ministries, and many "foreign Vietnamese," as Cao Giao called them—persons divided between their Vietnamese souls and their French or English culture, between their native roots and their jobs as translators, interpreters, or foreign guides and their salaries as employees of *Newsweek, Time,* or USIS.

When those at the top wanted to know "what people are

saying in town" they sent their messenger boys off to Givral, and some of the best-known Vietnamese journalists kept a corner of the place as a sort of branch office, as their permanent listening post.

Sometimes the news sent out from here was even true, but the grossest provocations were concocted here as well. During the big Communist offensive of 1972 the correspondent for *Le Monde* received from an old informant who frequented Givral, and who for years had put him on the track of stories that had all turned out to be authentic, a leak about a hard battle supposedly fought in the Delta between Vietcong and North Vietnamese units. My French colleague refused to believe it, until the event was reported to him in all its details and he was presented with a tape recording of a meeting apparently attended even by the NLF leader Nguyen Huu Tho and punctuated with bursts of gunfire and comments on what was happening. The tape, according to the informer, had been found in a bunker abandoned by the Vietcong after the North Vietnamese attack.

The whole thing was a fabrication. By whom it was never clear. By Thieu's espionage agents? By the Americans? Or by some dissident group in the Front, if it ever existed?

In March 1975 the same informant gave Paul Leandri of Agence France-Presse the news that the montagnards of FULRO had opened the gates of Ban Me Thuot to the Vietcong, and it was this piece of information that led to Leandri's death with a bullet in his head at Saigon's police headquarters.

Givral was also the den of a group of intellectual moderates, avowed opponents of any regime. Every so often one of them disappeared for a few days of interrogation, or for a few months in prison.

In the final months of the Thieu regime, at the time of Buddhist demonstrations for peace, Catholic demonstrations against corruption, and journalists' demonstrations for freedom of the press, Givral had become an excellent observation point, since individual protests, the delivery of petitions, and the end of every rally took place right there on the square, between the National Assembly and the monstrous monument to those who had died for freedom — Thieu's freedom obviously. Usually you received an anonymous phone call: "In an hour an officer will read a declaration against the government on the steps of the Assembly." And so you sat and waited at Givral, looking out as through the glass of a large aquarium, out of reach of Thieu's police, who would photograph you if you were in the square, smear grease on your camera, or pick you out of the crowd and teach you a lesson. This at any rate is what happened to Haney Howell of CBS television, who was cold-bloodedly given two karate blows in the chest by a plainclothes agent during a demonstration by the Third Force.

The terrace of the Continental had been the other great haunt of Saigon, though in recent times it had become increasingly shabby and more obviously a flesh market, so many were the prostitutes who came to park themselves at its tables. But the terrace of the Continental died with the Liberation. I think the last time it was crowded and all its armchairs with their red, yellow, and orange cushions were taken, was when a group of paratroopers came herding in in a final moment of insolence and fear, their rifles leveled at the empty square, immediately after the speech in which General Minh announced the surrender.

Givral instead survived—not as in the past, when it was impossible at certain crowded afternoon hours to find a table, but it survived. After a day or two of hesitation the old clientele reappeared with new stories, new gossip, and new rumors. Having counted the number of those who had fled with the American evacuation, the clique of avowed intellectual opponents continued to meet and whisper over a cup of *café filtre* or an ice cream.

With the Vietnamese newspapers and the offices of foreign companies closed, with most of the correspondents departed and most of those remaining more idle than before, Givral became the center for highbrow "obstinates." While outside Saigon was changing day by day, at Givral you still found middle-aged gentlemen wearing elegant colored shirts and fashionable leather belts and shoes— lawyers, doctors, and even many officers of the "puppet" army, who came there to hear "what people are saying in town."

One day at the beginning of June I happened to sit down next to General Le Minh Dao, who had commanded the 18th Division during the battle of Xuan Loc and had dropped CBU asphyxiation bombs on the Vietcong besieging the town. At Xuan Loc Le Minh Dao had sworn to fight the Communists as long as he had a drop of blood in his veins. But he had not fought and now, still in complete freedom a month after the Liberation, he had come to have coffee at Givral with his wife and an aide. The new authorities had even left him his car—they had only taken away his driver.

The Givral grapevine continued to broadcast innuendos and the most absurd and unlikely rumors concerning clashes between *bo doi* and former soldiers of Thieu who had taken to the jungle, about American planes that were coming at night to drop arms and supplies to the resisters, and so forth. It was said that the Hoa Hao and Cao Dai sects had come out against the new revolutionary authorities and declared war on the Vietcong; it was said that Marshal Cao Ky had landed in a small plane at Tay Ninh to place himself at the head of the anti-Communist guerrillas; that appeals signed by various generals of the former regime were being circulated in the city urging their soldiers to rejoin them in the jungle. People swore they had seen these leaflets, but I never succeeded in getting hold of one.

Once there was even a rumor that a flying saucer, used by the Americans as a radio station to maintain contact with the anti-Vietcong partisans, passed in the sky every night over Tan Son Nhut. The rumor also spread that the great American evacuation, during which many of Thieu's high-ranking officers were able to flee at the last moment, was part of a plan to retrain an army outside Vietnam that would later attempt a landing in the country. There was also talk one day of United States submarines putting saboteurs and agents ashore along the southern coast. Another time, while Mme. Binh, foreign minister of the Provisional Revolutionary Government, was absent from Saigon and on a trip abroad, it was said that she had been the victim of a purge inspired by Hanoi and that she had placed herself at the head of a dissident wing of the Front, ready to join the remains of Thieu's army to combat the supremacy of the northerners in the South. And in the middle of this conspiratorial climate some of Thieu's former officers told "Radio Givral" how they had been contacted by Communist colleagues in the Front to find out whether they were ready to put up an army against the North.

The only truth in all these stories and in many others of the same kind was the negative reaction by a portion of the city and by a certain class of Saigonese to the changes in the country. Every rumor contained the illusion—of those who fabricated it or spread it around—that some-

thing of the sort was true or at least possible. The jokes
told at Givral about the *bo doi* expressed the contempt of
city dwellers who feel themselves to be better and more re-
fined than country folk.

One of the jokes went:

"Did you know that the *bo doi* have sealed even the ele-
vators in the Banque Nationale de Paris?"

"Really? But why?"

"They thought they were the vaults!"

A couple of weeks after the Liberation, a rumor spread
among Givral customers that the *bo doi* were leveling their
sights on the bar, that they considered it a nest of counterrevolutionaries and were sending their informers, that
soon anyone seen there would be in trouble.

It wasn't true at all, but it was typical of these people to
think that the *bo doi* operated like every other previous regime in Saigon, and would use their spies, their *agents provocateurs* or whatever, to inform or misinform people
through the Givral grapevine.

The *bo doi* did not even contemplate such a thing, and
left the Givral problem, if it had ever been one for them,
to take care of itself like so many others. Givral was one of
the few places where in three months I never saw a *bo doi*
soldier or officer, a political cadre or guerrilla.

The ranks of the "obstinate" gradually thinned out. The
first to disappear were former officers called to be reeducated; then, with the banks closed, even the middle class
found ice cream more and more expensive. Still on the
whole Givral remained a small refuge for the old society
which, with much effort and few hopes, attempted to carry
on without relinquishing its old habits. But it was already a
society on sale.

Within a few weeks the book stall in front of the entrance to Givral grew to enormous proportions. During the
war years it had sold occasional detective novels, a few old
copies of *Playboy,* and the eternal *Quiet American* by Graham Greene, which had become required reading for every foreigner in transit, be he journalist, soldier, or mere
tourist. Now fed by the libraries left behind by the Americans, and by rich Vietnamese families departing at the last
minute with only a suitcase, the bookstall spread out along
all the plate glass windows of Givral with magnificent complete collections of French classics, translations of the finest
works of Vietnamese literature, the most important books
on the Indochinese war, on Communism in Asia, and so

on. Many still bore a rubber stamp reading "U.S. Air Force," "U.S. Navy," and "Property of the U.S. Government." They came from the embassy, from USIS, from the libraries and residences of the various American "advisers." Real bargains—but there were very few buyers.

All of a sudden, one Sunday in the middle of July, there was something like a last flareup of the old society along the streets of Saigon. Whole families of the well-to-do appeared everywhere, as though keeping an appointment with each other—the women in their most beautiful *ao dai,* the men in gaudy shirts, some even in jackets and neckties. For a few hours there was a classic promenade along Tu Do Street. Givral became so crowded you could not find a chair. People were smiling, Saigon's wealthy were coming out of hiding as though to take pride in their old ways for one last time, as though to delude themselves that nothing had changed, as though to hoist their banner once more in the face of their now vanishing world.

There had been two or three sudden and inexplicable flare-ups of this kind in the first weeks after the Liberation, a mutual show of bravado by people of a class that showed a creeping sense of doom.

At the table next to mine at Givral, over her third glass of gin and tonic, sat a beautiful woman who kept laughing and talking as though conversing with someone sitting across from her. But there was no one there. She was passing her hand through her black hair and moving her head back and forth in an excited dialogue with the void. Elegant, well groomed, she went on talking louder and louder in the midst of boys from good families with their girl friends, a "puppet" officer who was celebrating his last evening before reeducation by getting drunk, and a group of Chinese businessmen from Hong Kong who had been waiting for two months—and were to go on waiting—for a plane to take them out of Saigon. Outside the noses of a dozen beggars pressed against the glass.

"So now you've gone. Your wife is with you in the United States. . . . You've abandoned me because I'm twenty-three and old and ugly. . . . Five million piasters would have been enough, only five million, and I would have got out too. To get that money I went to bed with the Japanese. . . . Nine Japanese. But you, you could have got me out. You're a district chief, you're a colonel, you could have got me out, but you preferred your wife. . . . You could have paid the five million. You had it, you had it in the bank, but now the *bo doi* have

come and freed the city and the banks are closed and the
money is there, but it's not yours any more. Saigon is liberated and I can't get out. Me, your little Phung. I still have
fifty thousand piasters, but what then? Now I'm not even a
singer any more, that's all over too. But Vietnam is liberated—Saigon is liberated. . . ."

No one around her said a word. Givral plunged into an
embarrassed silence.

The Promenade des français

They thought themselves the soul of Vietnam. They had
been in the country more than a hundred years. They had
built roads, houses, palaces, churches, imparted their language, bestowed their *civilisation*. The Americans had come
and gone; but the French, though defeated twenty years
before, had remained, convinced that after all the fate of
others could not afflict them. "The last sleepwalkers in Saigon," Cao Giao used to call them.

Slowly, with every new day, they too realized that all
they had was lost.

First they lost their meeting places: the Circle Sportif,
the Circle Hippique, now put to revolutionary uses; the
golf course at Go Vap, transformed into a public park
where children ran over the greens and adults cut down
the trees for firewood.

Then they lost their old habits: coffee in the morning at
"Bo-da," lunch at "Ramuncho" or "Valinco," aperitifs under the slow fans on the terrace of the Continental.

All around them their world was changing, and soon
they even lost the hope of being able to remain in Vietnam.

The Revolution did not drive them away. It simply prevented them from leading their old colonial life.

At the end of June the planters in the Highlands began
to leave their large rubber, coffee, and tea plantations and
moved to Saigon. The Front's political cadres had told
them to stay on the plantations and continue to cultivate
them; but the workers accused them of being exploiters,
demanded new indemnities, no longer obeyed orders,
wanted to participate in the management, and refused to
call them *patron*.

French property went untouched by the *bo doi* and no one ever talked of confiscating it. But it soon became clear that the owners could no longer dispose of it at will as in the past.

On July 10 an important communiqué was issued by the Military Management Committee. It applied to the possessions of foreigners in general, but it was essentially intended for the French. After reaffirming the PRG's respect for the "legitimate rights" of foreigners, the communique established that:

— every foreigner authorized to leave the Republic of South Vietnam must obey the laws and policies of the PRG if he wants to take objects in his possession with him;

— foreigners are forbidden to sell, give, or otherwise transfer personal property or real estate in their possession, if this disturbs order and public safety;

— in order to protect the legitimate rights of the state and people, every Vietnamese citizen must have special permission from the proper authority to receive, in the form of a transfer or gift, or simply to manage, buildings, land, and any other kind of real estate or personal property belonging to persons of foreign nationality.

In practice, this meant freezing French property in Vietnam: it meant that every old resident who wanted to leave would have to obtain an unlikely permit to export his collection of Vietnamese art or his wife's jewelry.

There were about seven thousand French men and women in Vietnam at the moment of the Liberation: lycée teachers, development experts, young men who had come for a two-year tour of duty in place of military service, and long-term residents who had been rooted for decades in the country as heads of large and small firms, owners of huge plantations or of small restaurants and cafés.

They had all stayed, not only because President Giscard d'Estaing had been unable to evacuate them and had told them to remain; but above all because they were sincerely convinced that, having had no part in the war now ending, they had little to fear from those who were coming to take over from Thieu. To be French seemed a merit to them, and with no shame, to show they were not Americans, they ran up the tricolor of France on every one of their houses and on all their property on the morning of April 30.

For the old Vietminh, who had left Saigon in 1945 after

the unsuccessful August Revolution and the subsequent French repression, it must have been an amazing sight to see the flutter of "enemy" flags over their capital, which after thirty years they were reentering as victors.

They were not left to flutter long. A few days after the Liberation Ambassador Merillon, who had stayed at his post in great spirits, was summoned to the Foreign Ministry, where an official, without even bothering to introduce himself, told him the new authorities did not appreciate all that display of France.

"Those flags are an embarrassment to me as well," Merillon replied.

For the ambassador, whose position with the new rulers was proving increasingly difficult (on May 15 he received an invitation for the victory celebrations, but the time of the reception was wrong and he arrived to find Doc Lap Palace empty), the French themselves were becoming a growing embarrassment.

Every morning dozens of his countrymen lined up before the offices of the consulate to inquire what they should do, to protest, to demand that France organize an evacuation and send planes.

The number of those wishing to depart increased by the hour, but it was impossible to leave Saigon. The PRG refused to let foreign planes land at Tan Son Nhut, and had none of its own to offer for the resolution of a problem it did not consider urgent.

Only when the Red Cross and UNICEF started flights from Vientiane to bring medicine and humanitarian aid to Saigon did the new authorities allow the French and other foreigners to embark. (The South Korean and Cambodian diplomats left behind by the Americans the day of the evacuation also departed on these planes.)

Unfortunately these flights were seldom and unpredictable, and their arrivals and departures became one of the most discussed subjects in Saigon's foreign community.

Every day at five o'clock dozens of Frenchmen arrived at the Foreign Ministry—by bicycle, on foot, in cyclos—to check and recheck an old embarkation list on which their names were slowly being erased by the sun and rain.

Weeks went by in this way.

Strolling along Tu Do Street, which they insisted on calling Rue Catinat, walking alongside the cathedral and onto the Avenue Alexandre de Rhodes, gathering every day punctually at five in front of the wooden board of the Foreign Ministry, where a lively hunchbacked student working for the PRG would come post a slip reading "Today's flight is cancelled. Come back tomorrow"—this became the new habit of the French, their new promenade.

One day the name positioned number 15 on one of the "refugee" lists was: "Jean-Marie Merillon, French nationality, born 1926, passport No. 593."

Technically he was not expelled. The new authorities had simply asked him to leave.

He departed on June 5, amid a group of French teachers and nurses. His luggage was not searched, but as though to affirm the PRG's principle of not recognizing the diplomatic immunity of an ambassador who had been accredited to the "puppet" regime, the *bo doi* in customs opened the traveling bag that an aide was carrying for him.

7: Peace

In the Delta

The trip began amid bursts of laughter.

After weeks of waiting I had finally obtained, along with my friend Nayan Chanda, the first permit to leave Saigon and make a tour of the Mekong Delta. The press section of the Foreign Ministry had put at our disposal a car, a driver, a guide, and as chaperon Major Phuong Nam, the Vietcong with the paunch.

But as soon as we started out we realized that it was we foreigners who would have to give directions in the maze of Cholon streets. None of our companions knew the way: the driver was from Hanoi, the guide from Quang Ngai, and this was the first time in Saigon for both of them. As for Phuong Nam, who was born and raised in the Delta, he had been treading only jungle paths for the last thirty years and had no idea where Highway 4 began.

No sooner was this problem solved than we realized that Phuong Nam, looking worried, was feeling his chest, under his armpits, in the pockets of his trousers, looking for something.

"*J'ai oublié mon pistolet*," he said with ill-disguised embarrassment.

There was absolutely no need for it since we would not have to defend ourselves from anyone, but the idea of traveling under the protection of a Vietcong who had left his pistol at home amused everyone enormously, and in the end even Phuong Nam.

Phuong Nam was the good-hearted face of the Revolution. Gruff and paternal, he was a man who knew the joys of life. Good cooking was one of the things he appreciated.

"The Revolution," he once said, "is also being able to sit down peacefully at a street stall and have a bowl of good noodle soup."

Since 1945, when the French shot his father, Phuong Nam had been with the guerrillas—first in the terrible U Minh forest in the southernmost part of the Delta, then north of Saigon. He was now returning with us for the first time as a traveler to his own region. At the sight of the quiet expanse of fields with the little wooden peasant huts shaded by banana trees he said:

"If one day the Revolution doesn't need me any more I'd like to come here and till a little piece of land."

The revolution would probably not let him retire so easily. As I learned later in Hanoi, Phuong Nam was an important element in the Front's intelligence and counterespionage apparatus.

I had been to the Delta dozens of times during the war. But if it weren't for the jade green of the rice paddies and the fresh smell of mud where water buffaloes were rolling I would not have known where I was. I would not have recognized the landscape, its appearance had changed so much in two and a half months since the Liberation.

The military camps along the road, the concrete pillboxes at the heads of bridges, the blockhouses in the middle of fields had all been razed to the ground and swept away. The landscape was again an endless rice paddy, swarming with people at work.

We did not encounter a single roadblock or see a single group of soldiers along the entire eighty kilometers from Saigon to My Tho and beyond. Was this really the country in which a thirty-year war had ended only a short time ago?

Saigon at the time of our departure was absolutely calm, but rumors were still going round that the remains of Thieu's army were concentrated in the Delta, that bands of "obstinates" aided by the Buddhist Hoa Hao sect, were attacking convoys and engaging in bloody battles with the Liberation Army.

In the three days we spent in the Delta, first by car on the roads and then on foot from village to village, we did not hear a single rifle shot. When we aked various people if they knew of any ambushes or skirmishes in the region, the only rumor we were able to collect was one about "serious clashes" taking place in Saigon.

"The spreading of false news is the only weapon the obstinate have left," remarked Phan Van Thao, leader of the people's organizations in My Tho and political commissar of the city. "In this region every attempt at resistance has been eliminated. It's impossible for the obstinate to go on fighting without the support of the population. Counterrevolutionary elements have no way of hiding or surviving.

"Our security system is much more effective than Thieu's, because it's not based on police control but on the people's. For the peasants Liberation means peace, and counterrevolutionaries who want to carry on the war are immediately denounced."

Thao was short, with a broad face, strong cheekbones, close-cropped hair, and a large gleaming smile. He was one of those extraordinary characters you happened to meet in Vietnam—one of the "saints" who aroused conflicting reactions in me. My meeting with him was not accidental, it was one of the "surprises" Phuong Nam had carefully prepared. But that did not diminish its value.

When we went to see him in a rundown little villa in the center of town, I was sure I had never seen him before in my life. But Thao insisted he knew me, and began to recount details of things I had done two years before when, crossing the front lines with my friend Jean-Claude Pomonti of *Le Monde,* we had gone to seek out the Vietcong in an area a few kilometers from My Tho.

It turned out that at that time Thao had followed us step by step. He was the one who decided we should be treated as guests and not as prisoners; he was the one who gave permission for us to be taken to various villages and be briefed by political and military cadres. During the days we stayed in the liberated area, Thao, like one of the many peasants in the landscape of rice paddies, had been our shadow—silent, unobtrusive, so as not to be recognized, not to be photographed.

Then, in February 1973, the war was not yet over and, under the guise of a "merchant" Thao was soon to return to his clandestine work in the city of My Tho, in the midst of the townspeople and right under the noses of Thieu's police.

Born in My Tho in 1927, Thao had been Phuong Nam's classmate at the Lycée Lemyre de Vilers, later renamed "Nguyen Dinh Chieu." He had joined the partisans in 1945, but unlike other Vietminh who had regrouped in the North in 1954 Thao, on orders of the Party, had gone back to live in My Tho with his wife and three small children, in a house on Phan Thanh Gian Street.

In 1956, when it became clear that the elections and peaceful reunification of the country stipulated in the Geneva Accords would not take place, the Party asked him to make himself available to the Revolution once again, and Phan Van Thao "died." His family pretended to mourn him, his neighbors and acquaintances forgot him.

Actually Thao, after a brief period spent at a Resistance base behind the lines on the Plain of Jars, near the Cambodian border, had returned to live in My Tho. He had grown a mustache and wore glasses: he had become another person. His documents and identification papers, which had been easy to procure through the usual system of corruption, described him as one who had fought alongside the French forces against the Vietminh, now become a "grain dealer."

His first clandestine job was to select and train cadres in the city.

"We held our courses in a room we'd dug out behind a fake wall in a workshop," Thao said. "The police would have never found out. The only danger came from traitors, and at times we were forced to eliminate some. The worst period was during the Phoenix campaign."

Thao occasionally ran into his children on the streets of My Tho but they were now grown up and did not recognize him. He sometimes met his wife secretly, since she, an obstetrician in the local hospital, was also an underground cadre in the Front.

Told in this way, while we drank bitter green tea in a quiet room with young guerrillas walking past carrying papers and documents that they sometimes brought to be signed, Thao's story seemed unbelievable. How was it possible to hide for so long? What was the house like where he lived?

I asked him and that night we went to see Nguyen Tri Phuong Street, where Thao had lived until Liberation Day.

Not far from the beginning of Highway 4, somewhat hidden in the backyard of a school, on the second floor of a wooden house belonging to a teacher friend, Thao had a room. There was also a hollow space where he could hide if the police surrounded the house—under the stairs, behind a shelter of sandbags. A mat on the beaten earth floor covered the entrance to a tunnel which led to a drainage ditch, and from there on to a banana grove. It was Thao's safety exit.

I tried to imagine how Thao had lived. I wondered what measure time must have for a man like him. Twenty years. Twenty years of struggle, twenty years of living underground in one's own city, twenty years in constant danger of being caught.

"Yes, they caught me once in 1970, near Cai Be. It was the Americans who arrested me, but I had a friend who regularly paid off the American base commander and I was able to get free."

I couldn't understand. The Americans?

"Yes, yes, I was also captured by the Americans and I got away by paying 1,800,000 piasters," said the man who had been standing beside Thao ever since I met him.

"They arrested me in 1972 while I was crossing the Newport bridge, but they let me go after forty-five days. I'd
been buying stolen goods from the Americans for years,
and so I had a way of blackmailing them."

The man was Thao's second in command. His name was
Le Thanh Hien, he was thirty-seven years old, and up until Liberation Day he was a "puppet" captain in the Engineers Corps attached to the Military Geographical Institute
of the ARVN. At the same time Hien had been a Front
cadre since 1960: he had joined the army on orders from
the Party and had been in contact with Thao since 1967,
furnishing him copies of all maps and plans of American
and ARVN military installations in the region. Thao then
passed the maps on to the Vietcong military command in
the area.

In the course of the evening we spent together, Thao
mentioned that he was a cousin of Thieu's former prime
minister, Tran Thien Khiem, and that he had seen Khiem
a few days before the Liberation. This I could hardly believe.

"You foreigners don't understand what family relations
mean in Vietnam, and that's why you don't understand the
national reconciliation policy," said Thao.

"Khiem was with Thieu, he was an enemy, but there was
still the family tie. Khiem knew I was with the Front, but
he never denounced me.

"The night of April 25 I took my Honda and went to
see him at his home in Saigon. He was about to leave the
country and I told him to stay. The Liberation would soon
be here and he needn't fear for his life. But I wasn't able
to convince him. Khiem told me that by now he was in the
meshes of Thieu and the Americans, and he was afraid
that if he refused to leave the CIA would eliminate him."

My Tho and the surrounding region had been completely liberated on April 30, the day Saigon fell.

Though the area was not in the hands of the same Military Management Committee as Saigon-Gia Dinh, the
problems faced by the new authorities had been the same
as the capital: registration of "puppets," campaigns against
decadent culture, against "obstinate" elements, and so on.
Even the deadlines were more or less the same, but in general the Revolution in the countryside was harsher and
more thorough than in Saigon.

The capital had been treated with caution and discretion; all changes had been slow, gradual, and the *bo doi* who represented people's daily contact with the revolutionary power had been expressly trained to be patient, and were careful not to clash with the population.

It was different in the Delta. First of all there was no regular army there. Aside from a few units of *bo doi* who guaranteed security in the region, it was up to the local guerrillas, to the political cadres like Phan Van Thao who had lived for years underground in the midst of the population, to exexcise the new power. Unlike those in Saigon, the guerrillas in the countryside had not been eliminated, their troops were still numerous, their administration was functioning even while the "puppet" administration still existed.

In the countryside problems were simpler and the solutions more clear cut. People in the villages knew each other, knew each other's merits, faults, and responsibilities. Life had traditionally been a communal one, and so the people took more immediate, more enthusiastic part in what was happening than they did at first in Saigon.

For instance in the Delta the registration of "puppets" took place in the village squares, not inside old barracks or police stations as in Saigon. "Confessions" were not only written out on sheets of paper, they were made in front of everyone, and reeducation was a collective responsibility of the village, not of individual cadres assigned to the various classes.

In Nhi Quy, a small peasant community west of My Tho where we spent a day, *hoc tap* courses were held in a shed where farm equipment was stored at night. The "puppet" peasants of Nhi Quy, who in many cases had been forcibly drafted into the ARVN, sat on the ground amid bales of hay and rice-hulling machines. Five political cadres, peasants like themselves, gave the lessons from behind a dusty table, but around them stood the whole village. For hours children with younger brothers and sisters in their arms, old people, women, all watched and listened in. Those who did not find a place in the shed stood peering through the windows and door. The public often joined in the discussions and this exchange of ideas and experiences unfolded to the peeping of chicks shut up in a large basket and the grunting of fat pigs roaming around in the middle of people.

In the evening the "puppets" returned to their homes.

One area where the Revolution had gone further in the countryside than in Saigon was that of property.

In Saigon the rule was that only what belonged to foreigners and "puppets" who had left the country became "property of the people."

In the countryside things soon went beyond this: whatever the "puppets" had acquired by illegitimate means was considered subject to expropriation.

In one village, for example a police informer who had forced a peasant to sell him a field for a ridiculous price by threatening to denounce him as a Communist was brought before a people's tribunal, found guilty, and obliged to restore the land.

On Liberation Day in Quy Tan, a village we visited in the Cai Be hinterland, the population had entered the home of the village chief, confiscated all the money and jewels they found there and declared them "common property." The chief, tried as a "criminal with debts of blood to the people," was sent far away for reeducation.

His house, the only one in masonry, towered over the village. It was not touched; but a heated discussion went on for weeks among the peasants on whether to confiscate it or not. Those who felt it should be seized maintained that every brick in it belonged to the people, since for years local families had paid shares to the village chief to keep him from drafting their sons into the ARVN and sending them off to the front.

In Quy Tan, the end of the war had also brought about significant changes in the fields.

First of all, peasants went out to reoccupy the lands that the Vietminh agrarian reform had assigned them twenty-five years before. These were the only titles considered valid by the new authorities, despite the later counter-reforms of Diem and Thieu.

Then there had been actual land redistributions, in favor of "families of heroes," and of peasants who had abandoned the fields to join the guerrilla forces and had returned to their villages after Liberation Day with nothing to live on.

"What we redistributed was land recovered by the dismantling of puppet military bases and land ceded by rich peasants whom we asked to contribute to the Revolution," explained Chi Nhanh, head of the propaganda section of the Military Mangement Committee in My Tho.

The reconversion of land previously occupied by the

ARVN was still in progress three months after the Liberation.

The removal of land mines and the leveling of rice paddies were jobs assigned to "puppets" in the course of their *hoc tap*.

The way the rich had been asked to yield parts of their rice paddies was explained to me by the village leader of Quy Tan, himself a peasant who had joined the guerrillas in 1962.

"Immediately after the Liberation we convened people's assemblies with the participation of all inhabitants, and we explained that a hectare and a half, at most two hectares of rice paddy are sufficient to support an average family of seven or eight persons.

"Then we got everyone to talk about his problems. The poor peasant described what it meant not to have enough land, to have to go into debt by renting it, and those who had more rice paddy than they needed willingly gave up a part. Every time a rich peasant announced what he was pledging to the Revolution he was warmly applauded by the whole village."

According to the village leader's account, 150 out of Quy Tan's total of 350 arable hectares had been "spontaneously" ceded by their owners in this way for redistribution.

I believe that all this happened without threats or the use of force. The climate created by the Liberation, the growing social pressure to behave according to new rules and principles were enough to explain these "spontaneous" decisions.

After all, where owners did not give, the peasants took.

In the village of Quy Trinh, we were told, there was a certain Bac Im who had forty hectares of rice paddy. No one in his family had worked it for some time: one son was a "puppet" policeman in My Tho, another was in Thieu's air force at Bien Hoa. The land had been rented out.

After the Liberation, the tenants held a meeting and decided each would continue to till his portion, but would pay Bac Im only a fifth of the old rent. Bac Im could not refuse: the people's assembly in the village ratified this "just decision" by the tenants.

What did not happen in the Delta, at least not in the villages we visited, was the transfer of legal titles of ownership. Even where the peasants took possession of a new piece of rice paddy, the new authorities issued no legal document that declared them to all effects "owners."

This was no accident.

Front cadres, especially the higher ones, were well aware that the redistribution of land was a temporary policy, a concession that had to be made to the natural traditional aspirations of the peasants. Sooner or later the question of agricultural ownership would have to be faced in a completely different and radical way.

Though equalizing the availability of land, the new authorities in the Delta left the question of law vague so as to be able later to apply measures more in line with a new socialist society. No one in the South spoke of this society clearly yet, but no one doubted this would be the future of the country.

In Hanoi, where I later asked what the government's policy would be in this sector, they made no bones about it:

"There are two stages in the new phase of the Revolution and the building of socialism in the South: industrialization of the country and collectivization of agriculture," I was told by Hoang Tung, editor of the Party newspaper, *Nhan Dan*. He went on:

"Certainly to collectivize the Mekong Delta will be a problem. The peasants there are accustomed to different standards than peasants in the Red River Delta here in the North. We must take these differences into account. A simple leveling would be arbitrary. We will carry out collectivization together with agricultural mechanization, but we will certainly carry it out.

The *can bo* in the Delta did not yet speak of this policy. The word "collectivization" was still not used. The peasants were not even obliged to organize themselves in new cooperatives. But those that already existed were encouraged to expand and spread out.

Unlike Saigon, where the war had arrived only indirectly with the echo of cannon fire and its calamities, the Delta had been one of the great battlefields of Vietnam. The two armies had faced each other here, and for thirty years they recruited their soldiers among the peasants.

Passing through the fields, I saw no group of people that did not have someone crippled or disabled in it. Peasant families had lost their sons on one side or the other, and every ancestors' altar in every hut had among its slowly burning joss sticks either the photo of a son "sacrificed for the Revolution" or one in his ARVN uniform.

Every village had its stories of massacres and reprisals to tell. The peasants wanted to show us their underground tunnels, and the hiding places they had built everywhere for the guerrillas.

The Liberation in the countryside meant the end of all this, the end of the war. For the peasants peace meant being able to go into the fields at dawn when the land is moist and can be worked better, without having to wait for the end of the curfew; it meant not having to put aside a pig or a chicken for the "puppet" troops who came by and threatened to destroy the crops if they did not receive hospitality.

For some it meant finally being able to buy a new ancestors' altar, as Chau Van Dan had done. He was the peasant in whose hut I had slept two years before, and where Phuong Nam now took me as a surprise.

"My first house was burned by French colonialists. The second was destroyed by the Americans. And those holes," said Dan, pointing to the threads of sunlight falling down through the corrugated iron roof, "were made by Thieu's artillery after the ceasefire. Now at least I'm sure no one will come and destroy anything." Proudly he indicated a solid wooden altar, of fresh-smelling wood.

An old peasant with a black *ao baba,* a long pointed beard, and his white hair in a bun at the nape of his neck recognized me and come to say hello in Dan's hut. When I asked him what had changed in his life since the last time we saw each other, he replied:

"Now I look at a tree and I'm not afraid. I no longer think there's somebody behind it who might take a shot at me. A tree is a tree again. That's part of the Revolution too."

Hoa binh

Slowly Vietnam was getting used to it.

In the South, particularly in Saigon among the people who had feared it, the experience of peace was a pleasure which remained veiled at times by muffled doubts and subtle anxieties.

But in the North, in Hanoi, peace was everything. It was

joy, relief, hope, exaltation, pride. Peace was victory. Everybody's victory — they said — but above all their victory.

It was there in the North that the country's soul had been preserved; it was from there that the final resistance had been led; it was there that the country was now thinking of the future.

It was the end of July in Hanoi. On the front of the Government Department Stores, with their dusty and half-empty windows facing the Lake of the Recovered Sword, was a huge map of Vietnam. The whole country was colored red. Saigon, Ho Chi Minh City, was marked by a small yellow circle; Hanoi by a large five-pointed star. Between North and South, no difference, no border: the country was already one, and its capital Hanoi.

I had arrived aboard a "puppet" DC-4, repainted with the North Vietnamese colors and full of *bo doi* returning home on leave, holding in their arms the large fans they had bought at the thieves' market in Saigon as though they were dolls.

The impression of being in the heart of the new Vietnam struck me immediately. The city, the people, the attitudes, were the model for everything I had seen changing in the South. Whether common people or leaders, they all showed the self-assurance of those certain that nothing can change the course of history any longer.

"We've paid an enormous price for our independence. We've lost two million men and women in the war, we've lost our best cadres, our best trained youth. Had it been necessary, we would have sacrificed others.

"Up until the day of the Liberation of Saigon we did not exclude the possibility of an American intervention. We were prepared to resist that too.

"Now nothing more can happen. The problems we have to face now are trifles compared to those of the past. We have our political line, and we'll follow it," I was told by a member of the Central Committee of the Party, at the end of a long, night-time conversation. We sat under the light of a single bulb that hung from the ceiling of a large crumbling villa, presumably once the luxurious residence of some Frenchman.

To illustrate the surprising situation in which the country found itself one high official in the Foreign Ministry quoted a fifteenth-century poem that for the first time seemed to describe Vietnam's reality rather than its dream:

> In the sea there are no more sharks,
> On land no more wild beasts,
> The sky is serene.
> We can build a peace of ten thousand years.

Then he added: "Today peace is a fact. We shall no longer fight among ourselves, and it's hard to imagine another foreign invasion."

Under his windows, on Ba Dinh Square at the end of Dien Bien Phu Avenue, thousands of workers were toiling day and night to finish the mausoleum of Ho Chi Minh, a huge cube of gray stone and reddish marble.

Throughout the city the concrete cylinders sunk along the sidewalks to provide shelter for passersby during the bombings had been transformed into great vases of flower pots; the air-raid shelters built against the backs of houses and factories were being demolished and their bricks, recovered for some other purpose, were being loaded on wooden ox-carts that circulated in the center of the city amid thousands of bicycles.

The schools, dispersed into the countryside until the last day of the war for fear of American bombings, were returning to their old sites. The anti-aircraft batteries were being dismounted. The loudspeakers which once wailed sudden alarms now were used only in the morning, to broadcast reveille with revolutionary music. At that hour youths from the people's militia could be seen against the clear dawn sky, stretching their arms on the roofs of houses, and the streets would fill up with people doing exercises in front of their doorways.

So began the days, one the same as another in this simple, hard, modest, austere life, which little by little was also being imposed on Saigon.

Even peace brought its problems.

"What kind of man has the Vietnamese become? Years of war spent in the jungle, suffering, sacrifices, what have they done to the fighters? These are questions we ask ourselves, because it's important, it's urgent for us to reconvert," Nguyen Khac Vien said to me at his Institute for Historical Research.

During the war this thin, stooped man, left with only half a lung from an old tuberculosis, had directed Hanoi's propaganda to the Western world from an office with porthole windows. It was once the headquarters of a French shipping company and he had lined it with books.

For a whole afternoon he served me bitter green tea from a flowered teapot and spoke of the future:

"Now that the war is over we must make a triple revolution: a revolution in production relations, to create new and more socialist economic structures; a cultural and ideological revolution, to convert everyone's way of thinking; a technical and scientific revolution, to make up for the time we lost in the war."

As I saw them, lining up patient and orderly, in front of state restaurants for breakfast or squatting around the lake in the afternoon to suck on ice-cream sticks or walking in pairs through the center of the city, the women with long black braids down their backs, everybody dressed with radical simplicity in white shirts, black trousers, rubber or plastic sandals and all with the colonial pith helmet that through one of history's jokes had become the symbol of resistance, these Vietnamese seemed to me capable of any revolution in the world.

Hanoi was like a large peasant village dotted with old houses, French villas that now belonged to a remote past. The elegant facades, the stuccowork around the windows, the wrought-iron balustrades of the balconies in downtown Hanoi, no longer had anything to do with the life that was unfolding beneath them. They were like scenery for a play that had long ceased to be performed.

I had felt the same the morning I left Saigon. Aroused by the shuffling of the *bo doi* who at dawn went running in their undershirts through the empty streets of the city, I had looked out my window at Tu Do Street for the last time. The buildings, the houses, the hotels put up by the Americans struck me as immense, out of proportion with what the city was becoming. They were like the unimpaired ruins of another civilization.

The new Vietnam, in its way, would now build a civilization of its own. The "saints" would be the engineers.

In the sky over Hanoi as I returned home for the first time without leaving behind me a country at war, I thought of them, of those I had known, and of the thousands of others working anonymously in the rice paddies, in the forests, in the villages where columns of smoke from fires and bombs no longer rose.

Vietnam was theirs, and they had every right to it.

Glossary
and
Index

Air America: formally a private airline, but substantially funded with capital from the CIA, which, together with the State Department, rented its services in Vietnam. After the Paris Accords, Air America helicopters were used under contract to safeguard air transportation of the ICCS and of the quadripartite and bipartite commissions set up by the Accords.

Ao baba: the traditional dress of Vietnamese peasants, resembling pajamas and usually black.

Ao dai: the traditional costume of Vietnamese women. Wide trousers and a full-length tunic split up the sides to the waist.

ARVN: Army of the Republic of Vietnam. The South Vietnamese army, the army of Saigon.

Bao chi: press. The most common Vietnamese expression to describe journalists.

Bo doi: in the text this word is used, as it is now used in Vietnam, to signify "soldiers of the Liberation Army." *Bo doi* is to be distinguished from Vietcong in the sense that the first is the regular uniformed soldier, while the second is the guerrilla or partisan member of an irregular armed unit.

Cach mang: revolution.

Can bo: political cadre of the NLF.

Camp Davis: a camp inside Tan Son Nhut Airport, formerly used by the Americans. After the Paris Accords it became the headquarters of the PRG delegation in Saigon.

Cholon: at one time a separate city from Saigon and inhabited almost exclusively by Chinese. Today it is the Chinese quarter of Saigon.

CIO: Central Intelligence Organization. South Vietnamese espionage agency modeled on the American CIA.

DAO or U.S. DAO: United States Defense Attache Office. The office of the American embassy's military attache, located at Tan Son Nhut Airport in what had been the offices of the MACV.

Doc lap: independence. Doc Lap Palace, after having been President Thieu's residence, became the seat of the Saigon-Gia Dinh Military Administration Committee.

Dong: the currency of North Vietnam The official exchange varies from two to four dong to the United States dollar.

Freedom Birds: what American soldiers called the planes that took them back to the States after a tour of duty in Vietnam.

FULRO (*Front Unifié pour la Lutte des Races Opprimées*): organization protective of the montagnard tribes, always hostile to the Saigon government but actively supported by the American Special Forces for a brief period.

Geneva Accords: signed the night of July 20, 1954, after the Vietminh victory at Dien Bien Phu, these accords put an end to the French war in Indochina. They provided for the cessation of hostilities in all Vietnamese territory, and established a temporary demarcation line at the seventeenth parallel. Communist forces were to regroup in the North, forces that had been allied with the French in the South. General elections, which were to have taken place within a short time after the Accords, were never held.

Giai phong: liberation.

Hoa binh: peace.

Hoc tap: reeducation.

Honda: Japanese make of motorcycle, which in Vietnam became a general word for motorcycle.

ICCS: International Commission of Control and Supervision. Set up by the Paris Accords, its members were Canada, Indonesia, Poland,

and Hungary. After two months, the Canadian delegation withdrew and its place was taken by Iran.

MACV: Military Assistance Command, Vietnam. Also known as the Pentagon of the East. It was the general staff of the American expeditionary corps in Vietnam. After the Paris Accords, it became the headquarters of the American advisers remaining in the country and was renamed DAO.

NLF: National Liberation Front. The political organization of the guerrilla forces in South Vietnam. It included various other democratic groups besides the Communist Party.

Paris Accords: signed on January 28, 1973, by representatives of the governments of the Democratic Republic of Vietnam (Hanoi), the Republic of Vietnam (Saigon), the United States, and the Provisional Revolutionary Government (Vietcong), these accords put an end to the American intervention in Vietnam. Hostilities were to cease throughout the South. Once American troops were withdrawn, the Provisional Revolutionary Government and the Saigon government were to form, in a spirit of reconciliation and national harmony, a coalition government with three components, namely one in which the Vietcong, Thieu's Vietnamese, and the non-Communist opposition to Thieu or so-called Third Force would all be represented.

Article 1 of the Accords recognized the principle for which the Vietnamese guerrillas had fought for decades: "The United States and all other countries respect the independence, sovereignty, unity, and territorial integrity of Vietnam as recognized by the 1954 Geneva Agreements on Vietnam." By subscribing to this principle, the United States renounced what had been its justification for military intervention in the country, namely to defend the South from North Vietnamese aggression. This acceptance of the principle of Vietnamese unity led to another consequence: if North and South were a single country, the northern troops in the South could not be considered "foreign," and their withdrawal could not be likened to the withdrawal of American troops. Contrary to Thieu's wishes, the United States agreed to allow the Paris Accords to omit mention of the withdrawal of the North Vietnamese divisions. Their presence was now taken for granted.

Piaster: the currency of South Vietnam. The official exchange before the Liberation was 755 piasters to the American dollar.

PRG: Provisional Revolutionary Government. Constituted on June 6, 1969, it is the government of the National Liberation Front, the government of the guerrillas, of the anti-American resistance.

PX: Post Exchange. Its merchandise was tax-free and sold only to American citizens.

Rangers: special corps of ARVN commandos.

Tan Son Nhut: the Saigon civil and military airport.

Third Force: generic expression used to designate, especially after the Paris Accords, all the various non-Communist organizations in opposition to the Thieu regime.

Tu do: freedom. Tu Do Street is the principal thoroughfare in Saigon. In French times it was called Rue Catinat.

Vietcong: Vietnamese guerrillas at the time of the anti-American resistance. The term, which simply signifies "Vietnamese Communists," came to be derogatory in American usage, especially in its abbreviated form "VC." In this book the word is used until Liberation Day as equivalent for partisans, guerrillas, freedom fighters.

Vietminh: Vietnamese guerrillas at the time of the anti-French resistance.

Weapons, planes, and military vehicles:

A–37: American-made jet plane used as a fighter

bomber by the Saigon air force.

AK–47: Chinese-made rifle, the standard weapon of Vietcong guerrillas and *bo doi*.

B–40 rocket: with its newer variation, the B-41, it was the standard antitank rocket used by North Vietnamese troops and Vietcong guerrillas. Transported by hand by a single person, it was fired from a rocket-launcher not much larger than an ordinary rifle.

B–52: American transport superbomber.

C–141: American air force transport plane. One of the largest in the world.

Cobra: small American helicopter armed with rockets, supplied to the ARVN and the American forces.

DC-3: American-made propeller-driven plane, used to transport passengers and cargo.

F–5: American-made jet plane, much faster and more sophisticated than the A-37, used as a fighter bomber, along with its F-5E version, by the Saigon air force.

Ilyushin: Soviet-made passenger jet.

Jolly Green Giant: the largest helicopter for transporting troops and material supplied to the American forces.

L–119: small American-made plane used for scouting by the Saigon air force.

M–16: American-made rifle, standard weapon of the ARVN. Can fire automatic bursts or single shots.

M–41: American-made light tank supplied to the ARVN.

M–113: American-made armored troop transport vehicle supplied to the ARVN.

Mig: Soviet-made jet fighter supplied to the Hanoi air force.

Molotova truck: troop transport truck of Soviet model, but also made in China, supplied to the Liberation Army.

130-MM. Cannon: the longest-range artillery supplied to the Liberation Army.

"Strella" missile or SA–7: Soviet-made, heat-seeking ground-to-air missile supplied to Communist troops. Made its first appearance in Vietnam during the 1972 offensive, and proved highly effective against low-flying planes and helicopters.

T–54: Soviet-made heavy tank supplied to the Liberation Army.

References in boldface are to the caption numbers identifying photographs.